I0022872

Absolute

Disaster

---

99 things you should know
about natural disasters

JAMES SHEPHERD-BARRON

KISSYFISH BOOKS

London and New York

Absolute Disaster

The KissyFish Book Company
Mains of Geanies
Fearn
Scotland IV20 1TW

info@kissyfishbooks.com
First published in Great Britain, January 2017
© James Shepherd-Barron 2017

The right of James Shepherd-Barron to be identified as author of this work has been asserted by him in accordance with the UK Copyright, Designs and Patents Act 1988 and the US Copyright Act 1976.

ISBN: 978-0-9927201-2-4

British Library cataloguing-in-publication data
A catalogue record for this book is available from the British Library.

All rights reserved. No part of this publication may be reproduced, stored in a retrieval system, or transmitted in any form or by any means, in part or in whole, electronic, mechanical, photocopying, recording, or otherwise, without either the prior written permission of the publisher or a license permitting restricted copy in the United Kingdom only, or her Dominions and Territories overseas.

This book may not be lent, resold, hired out or otherwise disposed of by way of trade in any form of binding or cover other than that in which is published, without the prior consent of the publisher.

Research facilities for preparation of this book were generously provided by Crown Agents and supported by the International Feinstein Center at Tufts University, USA. Contents do not necessarily reflect the official position, policies or views of these institutions, however, nor does information, designation, and presentation of the material necessarily reflect the views of the organisations and entities referred to. The views expressed herein reflect those of the author alone.

Cover photograph courtesy of www.earth.net

in which
a disaster management consultant
(and disaster epidemiologist)
tells the story of natural disaster;
explores how people die
of mostly avoidable causes;
and suggests how such outcomes
might be prevented in the future,
while challenging some
long-held assumptions
in the process.

Dedication

To Kat,
and my very special God-daughters
Sophie, Em, Bug, Banana, and Frankie.

Author's Note

THIS BOOK IS NOT SO MUCH ABOUT natural hazards and their ability to unleash awesome destructive power, but about their sometimes disastrous consequences and how they are managed. This approach expands on what would traditionally be referred to in schools of international health and disaster management as *Disaster Epidemiology*, a field which sounds horribly medico-centric and which you might well be coming across for the first time. Don't worry; you're not alone.

If risk is a measure of uncertainty, 'disaster epidemiology' is a measure of predictability.

To know how people are affected by natural hazards is not of much use if you don't really know how to apply this knowledge when trying to reduce disaster risk, build resilience, respond to disaster, and when doing your best to avoid unnecessary suffering later.

What this means in practice is that the field of disaster epidemiology is actually about the appliance of science. After all, superficial understanding of what the numbers are telling you about hazard, risk, vulnerability and predictability, combined with inadequate management before, during, and after a crisis, can end up killing even more people in the weeks, months and years afterwards than during the disaster event itself.

And then there is our moral obligation to understand what could have been done better, so that the same – perfectly avoidable – thing doesn't happen again sometime, someplace else.

As is the nature of all scientific enquiry, however, there is danger in extrapolating the results of experiment and observation from one place or time to another, and in so doing, of merely replacing one half-truth with another. The 'truth', in other words, is highly dependent on the context and who is doing the analysis.

This is particularly evident within the discipline of disaster epidemiology where understanding what is going on in real time as a disaster unfolds is nigh-on impossible when people are either too busy surviving and responding to allow time for rigorous investigation, or definitions are too vague to be universally applied. Almost all the 'facts' discussed in this book come heavily asterisked as a result.

A Tropical Cyclone, for example, tends to create more damage on one side of its path than on the other, but this might not be the case on every occasion. Also, what appears to be a trend might be nothing more than a statistical anomaly ... just noisy numbers getting in the way. Statistical analysis, after all, can only point out a correlation; we need the physics to understand causation and attribution. The number of reported disasters appears to be reducing, but this might be the result of changes in the way disasters are reported and recorded rather than in any actual change in the long-term trend.

I have preferred, therefore to use the term 'misperception' rather than 'fact', as a misperception better reflects the uncertainty within our natural world; the vagaries of human behaviour; and the mushiness of much of the data used for disaster preparedness and response planning. Misperception allows room for manoeuvre.

That said, none of what follows is made up. Each of the misperceptions in this book reflect my own observations in the field, triangulated with evidence from peer-reviewed scientific journals or from the reams of unpublished grey literature that litter the shelves of NGO planning departments. As a minimum, every misperception is endorsed by the views of at least two experts other than me.

Nevertheless, as author, I take full responsibility for any mistakes you may feel I have made, and invite you to contact me through the publisher (info@absolutedisasters.com) so that I might make amends in future editions as appropriate.

Finally, it is difficult to ignore one of the fundamental drivers of disaster risk – climate change – when discussing natural disasters. But this is not a book about climate change ... for that, it is probably best to refer to ongoing deliberations by the Inter-Governmental Panel on the subject[1] or the blogosphere[2]. It is instead a book about little-known and often misunderstood interplays between naturally occurring hazards, risk, and human frailty.

I hope you are as surprised by some of the misperceptions discussed here as I was when researching them, and that this stimulates you to delve deeper into where the myths and maths of un-natural disaster collide.

James Shepherd-Barron
New York, January 2017

---

[1] See: www.ipcc.ch
[2] See, for example: www.realclimate.org

Definitions

[disaster epidemiology]: ~/ˈdɪˈzɑːstə/_ˌɛpɪdiːmɪˈɒlədʒi
noun; sic.verb;
the art and science of measuring and investigating determinants and
trends in natural hazards and disasters across time and space; their
impact on defined groups of people; and prediction of future
consequences for prioritisation of humanitarian action[3].

[catastrophe]: ~/ˈkəˈtastrəfi/
noun;
a hazard event resulting in widespread death and destruction to the
extent that day-to-day functioning of governance has been
overwhelmed; everyday societal functions have been sharply and
simultaneously interrupted; and external help is not available.

[natural disaster]: ~/ˈʌn,natʃ(ə)r(ə)l _/dɪˈzɑːstə
adj.; noun;
a seemingly natural hazard event resulting in great damage and loss of
life.

[disaster risk management]: ~/ˈdɪˈzɑːstə/_ˈrɪsk-ˈmanɪdʒm(ə)nt
noun; sic.verb;
process of controlling systems or people exposed to danger before,
during, and after disaster.

---

[3] This is the author's definition. It extends the traditional public-health version to include
the study of natural hazards and the implications of their impact for risk reduction and
disaster management.

To test your knowledge
before, during, or after
reading this book,

take the Quiz

which can be found at

www.absolutedisasters.com

This site is also a blog, so

feel free to leave a comment
as we can always learn from each other.

Table of Contents

Introduction

WHEN THIS BOOK – and the online media package that goes with it – was just an idea wafting around in the back of my head, I pondered long and hard before putting pen to paper wondering if anyone would find such a book in any way useful?

For a start, it was bound to contain words like *epidemiology*, a word so ugly that even public health specialists can't pronounce it half the time, while almost everyone else assumes it refers to the study of not-so-exotic skin diseases. It would also be dealing in intimate detail with the more hideous realities of death and destruction. Not, I thought, the sort of subject matter to grab people's attention.

I also didn't really know who I would be writing it for. Whose attention would I be seeking to get, exactly? And why? Disaster management professionals and graduate students would probably know everything they needed to know already, wouldn't they? But those non-professionals who are nevertheless intimately involved with managing disaster risk such as Mayors, Ministers and Ambassadors – those whose duty it is to protect us, in other words – probably wouldn't, I thought, and could possibly benefit from such insights?

And so would a lot of the people running around in the hurly-burly of an actual disaster response ... volunteer aid workers, civil servants in line ministries, donor representatives, UN staff, first secretaries in embassies, that kind of person. Certainly the media never seemed to get it right, with the same tired old clichés being trotted out by breathless journalists disaster after disaster.

That those who potentially live in harm's way, the public, might want to know about the *epidemiology of disaster* never seriously crossed my mind. Surely the geology, hydro-meteorology, behavioural psychology, public health, and statistics involved would be a top-ten-turn-off for them, wouldn't it? And anyway, I kept thinking to myself, is any of this really going to make a difference?

Despite these misgivings, a rough outline of what I thought needed to be said based on my own observations and experiences from over twenty years in the field began to take shape. But where to start? I saw myself more as a practitioner than an academic. I couldn't escape the day job, either, as I was working as a regional disaster management adviser for the UN in Bangkok at the time, and such job descriptions don't come with a lot of spare time built in. But, with what little I did have, I started amassing a data dump of research papers that looked as though they may be relevant.

The idea began to take physical form when, aged 42, I went to take a belated Masters' degree in International Health at Copenhagen University's famous school of public health, the Panum Institute.

I was hooked from Day One. All the humanitarian work I had been doing in disaster zones like Rwanda, Iraq, Sudan, Pakistan, Indonesia and Nepal suddenly fell into place.

Why? Because I could suddenly relate my years of field experience to the academic theory. What had previously been a soft and noisy jumble of obscure hieroglyphics began to turn into information, and with that information came knowledge. As the course progressed, the veils slowly fell away and knowledge morphed into understanding. I realised, too, there were underlying causes behind the disasters I had worked in that were more complex than had been imagined at the time. Patterns in the data were at last telling me something, and allowing me to relate my experiences directly to the application of evidence-based decision-making.

As the months went by – three of them learning the dark arts of epidemiology in India at the famous CMC Velore, with my 'practicals' conducted in a nearby leper[4] community – it became clear that I was not alone in having noticed the way people were dying was repeating itself time and again, and nobody seemed to be asking why.

---

[4] Contrary to popular belief, Leprosy is not very contagious, rarely kills, and, being a *mycobacterium* distantly related to TB, is treatable with antibiotics.

An earthquake in Turkey had just killed tens of thousands, and a few years later a similar sized event in Iraq killed even more. People died from more or less the same cause: falling masonry. But were there other reasons to explain how they died, reasons that could have been prevented? How many hadn't been crushed, for example, but asphyxiated because they had inhaled brick or concrete dust? How many were pulled dusty and dazed from the rubble only to die later from secondary effects like kidney failure, or heart attack? How many were paralysed in the course of their rescue, or had limbs amputated unnecessarily purely because there were too few resources available to look after them properly?

We know very little about how people *really* die in disasters. We hear of people being buried alive in a landslide; of being crushed to death in an earthquake-induced building collapse; or being drowned in a flood. But is this true? Is this really how they died? And if it isn't, if such generalisations are messing with the truth, are we taking the correct preventive measures to stop such things happening again in the future?

A book like this, I thought, would help us explore the numbers, and in so doing, help us all understand what is going on. As my researches gathered momentum, it became ever-clearer that a great deal of what we are told about natural disasters can be a little economical with the truth. One popular misconception will tell us, for example, that the number of natural disasters occurring around the world is increasing when the evidence suggests otherwise.

But it would also have to explain that this doesn't tell us very much if those that do take place are affecting more people, or that the natural hazard events causing them are increasing in magnitude or intensity. It would have to embrace the notion that global statistics about the total number of those killed or displaced won't mean much if populations are expanding, or that certain parts of the planet are ravaged more than others.

In challenging some long-held misperceptions, the chapters that follow demonstrate how, if we're 'on' with the trend, we're too often 'off' with the message, in part because we continue to confuse terms like *hazard* with *disaster*, *frequency* with *intensity*, and *vulnerability* with *exposure*.

Worse than all this, though – as some of the Reality Checks in the next section point out – when we do respond, we often don't respond properly. After all, if we don't know the underlying cause of death and injury, how can we know what investment has the greatest potential to save people from dying and suffering unnecessarily? How can we save lives if we don't understand how they are threatened in the first place?

Given that we need flaky data like a newborn baby needs a whisky and soda, this lack of insight means we continue to draw the wrong conclusions and make stupid decisions because we are hostage to the assumptions and half-truths of the past. It's like a scene from the movie *Groundhog Day* where Bill Murray learns nothing form the previous day's events and is thereby condemned to repeating the same mistakes over and over again.

Nevertheless, despite knowing that dealing with aspects of disaster is like wrangling a snake – the more one twists and turns, the more slippery the challenge of knowing what works becomes – patterns in the numbers are telling us things, and just might be pointing the way to what we could and should be doing better. Knowing how many people died in a disaster is no longer enough. And nor is responding with the bare minimum of taps, tablets and tents.

Reality Check

THE CALCULUS OF CALAMITY CHANGED when *Ebola* erupted from the jungles of West Africa in early 2014. The epidemic which followed changed the way we think about natural disasters, and even the way we calculate risk. More directly, it forced the disaster management community to change the way preparedness, response, and recovery operations are managed.

Why was Ebola so different? Partly it was because the speed and virulence with which this terrifying virus emerged to kill so indiscriminately scared us all witless. But a lot of it was because the world woke up to notice that it was ineptitude and indifference as much as the disease itself that allowed it to escalate into a catastrophe when it really didn't have to. As with so many of the disasters that came before, it was human behaviour, not nature *per se*, that allowed people to die in their thousands, many of them from quite avoidable causes.

Why, when we knew perfectly well what needed to be done to stave off impending calamity, was this allowed to happen?

One of the main reasons was that those in charge at the beginning of the outbreak did not have the breadth of knowledge or experience to see the problem for what it was ... a full-on, slow-onset, large-scale natural disaster requiring a full-on, large-scale international response. The Minister of Health in Sierra Leone just didn't know what was required to mobilise resources at the sort of speed and scale used just months before for *Typhoon Yolanda* in the Philippines or for the *Haiti Earthquake* in 2010. If she did, she saw such mobilisation as some kind of threat to her country's status and therefore chose to remain blind to the options available.

Those who could have woken her up to the enormity of what was going on in the World Health Organisation failed to do so. As a result, the management architecture was incorrectly configured and inappropriately resourced. This meant that those in charge were reacting to events, when they should and could have been getting ahead of the disease.

The national 'Ebola Operations Centre' established to manage the extensive control measures needed consisted of little more than two flip-charts, one without paper, and a pile of ink-less pens strewn across a dusty table. There was nothing to show that this small room, crowded with empty chairs, was an 'operations centre' for anything, let alone an unfolding national calamity. There were no maps and no organigrams on the wall to show who was responsible for doing what, where, and when. There were no graphics charting the progress of the disease. Daily coordination meetings, micro-managed by the Minister of Health herself, routinely descended into farce, with heads of the five command and control pillars ducking and diving in their frantic efforts to avoid having to make decisions.

What she and the United Nations Country Team advising her failed to recognise was that a natural disaster, whatever its cause, requires a multi-sectoral and multi-disciplinary response coordinated across the entire humanitarian system, not just medico-centric and defensive mis-management from political appointees jealously protecting their privileges.

In part, too, drama was allowed to turn into crisis because heads of UN agencies, country directors of non-governmental organisations, and local politicians have always found it difficult to admit that the real drivers of natural disaster are competition, vanity, power dynamics, and politics just as much as more legitimate causes such as inadequate resourcing, poverty, urbanisation, climate change, or population growth.

None of this was helped by the fact that outbreaks of communicable disease are not classified as natural disasters and are therefore not registered as such on the world's disaster databases. This simple and deliberate omission tends to reinforce the notion that *population health* is another of those aspects of life over which we have no control, and is something apart; something beyond our lay comprehension that only health professionals can deal with.

Ebola destroyed that illusion once and for all by clearly demonstrating that other professional disciplines such as anthropology and psychology, politics and economics, media relations and information management, were every bit as important as disease control and community mobilisation. As was said at the time, the challenge was not the disease, but *fear* of the disease.

Worse though – at least as far as Sierra Leone was concerned – was knowing that the guidelines and protocols on how to deal with such an event across all these different disciplines had been drawn up and ratified just eighteen months before as part of the lessons learning exercise that followed the deadly Cholera epidemic of 2012. I know, because I led the team that produced it[i].

All the more galling for me, then, was to find a copy literally gathering dust on a shelf in the Health Ministry when I returned in July 2014 as the Minister of Health's Special Adviser, sent out by the UK Government's Department for International Development (DFID). Within days of my arrival the problem become clear, prompting me to send the following message to London:

> *"The Government of Sierra Leone is not alone in treating Ebola like any other cholera outbreak which it assumes can be contained by traditional measures of isolation, treatment, and community outreach. As a result, they, the UN, and especially The World Health Organisation are failing to see it for what it is: a full-scale natural disaster, every bit as deadly as the 2005 earthquake in Pakistan or the 2013 hurricane in the Philippines.* **The epidemic is a slow-motion tsunami, the only difference being that the havoc being wrought is invisible and is taking place over months rather than minutes.** *All predictions point to it killing just as many people."*

The bit of text I have highlighted here took a further ten weeks before it appeared in the Whitehall briefing document which galvanised the response. By then, the damage had been done.

⟡

I arrived in Sierra Leone just weeks after spending six months in Manila advising the UN Country Team and the Government of the Philippines on shelter aspects of their recovery from the world's largest Tropical Cyclone, *Typhoon Yolanda*. A few months later, I found myself on the Turkish-Syrian border, once more with DFID from where I was then dispatched to the British Embassy in Kathmandu after Nepal was devastated by a series of earthquakes and landslides.

Four countries in a little over twelve months is not unusual for a disaster management consultant like me; just enough time to build a relationship with those you are advising, and then move on, hoping that you have made a difference. Despite the Ebola debacle, the three Reality Checks that follow hopefully demonstrate that my particular field, that of *disaster epidemiology*, sometimes does make that difference.

✦

While catching up on my reading on a long-haul flight from New York to Seoul, I learned about how people die in earthquake-induced building collapses, specifically about asphyxiation and the role played by dust inhalation.

I hadn't even got off the plane when my phone rang. It was the office, telling me to take the next available flight to Kobe in Japan rather than return to Bangkok which I was planning to do. The mega-tsunami of 2011 that killed over 26,000 people had taken place only a matter of weeks earlier and I was now to represent the UN at a Planning Workshop with the Japanese Ministry of Health. This sort of last-minute scheduling change was not unusual in the humanitarian world, so I sent a few hurried e-mails postponing various meetings, picked up my new ticket, and checked in for the next available flight to Kobe.

The three-day meeting was fascinating. At some point during the second day, I had argued quite vociferously that using 15,000 troops to find 5,000 missing bodies after a tsunami was perhaps not the best use of resources when, a) tens of thousands of people needed urgent shelter, and b) the bodies of approximately one-fifth of tsunami victims are never found, having either been obliterated by the millions of tons of churning coral, rocks, and rubble that constitutes a tsunami, or because they have been washed out to sea to become turtle food[5]. Interestingly – and perhaps coincidentally – the county's civil defence force was re-tasked to clear rubble and build shelter a few days later.

---

[5] All over the world, communities affected by the 2004 tsunami refused to eat locally caught fish for months after the disaster.

Lunch on the third and final day was a formal affair and took place in the dining room of Kobe's National Earthquake Museum next door to the conference centre. As it happened, my accommodation was being sponsored by the government so was in the same building. Having noticed the early warning system by my bed and the helmet hanging behind the door, and respecting what had happened in the city in 1995, I began to talk about earthquakes. It was, after all, a sub-sea, mega-thrust earthquake that had triggered the tsunami we were there to discuss.

Encouraged by what I had gleaned from my data dump about earthquakes, cement dust and asphyxiation while travelling to the meeting three days earlier, I was keen to know why a twenty dollar helmet did not contain a twenty cent dust-mask. I thought if anyone knew the answer to this question it would be the Japanese, especially their public health officials from Kobe, and especially in the country that seemed to wear dust-masks all the time anyway. Much to my surprise – and much to their embarrassment – they did not know the answer to this. But we spent an interesting half-hour discussing the contents of the paper I had so recently read, before returning to more germane topics.

I thought no more about this until, nearly three years later, and when working in the Philippines on the Typhoon Haiyan/Yolanda response, I bumped into the Red Cross delegate who was also at that lunchtime discussion. He told me that the Japanese government had looked into the matter following our discussions, and had just recently passed a law making it obligatory to insert a dust-mask into every helmet behind every hotel door in the land.

⟡

The next opportunity for my researches to influence government policy happened about eighteen months later. I had been talking to one of the laboratories at Columbia University in New York looking at new ways of determining whether cholera vibrio were present in drinking water. The idea had something to do with genetically modified yeast whose implanted tomato genes would turn red in the presence of cholera … interesting, ingenious, and potentially life-saving research.

In the midst of these discussions, I was dispatched to Sierra Leone to advise the President's office in Freetown on how best to prepare for, and manage a cholera control programme. It was late 2012 and this poor, broken country was suffering yet another devastating cholera outbreak. In my conversations with Columbia, we had discussed the role of technology in predicting just such an event, and it involved satellites as well as their 'red yeast'.

Essentially, the idea hinged around the fact that satellite imagery can be used to detect algal blooms in estuaries in certain parts of the world where cholera is endemic. This includes the West African coast where marine algae turn up as bright red blotches on images taken by infrared cameras in space. Since many major cholera epidemics start in such estuaries and appear to follow such blooms a couple of weeks later, it is possible that remote sensing by satellite could be used to predict where and when these might happen.

Algal blooms come about when a 'perfect storm' of particular environmental conditions are met. These include raised surface sea-water temperature, reduced salinity, increased nutrient concentration, and contamination with human faeces. Depending on rainfall patterns inland, these conditions come about every eight years or so and just happen to be the same conditions that stimulate the production of cholera vibrio, of which there are over 130 different types, and all of which live in the sea.

Initially, the President's health adviser – later to become the Minister of Health dealing with the Ebola epidemic – was sceptical. But when I put her in touch with the International Strategy for Disaster Reduction and the UN's remote sensing office, UNOSAT, in Geneva, and they confirmed that remote sensing of this sort was indeed possible, an amendment was made to the country's disease surveillance and early warning protocols for cholera outbreaks. The system has yet to be tested in anger, but let's hope that the few days of additional warning time this technology could bring is enough to prevent a repeat of what happened in 2012 when 836 people died.

✦

Thirdly, and more recently, government emergency response policy to typhoons in the Philippines was changed following a presentation I made in May 2014 to the Department for Social Welfare and Development, in Manila.

The maximum Category-5 super-typhoon known internationally as *Haiyan* but locally as *Yolanda*, had smashed into the southern Philippines six months earlier at 5 o'clock in the morning on Friday 8th

November 2013. With sustained wind speeds of 280 kilometres per hour (175 mph) and gusts of up to 378 kph (235 mph), this was the strongest and largest tropical cyclone ever to make landfall. Over 6,500 people had died from the impact of wind-blown debris, from drowning in the storm-surge pushed ahead of this monster, and later from injuries and infections. Over six million people had been made homeless in the course of a few hours, all that they owned scattered to the four winds. Over thirty million coconut trees had been uprooted and lay flattened across an area the size of the whole of the United Kingdom.

By the time I arrived in Tacloban, the coastal town hardest hit by *Yolanda*, the radio waves were full of talk – as they always are a few weeks after such types of disaster – about the threat posed by cholera and typhoid. When I met the Mayor, a tall and elegant man called Alfred Romualdez, this was his main preoccupation. In our first meeting, ostensibly to talk about tents, tarpaulins, and the need to relocate people away from coastal danger zones, I spent most of my time explaining to him how vaccination against cholera was expensive and unnecessary given that an outbreak was extremely unlikely. His time and money would be better spent, I said, on reiterating to his people the virtues of hand-washing with soap and on chlorinating the town's water supply. I told him, too, how an outbreak of malaria was also extremely unlikely, at least for the next few months, and that he should be more concerned about those scrambling through the wreckage of their former homes contracting tetanus or being exposed to the longer-term threat posed by asbestos in the dust.

Our next meeting took place at midnight on Christmas Eve. I had joined most of the international aid community at a 'midnight mass' in the town's small cathedral, not so much to celebrate Jesus's birth but to commemorate those thousands who had died just a few weeks before. The cathedral's roof had blown off in the typhoon and had been patched up with donated tarpaulins which were now flapping noisily in the winds of yet another approaching storm. Rain was pouring down the walls to flood the aisle, and we stood to sing carols ankle-deep in running water. Everyone in the congregation had lost a friend or relative, yet here we all were amidst the 'smells, bells and candles' clapping and singing. The service epitomised the *"tin dog"* (can-do/stand tall) spirit of Tacloban's survivors and had been a very emotional experience, even for those who were not particularly religious. Alfred grabbed me as I was leaving and asked me to walk with him to the small reception he was holding at the Town Hall. As we walked through the dark and mud-encrusted streets, I told him about

25

how cyclonic winds in the Northern hemisphere are much more powerful, and cut a much wider swathe of damage over the ground, north of a typhoon's track than to its south. The immediate practical implication, I explained, being that, when there are not enough resources to go round, focusing initial relief efforts on windward areas to the north of track, including along exposed low-lying coastal areas vulnerable to the effects of storm-surge, is likely to have the greatest impact, as it is here that the potential for preventing a second wave of death is greatest.

Alfred attended a meeting a few months later in Manila where he heard me present the same theory, this time with some preliminary evidence from a shelter cluster survey commissioned to corroborate what I had been talking about. He came up afterwards to thank me again for these insights and explained to the ministers present how this was indeed what had happened in his town, Tacloban. Despite the regularity with which the Philippines is impacted by life-threatening storms, none of them were previously aware of any of this. To cut a long story short, the Department of Science and Technology duly confirmed the cluster's findings – now triangulated by separate data from the health cluster which came to the same conclusion – with the result that initial search, rescue and relief efforts in the Philippines now routinely concentrate resources to the north of a Typhoon's track.

I often reflect on how privileged I am to have travelled the world in the course of my humanitarian work and, in so doing, to have accumulated this sort of knowledge.

These three stories also confirmed for me that long-held disaster myths needed challenging. Many of the senior government decision-makers I was fortunate enough to be meeting in the course of my day job appeared to be benefiting from this sort of information, too, as were all those working around me who I had wrongly assumed already knew all this stuff.

It was becoming clear that *disaster epidemiology* in the widest sense of the term was somehow resonating in a way it hadn't before.

Initially, I didn't intend to spend much time looking at trends in such things as 'frequency of disaster' or to make more than passing reference to that hot potato called *Climate Change*, despite it being one of the fundamental risk drivers on the planet; I thought there was enough out there already on these topics … in fact, it was hard to open a newspaper and not read about them. Instead, I wanted to tell the story of natural disasters: What they are, and what they're not; who dies, who doesn't, and why. I wanted to explore the darker, unknown side of what happens when natural hazards collide with human indifference to cause catastrophe. I wanted to know why, when we know exactly how to stop people dying unnecessarily, we continue to allow natural disasters to happen in the first place.

I wanted to challenge the half-truths and misperceptions that still tend to define humanitarian action today.

Thinking this would be a relatively iterative process focused mainly on what they call *international health*, it quickly became more than that, as to truly lift the lid on what was going on meant engaging in aspects of management, economics, and even philosophy and psychology that I hadn't thought hard enough about before. For example, disaster management is expensive and costs the same whether it is done well or done badly. Done badly, however, the cost is measured in wasted lives not just wasted money. And, if there isn't enough money to save everybody, who do you save? Does life have a price? Is charity always a good thing, or does it have unforeseen consequences which can actually do harm? Do people understand the risks facing them, and, if they do, do they make rational choices about how to protect themselves and their loved ones? Should humanitarian funds be used to deal with the after-effects of disaster when the government has already been provided with adequate funding to prevent the disaster from happening in the first place?

All these make up what the disaster management community refers to as the *humanitarian dilemma*. But dealing with the aftermath of disaster is no morality play. It is brutal. Disaster managers make life and death decisions all day, every day, and as a result end up "playing God" more often than they would like. When all is said and done, if charity represents how people would like the world to work, then *Absolute Disasters* demonstrates how it actually does.

Unnatural Disaster

1 *The frequency of natural disasters is decreasing, not increasing.*

Hardly a day goes by when we are not assaulted by imagery of one type of disaster or another unfolding somewhere on the planet. Given the voracious appetite of modern 24/7 news media and the number of potentially hazardous events being unleashed by Mother Nature – somewhere in the order of 4,000 earthquakes, 8.6 million lightning strikes, and 50 meteorites impact our planet every single day, for example – the only surprise is that more of these events don't kill more people. Yet, despite the headlines, the number of natural disasters taking place on our planet every year is actually declining.

This seems to come as a surprise to most people. What we have to realise when trying to understand trends and patterns in the disaster data is that it is one thing to say – as most formal analyses on the subject of natural disasters wrongly tend to do – that disasters are becoming more frequent, but it is quite another to say that natural hazard events are occurring more frequently. There is, after all, a big difference between the number of natural hazard events taking place (the denominator) and how many of these events go on to become disasters (the numerator). Confusing the two terms merely serves to convey a false impression of what is going on, especially when, in its quest to inform and entertain, the media give the impression that there are far more going on than actually are, and when, in their need to raise funds, relief agencies say the same. The fact is, those who should know better too often allow myths to get in the way of the maths.

The world experiences an average of 385 natural disasters every year.

Despite wildfires, heat waves, floods, and even asteroids seeming to be in the news constantly, the number of natural hazard events posing a threat to human life has remained more or less constant at around 4,000 per year according to the London School of Economics. Of these, the world experiences an average of 385 natural disasters every year, or slightly more than one disaster per day. At its peak, the annual average was 450[6].

---

[6] Based on data from the international EM-DAT disaster database at the Catholic University of Louvain in Brussels, Belgium, and using decadal averages i.e the five years before and after the peak year of 2002, and the 10 years prior to 2013.

Approximately one disaster per week requires significant external support and might warrant a passing mention on the evening news, and two per year require worldwide mobilisation of humanitarian resources, thereby meriting rather more airtime. Mega-disasters[7] – the ones like Haiti's earthquake in 2010, or the Philippine's typhoon in 2013 that dominate the news for days or even weeks – thankfully occur even less frequently, taking place at the rate of one every two or three years.

Number of Worldwide Natural Disasters Reported
(50 years 1965-2014)

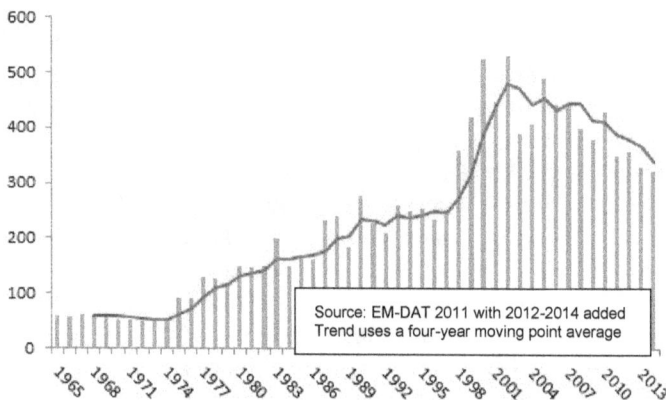

Source: EM-DAT 2011 with 2012-2014 added
Trend uses a four-year moving point average

The curve in the graph above appears to show a clear decrease in the annual number of disasters over the past decade or so, with a year-on-year reduction in all but one of the last 10 years and eight being below the decadal average. Not only that, but with 335 recorded disasters, 2013 witnessed the lowest number of disasters since the turn-of-the-century, being 75 less than the decadal average of 410 and nearly 200 less than the record number of 530 set in 2002. Although the number of events during the past decade might be nothing more than a statistical anomaly – what is ten years in geological time, after all – it seems clear that the number of disasters per year peaked around the turn-of-the-century and has been decreasing ever since.

If we unpack the data since the year 2000 a little further, we see that, with one notable exception, all trends in the incidence of different

---

[7] 'Mega-disasters' are catastrophes of exceptional magnitude which cause unprecedented death, destruction, or displacement. This would imply over 100,000 people dying in a single event or more than 1 million being displaced over slightly longer timescales. It might also include slow-onset but large-scale events such as a famine.

categories of natural disaster reflect this overall decline. With the exception of floods[8], the frequencies of other types of natural disaster have been reducing.

Perhaps even more surprising is that, although there were more floods during this period, there were correspondingly fewer storms, meaning that there was no net increase overall in weather-related events.

2. *Risk reduction measures are paying off.*

The causes behind declines in frequency of natural disaster are complex, and are quite different for different types of disaster and across different regions. In general, however – and accepting that the current state of scientific research on the differential impact of disasters on prepared and un-prepared communities does not allow for much in the way of causal association – there are probably three main reasons for this:

The first is that risk reduction measures being taken by governments in disaster-prone areas are paying off. The same number of natural hazard events – or more – is resulting in fewer disasters because people are better prepared than they were before, especially in the areas of physical infrastructure, early warning, stockpiling, and first aid training.

The second is that pro-poor development policies only indirectly related to managing disaster risk – such as education, for example – have had more of an impact on reducing human vulnerability than previously assumed.

And the third is that public health programmes not directly related to disaster preparedness may be exerting a more significant effect in the medium and long term on those affected by natural disaster than we previously knew. Where pre-disaster immunisation coverage rates for Tetanus are high, for example, very few people are likely to die from this otherwise fatal disease when disaster strikes.

---

[8] Detailed examination of EM-DAT data over the last five years indicates that the number of floods may actually also have decreased despite the fact that they still account for about 145 of all disasters around the world per year.

3   *'Disaster Epidemiology' is about much more than population health.*

This book challenges and expands the traditional definition of *disaster epidemiology*, a discipline which, until now, has been mostly concerned with the impact of ill-health on disaster-affected populations.

Measuring the scale of disaster by knowing how many people died might give us a rough guide as to the severity of the problem and heighten the drama of an event for the casual observer, but it does not help those involved with managing disaster risk in determining the overall impact in terms of direct and indirect effects over the short, medium, and longer term. Nor does it help in defining the underlying causes and associations. And, if the detail is poorly understood, the wrong prevention, mitigation, response, and recovery strategies are likely to be the result, meaning that we learn nothing and more people are affected who could otherwise be saved next time.

Governmental and non-governmental agencies have always been pivotal in disaster planning and response, and are increasingly seeing the need for a more evidence-based approach to the way disaster risk is managed, based on the wide but fragmented body of knowledge which has accumulated through case studies, post-disaster evaluations, and lessons learning exercises. *Disaster Epidemiology* is the relatively new and emerging discipline which provides that evidence.

An average of 357 people per day die somewhere in the world from the impacts of natural disaster.

Despite being primarily concerned with public health aspects of disaster, the discipline covers additional aspects of the planning and operational process, from supplying global level trend analysis; through supporting post-disaster needs assessment at national level; to informing first responders of those applications which are most appropriate and most cost-effective at the local level; and even by suggesting which management processes render the overall prevention, response, and recovery effort more effective.

It is, in other words, more than just about death and destruction.

Death and destruction does not occur randomly but in patterns that can be predicted. Disaster epidemiology is therefore not just about determining how, when, and where people died or were otherwise affected in a disaster. Nor is it just about destruction and money. It's about the art and science of investigating patterns in natural hazard events in time and space, and defining their impact on specific groups of people in order to prevent such things from happening again. Given the likely future consequences, it is also about prioritisation and making the best use of scarce resources before and after disaster strikes.

An average of 357[9] people per day die somewhere in the world from the impacts of natural disaster. This is in addition to those who will die anyway from other causes. Today in Bangladesh, for example, 83 children from the age of 1-17 will die from injuries un-related to natural disasters: Nearly 50 will drown, 9 will die in road traffic accidents, and 7 will die from some form of animal bite. Another 36 will be disabled having had amputations that could have been avoided had correct first aid been provided at the scene of the accident[ii]. These figures provide some sort of everyday baseline against which the one-off and extraordinary impact of natural disasters can be measured.

Similarly, disaster epidemiology should record the number of hazard events taking place in a specified area (the state, the country, or the world) and *then* the number that go on to become disasters. But we don't. We only hear about the number of disasters in a certain place or over a certain time. Furthermore, it is never made clear what proportion of those exposed is actually affected, and it is this proportionality that helps planners understand where the priorities really lie. Twenty houses destroyed, for example, might be devastating for the twenty families involved but would prompt a different response if they represented 50% of a village with 40 houses than if they represented 0.1% of a town with 20,000. This is why *damage density* is as important as absolute damage.

This failure to apply the basic rules of scientific investigation can give a false sense of what is going on around us. We really should know the answer to the question, "Are there more hurricanes?" before asking, "Are there more people being killed by hurricanes?" for example.

The impact of a natural disaster is measured in terms of death, injury, economic loss, and a rather woollier metric about 'affected' populations[10]. The causal factors will not all be health related, however. Compliance with zoning regulations and building codes are as much a risk factor for avoidable death and destruction in an earthquake, for

---

[9] 280 reported and officially recorded by CRED + 65 from lightning (un-reported) + 12 from unreported landslides.

[10] An 'affected population' consists of all those who, at least for a time, lost − or lost access to − some or all of their homes, crops, animals, livelihoods, or health as a direct or indirect result of a natural hazard event.

example, as are whether or not evacuation drills have been included in the school curriculum. This means that disaster epidemiology cannot confine itself to the health sector only, but must provide insight into the totality of cause and effect within and between all sectors; from nutrition to education; from shelter to food security; from water and sanitation to communicating with communities; and from early warning to prevention.

Shelter, for example, is often ranked by disaster-affected populations as their number one priority after access to safe drinking water. Typically this will take the form of a tarpaulin or a tent in the first phase of response supplemented by salvaged building materials. It's not a matter of dignity; it's a matter of thermal protection. Even in freezing weather, a suitably insulated tent will prevent people dying from the cold. But, with such forms of temporary shelter come other hazards: If inadequately ventilated, people die, and

Each disaster has its own profile and pathology. in large numbers, from the fumes of kerosene-burning stoves and from the burns sustained when they are knocked over. Wood-smoke causes acute respiratory infections. And living huddled under blankets gives rise to skin diseases. The extent to which shelter is adequate or not can be measured in terms of adverse health outcomes such as these.

Each type of disaster has its own profile and pathology, though, and these similarities and differences are crucial when it comes to planning, designing, and implementing prevention activities and in executing response programmes. For example, knowing that *attack rates*[11] for those diseases found amongst disaster victims in each different type of disaster can help determine what kind of supplies, equipment, and personnel are most urgently needed is useful, but knowing that ingestion of cholera-laden seawater into the lungs after a tsunami gives rise to a particular kind of pneumonia; that inhalation of concrete dust after an earthquake gives rise to another; that dialysis is required to treat crush injuries after a landslide; or that snake bite is potentially one of the biggest killers of children in a flood is just as important.

This basic science of disaster epidemiology consists of four analytic components – the 4P's – which are common to all forms of disaster-related investigation:

---

[11] 'Attack Rate' refers to the number of people infected with a disease divided by the total number of people exposed. If 70 people are taken ill out of 98 in an outbreak, the Attack Rate is 70÷98 = 0.714 or 71%.

- **Prevalence**[12] of natural hazard events
- **Patterns** of distribution and magnitude in time and space
- **Physical** and behavioural causes that transform a naturally occurring event into a disaster
- **Price** in terms of the opportunity cost of not taking alternative preventive measures

Each of these components confers an important message about the profile and pattern of each type of disaster which may then suggest counter-measures that prevent or, to some extent anyway, mitigate their effects.

4 · *Natural Disasters are far from 'natural'.*

A 'natural' disaster is a naturally occurring hazard event which just happens to kill people. To be officially recorded, it must kill ten or more, or cause significant damage[13]. A tornado sweeping through the American mid-West without killing anyone or causing significant damage won't be logged as a disaster.

The term 'natural disaster' is somewhat ambiguous in that it is particularly difficult at times to distinguish between what is *natural* and what could be deemed to have been *man-made*. The devastating toll on Haiti of four hurricanes in 2008 was primarily the result of natural phenomena, for example, but their impact was undoubtedly exacerbated by years of de-forestation and poor governmental policy-making. In fact, in that year, severe hurricanes struck both Haiti and Cuba, but while 698 people died in Haiti, only 7 fatalities were reported in Cuba[iii].

The term is also ambiguous in another sense, in that it is particularly difficult at times to distinguish between a *man-made* and a *technological* event. The distinction between natural disasters and those caused by

---

[12] In epidemiology, prevalence is the total number of cases of a disease in a given population over a specific period of time. In disaster epidemiology, prevalence is the annual number of a specific category of disaster (globally or in a specified region) averaged over the past 10 years (author's definition).

[13] According to CRED, a natural hazard event is considered to be a disaster if at least one of the following criteria is fulfilled: Ten or more people are reported killed; 100 people are reported as being 'affected'; a state of emergency has been declared; or an appeal for international assistance has been made.

humans is therefore somewhat blurred, especially when a single hazard event such as an earthquake triggers a secondary event such as a tsunami which goes on to knock out a nuclear facility or petro-chemical plant, the spilled fuel-oil from which then goes on to cause widespread fires and poison the environment.

Another definitional problem is the relationship between *sudden-onset* and *slow-onset* events. While floods, hurricanes, and earthquakes occur with little advance warning, it may take months or years for droughts or environmental degradation to overwhelm those living in the affected area. While the difference between the two makes intuitive sense, there is no consensus on where the dividing line between sudden- and slow-onset disasters is to be drawn. For example, flooding, even though it is usually considered a sudden-onset disaster, sometimes occurs over a period of weeks or months, as in Pakistan in mid-2010.

All disaster deaths are ambiguous, too. What is meant by this is that mortality studies focus on people who clearly died or were injured as a direct result of a specific hazardous event. But many deaths occur months or even years after that same specific event from indirect causes, like emphysema from inhaling asbestos fibres in the dust after an earthquake, or suicide from mental stress having been displaced far from known communities. Because establishing cause and effect in such cases is highly subjective, these deaths remain unnoticed and become part of the disaster's hidden cost.

In almost all cases, a complex interplay between these physical factors and the way people behave is what actually determines who lives and who dies.

5   *'More people' does not necessarily mean more people in harm's way.*

The same number of hazard events of similar intensity in one place in any given year will surely result in more disasters if the population in that same area has expanded. We assume an expanding population means more people potentially exposed, and that these extra people are just as vulnerable as before. But they are *not* necessarily more vulnerable, and therefore not necessarily more *at risk*. They might have taken robust measures to prevent or at least mitigate the threat posed by the hazard they knew was facing them ... by building basement shelters, for example, in known tornado-prone areas, or seismic-resistant hospitals in areas of known earthquake risk. Or they might have become more resilient by teaching each other how to treat physical injuries amongst their neighbours should the worst happen.

6   *Disaster responses cannot wait for perfect data.*

In epidemiology, the process of identifying the underlying cause of a disease is a multi-step process. The first step is to determine whether an association exists between exposure to a factor such as a bug or a person's particular behavioural characteristic, and progression of the disease in question. If we find there is indeed an association between exposure, susceptibility, and development of the disease, is it necessarily a causal relationship? No, because not all associations are causal.

The second step, therefore, is to try to derive appropriate inferences about a possible causal relationship from the patterns of the associations that have been found. The third step is to see whether there is a trend in its distribution. Disaster epidemiology applies much of the same basic science to hazards as well as disasters and their aftermaths.

Unfortunately, however, the data around disasters are soft and noisy. This means that the scientific methodologies used to collect and/or crunch the numbers are either weak, or the analysis more subjective than they should be, or both.

Richard Feynman, one of the world's best-known physicists back in the 1960's, was as much philosopher as he was theoretical physicist. He used to say that "science is believing the ignorance of experts." He was also vocal about the way society increasingly expects science to do something it cannot. That is, to characterise highly complex and dynamic systems in terms of linear, unambiguous causes and effects that 'left-brained' thinkers[14] such as engineers and doctors can understand, replicate, and apply in the real world. Given that there are many engineers and health professionals in the disaster business, this lack of linearity can confound those trying to apply the evidence in the best way possible when all around is chaos.

Natural disasters are some of the most complex and dynamic 'systems' imaginable, and their effects might not be felt for years after the event. Capturing scientific data is not only complicated at the best of times, but almost impossible in the hurly-burly of a full-on disaster

---

[14] Left-brained people tend to be more analytical, logical, mathematically and scientifically inclined, concise, and detail oriented.

response. Many aspects of disaster, by their nature, don't lend themselves to study. The lack of time and money to organise surveys, the high turnover of aid agency volunteers, dynamic population movements to, from, and within disaster zones, and competing life-saving priorities, all make it difficult to conduct quality research in such settings.

This means that data-sets are limited. And the smaller the data-set, the less truly representative it will be, and therefore the greater the leap of faith required when extrapolating from them, let alone making decisions based on them. But statistics deal in probabilities, not certainties. And, where there is probability, there is always the possibility of the unlikely. Nevertheless, this makes it difficult to apply the scientific rigour required for academic publication.

Natural disasters are some of the most complex and dynamic systems imaginable.

Much of the evidence that does exist lies un-published as so-called "grey literature" in the dusty cupboards of university faculties, NGO programme departments, and reinsurance companies. Conflicting information and false conclusions litter the disaster landscape as a result. This is what Vin Scully meant when he said, "One should use data the way a drunk uses a lamp post … for support, but not for illumination". Numbers, then, are little more than guides and can sometimes be interpreted to mean whatever the observer wants them to mean.

Furthermore, any trend analysis is highly dependent on which definitions are applied at each stage of the investigative process. This is especially true in the field of the 'disaster sciences' where ambiguities abound and the talk is about trends and patterns in data sets which are comparatively limited given the millennia over which natural hazards have been evolving.

The downturn in frequency of natural disasters talked about in this book may be real and may reflect real underlying causes, or it may be nothing more than random statistical noise in the same way that tossing a coin can randomly come up 'tails' five times in a row. It is therefore better to look for trends rather than precise figures in disaster data. Partly, this is because the definitions used are vague. Partly, too, it's because figures are culled from newspaper reports, NGO surveys, and insurance company returns, as well as from statements made by government departments, all of which can be wildly inaccurate.

7 *Natural disasters are becoming less, not more, deadly.*

Patuakhali is a fairly typical fishing village in the flood-prone coastal sunderbans of Bangladesh. Like all other villages in this vast delta of the Brahmaputra river, it is periodically threatened by man-eating tigers. During the cyclone *Sidr* disaster response of 2007/2008, it was pointed out to the village chief that over 300 children die from diarrhoea around the world every hour, many of them as a result of flies transmitting bugs when landing on exposed food and insufficient washing of hands with soap. Understandably more concerned with the immediate threat of being eaten, the village elder seemed less than impressed. However, after a thoughtful pause, he remarked, "if this is true, one fly has the potential to kill more children than all the tigers in Bangladesh". The point about this story is not the flies or the diarrhoea, but to point out that, despite appearances, some threats are perceived to be more deadly than others.

The average number of deaths per disaster now stands at 228, and is falling steadily.

What the story does not point out is that the number of people dying in this part of the world from the direct and indirect effects of the tropical cyclones that sweep in regularly from the sea has reduced markedly over the years. Nor does it point out that this is true of the world in general, as natural hazard events everywhere are becoming significantly less deadly as people learn how to mitigate the risks facing them.

In the past decade, more than 2.2 billion people worldwide were affected by 4,484 natural disasters. These disasters killed close to 840,000 people – equivalent of one third of the planet's population – and cost at least $891 billion in economic damage. These disasters have claimed an average of somewhere in the region of 100,000 lives per year[15] over this time. It is interesting to note, though, that the average number of deaths per disaster has been steadily decreasing over this same period[iv] and now stands at 228. As with all global figures, these numbers hide the fact that in rich countries the average number of deaths per disaster is 23, while in the poorest the average is 1,052[v].

---

[15] Actually the figure fluctuates between 98,816 and 108,705 depending on whose data you are looking at.

Of course, these figures are in themselves rather meaningless, as they tell us nothing about trends or disaster impact at country level ... the level at which action is decided and taken. But it does remind us that this is equivalent to a packed jumbo jet crashing every day, killing everyone aboard. It also provides some sort of perspective, as they amount to less than a twelfth of those dying from malaria or the number of children drowning around the world every year.

To lend even more perspective, we must remember that disease epidemics have killed by far the largest number of people of any disaster type during the past two millennia. Smallpox was responsible for an estimated 300 million deaths during the 20th Century alone, while a similar number of deaths are attributed to the Bubonic Plague epidemics that occurred in the 6th Century, the 14th through the 18th Centuries, and the mid-19th through the mid-20th Centuries. The Spanish flu pandemic of 1918-1919 killed an estimated 50-100 million people worldwide in only two years.

Apart from epidemics, other types of natural disaster caused 62 million deaths throughout the world during the 20th Century, with 85% of those deaths occurring during the first half. The largest improvements came from declines in mortality due to droughts and floods, which, together, were responsible for 93% of all deaths. Over half of the deaths associated with natural hazards from 1900–2004 were due to drought.

Overall, earthquakes are the largest cause of death from natural disasters[16], accounting for approximately half (58%) of all disaster-related fatalities worldwide, whereas floods account for one third (32%) and storms another third (31%) respectively. Over the past fifty years, about 85% of the 1.5 million deaths from earthquakes worldwide have been caused by the ten largest[vi]. In 2010, for example, five times as many people died in a single day in the Haiti earthquake than in all the disasters around the world during the whole of the year before *and* the year after.

In 2010 – the worst year for natural disaster since 1983 in terms of the numbers killed around the world – 344 out of the 373 recorded disasters (92%) were weather or water-related. The 182 reported floods affected almost 180 million people and killed more than 8,100. This is almost double the average number of people affected every year by floods.

---

[16] Seismic events killed an average of 50,184 people per year during the period 2000-2008.

2010 was also a particularly deadly year for those affected by landslides and avalanches, which together killed 3,258 persons compared to an average of 763 persons killed per year in the preceding decade.

The largest six events accounted for more than half of all disaster-related deaths during the past decade.

Despite the recent spate of deadly extreme weather events – such as the 2010 Russian heat wave, floods in Thailand, and the near record-breaking 2011 tornado season in the US – the number of people dying or being injured by extreme weather events has declined by more than 90% since the 1920's in spite of a four-fold rise in population and more systematic reporting of such events since then. And in East Asia and the Pacific, two of the regions most exposed to weather-related hazards, the risk of dying from weather-related events has fallen by one third since 1980[vii].

The risk of dying from a weather-related event has fallen by one third since 1980.

According to the World Bank, these reductions in all-cause mortality are largely down to the success of mitigation measures such as more accurate long-range weather forecasting, more sophisticated early warning systems, better education, and the building of more robust infrastructure. They are also attributable to increases in thermal protection afforded by access to fossil fuels, improved agricultural practices (including irrigation), better disaster preparedness, and more rapid delivery of humanitarian aid by ever-increasing numbers of international relief agencies[17]. These improvements, which occurred despite increases in the populations at risk, can be attributed largely to the combination of greater economic development and technological change. Together they enable society to protect against and cope with adversity in general, and extreme weather events in particular.

Seven out of the top 10 countries in terms of people killed by natural disasters are located in Asia, and accounted for 83% of global reported disaster mortality, while the other three countries are located in the Americas. However, when looking at disaster mortality relative to the number of inhabitants in the country, it is the African continent that appears in the top ten ranking.

---

[17] The number of registered international relief NGOs has risen from less than 1,000 in 1945 when the UN was formed, to over 40,000 currently.

8   *On average, less than 100,000 people die each year around the world from the immediate effects of natural disaster.*

According to the World Health Organisation's collaborating centre for disaster epidemiology at the University of Louvain in Belgium, natural disasters have claimed an average of 98,816 lives per year over the last decade (although some other universities and insurance companies have put the figure slightly higher). To give you some context, this is about one fifth of worldwide deaths from malaria every year, and one twelfth the number of children that drown. For reference, Ebola in West Africa killed just over 11,000 people during the course of the 2014-2015 epidemic.

9   *The numbers of those displaced by the effects of natural disaster is not increasing ... not yet.*

We often hear about the millions of people 'affected' by disaster. But what does this mean? There is a massive difference, after all, between floodwaters washing away a bridge to make movement difficult, and a landslide burying an entire village. Yet both communities are deemed to have been 'affected'. Some people will have been affected for a few weeks or months, some for years, and others forever. And some of those affected might actually have been affected positively ... the farmer whose land is rendered more fertile by the soil deposited from upstream during a flood, for example.

One in ten of the world's population has been affected by disaster over the past decade.

Displacement, on the other hand, even for relatively short periods of time, can have serious long-term implications for health and livelihood, and probably constitutes a more realistic measure of a disaster's impact than the rather looser term 'affected'. Being affected by disaster does not necessarily result in displacement. In 2011, for example, natural disasters triggered the displacement of over 15 million people which was less than 15% of those affected. In 2010, the figure was 42 million, the figures lunging from peak to trough depending on whether or not a mega-disaster has occurred.

Somewhat paradoxically, while major investments in disaster preparedness and response over recent decades have resulted in a decline in the number of fatalities per disaster, population growth and relocation – often into areas of greater risk – have seen more people overall being *affected* by disasters. Furthermore, while the numbers of those affected appears to be rising worldwide, the numbers displaced appears to be reducing[viii].

Over the past 50 years, an average of roughly 130 million people have been affected every year by natural disasters[ix], the vast majority of whom (98%) are from nations of low or medium human development. This is seven times more than the number of people affected by conflict over the same period. This statistic hides the fact that the number of people affected by natural disasters each year nearly quadrupled between the 1975-1984 decade and the first decade of the new millennium[x]. In the past decade alone, more than 2.2 billion people – equivalent to one third of the planet's population – have been affected by natural disasters of one type or another; 44% by floods, 30% by drought and 4% by earthquakes. In the 1960's, 1 in 138 people worldwide were affected by natural hazards, compared to 1 in 28 in the last decade.

In Asia, where 80% of the world's disasters are concentrated, the number of people directly impacted by natural hazard events has dropped, decade-on-decade, by almost one billion, owing to measures like the Indian Ocean tsunami early-warning system. Timely evacuations in the face of accurately forecast major storm systems have also enabled the Philippines and India to save thousands of lives.

Meanwhile, Turkey will have earthquake-proofed every school and hospital in the country by 2017. Ethiopia has developed a sophisticated data-management system to help guide its efforts to address not only drought but also other natural hazards. Both countries – and many others – have incorporated the study of disaster risk into their school curricula and carry out regular first-responder and evacuation drills.

That said, there is no room for complacency as the drivers of disaster risk – improper land use, urbanisation, poorly implemented building codes, environmental degradation, poverty, climate change, and, most important, weak governance by inappropriate and insufficient institutions – still abound. More can be done. In the last 44 years, disasters caused by weather, climate, and water-related hazards have led to 3.5 million deaths. With the correct mitigation measures, most of these lives could have been saved.

10 More people are killed in un-reported 'mini-disasters' every year than by the big ones we hear about.

Hidden in the glare of TV spotlights that congregate in mega-disaster zones, there is a world of smaller lesser-known emergencies that we never hear about because they are considered too small to be registered in global databases. Small-scale disasters might be high intensity hazard events of short duration, or low intensity events of longer duration, but which, whether they occur in densely or sparsely populated areas, nevertheless kill fewer than ten people or affect less than one hundred. In 90% of recorded natural disasters, more than 10 but fewer than 50 people are killed. In two thirds of natural disasters, fewer than five people are killed[xi]. These mini-disasters get less attention, but they add up to greater combined losses.

Take the case of Colombia, where researchers catalogued more than 19,000 small and moderate natural hazard events through the last 30 years that, even though they did not meet the international criteria for a disaster, nevertheless took lives and destroyed assets and infrastructure. In fact, while only 97 disasters were recorded during the same thirty year period, the total loss in financial terms of these smaller events, few of which even made it into the national press, far less the international media, was greater than all of the high profile disasters taken together[xii].

Fewer than five people are killed per event in two thirds of the world's natural disasters.

There is a growing body of anecdotal evidence to say that the frequency of these types of event is increasing, and there are NGOs on the record as saying that they are responding to more and more of these types of disasters around the world[18]. But is this a solution in search of a problem? Are there more hazard events and/or more people in harm's way? Or, is it just that there are more NGOs seeking more events to

---

[18] For example, Save the Children UK, whose humanitarian director said in 2011, "Year on year, we are responding more frequently and on a larger scale to an increasing number of disasters".

respond to? With the observational data currently available – which suggests that neither the overall number of natural hazard events *nor* the disasters they give rise to, have risen – there is only one viable conclusion: we are observing, and consequently responding to, more mini-disasters that had previously gone un-noticed.

11 — *Natural disasters are not random events.*

There is a structure to the location, timing, and magnitude of natural hazards, especially seismic events which, for the most part, take place on or near known fault lines in the Earth's crust. Equally, while it is difficult to predict the path a tropical cyclone will take, we know one cannot form within 5° latitude north or south of the equator. This implies that 'natural' disasters are not as random and unavoidable as we are led to believe, and cannot be randomly distributed around the world.

An average of 1,052 people die in any given disaster in a poor country, compared to just 23 in a rich one.

Furthermore, disasters, when they come, strike the poor and marginalised disproportionately – especially women, children, the disabled, and the elderly – so are not randomly distributed across populations. The poor are most 'at risk' in a natural hazard event because they are the ones that are least able to afford earthquake-, flood-, or wind-proof housing. The poor are less well educated about appropriate life-saving procedures, too, and have little option but to live in marginal land, vulnerable to inundation and landslide.

And it is women who suffer the most when disaster strikes, simply because they're women, and women make up 70% of the world's poor. They have less access to financial resources, land, education, health and other basic rights than men, and are seldom involved in disaster preparedness decision-making processes.

Low income countries are also disproportionately affected. Almost all of the most deadly events occur in middle income or developing countries. An average of 1,052 people die in any given disaster in less developed countries, compared to just 23 per disaster in developed countries. Higher-income countries experienced 56% of disasters but lost 32% of lives in 2014, while lower-income countries experienced 44% of disasters but suffered 68% of deaths.

This discrepancy can partly be explained by the fact that earthquake deaths in particular can be prevented by engineering approaches that are widely applied in wealthy countries, but rarely found in the developing world. This would suggest that levels of economic development, rather than exposure to hazards per se, are major determinants of avoidable death.

12   *Natural disasters are not 'Acts of God'.*

Melissa Leo plays a civil rights lawyer helping find someone's missing brother in post-Katrina New Orleans in the elliptical TV mini-series, *Treme*. Her 'preachy' husband, played by John Goodman, at one point delivers a venomous diatribe that concludes with the immortal line, "that was no goddamn natural disaster ... that was a goddamn man-made catastrophe !!!" Unusually for Hollywood – which has never been known for letting history or science get in the way of a good storyline – John Goodman is expressing a fundamental truth: all so-called 'natural' disasters are, to a greater or lesser degree, derived from the action or inaction of man, and therefore cannot be considered entirely of nature's making.

Natural hazards such as earthquakes, floods, volcanic eruptions and landslides usually spring to mind when the word 'disaster' is mentioned. Yet these events are in fact only natural agents that transform a vulnerable human condition into the death and destruction that constitutes a disaster. This is the same as saying that disasters are defined by what they do to people. Otherwise, disasters are nothing more than interesting geological or meteorological phenomena ... accidents waiting to happen, if you like.

Our emotional reaction to disaster may be exaggerated by a perceived lack of control over what many, including insurance companies and the more religious amongst us, tend to think of as 'Acts of God'. But natural disasters, despite the adjective, are far from natural; death and destruction results from human acts of omission or commission ... a water well contaminated by salt water during a storm surge because it had no protective wall or cover, or building homes in zones known to be vulnerable to landslide, for example. Hazards are natural, disasters are not.

A hazard only becomes a disaster when a naturally occurring phenomenon kills enough people to get noticed. If, say, a massive earthquake were to occur in the middle of the largely uninhabited Gobi

Desert this would hardly constitute a 'disaster' as only a few yaks would be around to get hurt. Since a natural hazard event does not therefore automatically lead to a disaster, we must infer that natural disasters are not 'natural' at all, but somehow created by us, either because we're unable to live our lives out of harm's way, or because we have failed to protect ourselves fully from the hazard. If we do live in harm's way, it's not that there is no other option; it's that those whose job it is to protect us, our Ministers and Mayors, have chosen to spend our money on something else.

If we were being entirely logical, then, we would have to conclude that all disasters are theoretically avoidable, since good governance and good management would be all that's required to prevent avoidable death and destruction. After all, hazards are well understood phenomena, and the science has existed for some time for us to understand their mechanisms and to know with some certainty where and, to a lesser extent, when they will strike. These acts can be prevented, or at least their effects mitigated, and usually at very little extra marginal cost. As Andrew Coburn said very eloquently in his forward to Cambridge University's 2011 paper on human casualties in earthquakes, "The forces wrought by nature are formidable, and yet there are ways that these forces can be understood, withstood, and accommodated. There are success stories where infrastructure has been built strongly enough to withstand the energy unleashed on it, and the preparation has been sufficient to organise people to protect themselves". There is no reason why societies everywhere – from the wealthiest in New York to the poorest in the Philippines – cannot invest in infrastructure that has enough redundant capacity to withstand forces beyond those required for the every day.

Disasters can be prevented, usually at very little extra marginal cost.

There are occasions, of course, when we have not exactly helped ourselves. The destruction of mangrove forests and coral reefs off the coasts of South-East Asia, for example, has dramatically increased exposure to tsunami and storm surge. And the clear-cutting of mountain forests exacerbates soil erosion and thus, as in Pakistan, the magnitude of floods, and, as in Indonesia, the number of landslides.

So, with disasters being viewed by many people as 'Acts of God', you don't have to be an atheist to realise that the reality is somewhat different. A hazard like a volcano could conceivably be considered an 'Act of God' but a disaster is what happens when the volcano erupts, spewing lava, gas and ash over people to ill-informed or too slow – like the inhabitants of Pompeii – to get out of the way. As *Disaster Misperception # 33* will tell you, it's a rare volcano that erupts without warning nowadays, with those living on its slopes given ample warning to evacuate. Nevertheless, when you hear the word 'disaster', this means you are hearing about people too poor to take action to prevent or mitigate the effects of the hazard before it transforms itself into a harmful event.

But, as humans, we take comfort in a certain fatalism. Far too many people – particularly poor people in the developing world – continue to think that floods and earthquakes can be nothing but 'Acts of God' and, by extension, cannot be avoided. This passivity relegates people who could help themselves if they only knew how to becoming nothing more than pathetic, helpless victims; a mind-set that worries the UN Secretary-General Ban ki-Moon who recently stated, "Almost as dangerous as the cyclones or earthquakes themselves is the myth that the destruction and deaths they cause are somehow unavoidable."

13   *Emergency, Disaster, Calamity and Catastrophe don't describe the same thing.*

Emergencies, Disasters, and Catastrophes (or Calamities) are separate, distinct events with each requiring their own strategies of response. Disasters are distinguished from everyday emergencies by the fact that day-to-day functioning of governance has been overwhelmed. Calamities are even worse, in as much that most, if not all, infrastructure has been destroyed; officials are either dead or unable to perform their usual roles; everyday societal functions have been sharply and simultaneously interrupted; and help from nearby communities cannot be provided.

14   *The 'compounding' effects of a natural disaster are becoming more complex.*

Are natural hazard events occurring more frequently, or less so? As this book repeatedly points out, the rhetoric suggests the former while the evidence points to the latter. Or, at least it used to. What is happening now, though, is that floods and droughts, and hazards like landslides that accompany them, are interacting: more of one is now beginning to mean more of the other.

Climate change appears to have more or less doubled the odds of the warm, dry conditions that intensify and prolong periods of drought. Many drought-prone parts of the world such as California are experiencing records of low precipitation and high-temperature. At the same time, extreme wet periods also appear to be increasing, mostly because a warming atmosphere carries a larger load of water vapour.

Rather counterintuitively, this makes the spectre of simultaneous flooding and drought more and more likely. The more rainfall there is, the more water will be lost as run-off, thereby increasing the risk of flooding. The most likely scenario in such circumstances is that we suffer from too much water falling too fast where more rain is delivered than aquifers can absorb and reservoirs can store. Intensity of this rainfall will increase pore water pressure in unstable soils, thereby increasing the likelihood of landslides. Add in the fact that bone-dry tinder and poor forest management practices are creating conditions that fuel wildfires, and that drought and wildfires have hardened the ground, and a paradox arises where the potential risk from all these hazards increases.

Rainfall from tropical cyclones increases landslide risk and wildfires increase flood risk.

Nobody is arguing that the droughts we are experiencing today around the world in Africa, the US, Russia, or Australia are caused by climate change alone, or that all weather-related disasters have a link to climate change. However, the evidence is clear that many areas of the globe are experiencing increasing risks from weather and climate-related hazards. What this means is that the odds of specific extremes being experienced in specific places is increasing. We should expect warmer winters and hotter summers; drier dry ears and wetter wet years.

15 *Sexual violence increases in the wake of a natural disaster.*

Insurance companies make their money by knowing something we don't: Human beings don't perceive risk rationally. Martin Hartley, Chief Operating Officer of one such company put it very clearly following the Paris terror attacks of November 2015: "The risk is made to seem far worse than it is by its perceived magnitude, not by its probability."

The spatial distribution of natural hazards, their intensity, timing, and frequency are largely a matter of physics. Understanding who dies, when, and how is a matter of epidemiology. But impact is a function of human behaviour, and is therefore a matter of psychology.

Humans behave in predictably unpredictable ways when faced with a natural disaster. If told of an impending tsunami and the need to evacuate, it is said that Californians will go down to the beach to watch. Certainly, only half of those ordered to evacuate as super-storm *Sandy* approached the low-lying coastal areas of New York did so. How many people in Japan in March 2011 were swept to their death by the overpowering tsunami because they spent too many precious minutes gathering up their belongings or, in some cases, started to climb hillsides only to turn back to get a stouter pair of shoes. They didn't know enough to be able to assess the real risk for themselves, perhaps? Or they had had too many false alarms before? Or previous survivors told them not to worry unduly?

Anti-social behaviour such as looting or rioting is extremely rare in the immediate aftermath of a natural disaster. Most people respond spontaneously and generously, both in the affected area and when making donations or volunteering from the other side of the world.

However, when safe water and food run short, people quickly resort to violence in order to secure their means of survival. You can see this during food distributions in refugee camps when supplies are either low or rumoured to be low, and when *Human* helicopters drop food into unsecured areas. In both cases, *beings don't* the fittest young men around get an unfair proportion of *perceive risk* whatever is available and, if they distribute it at all, share *rationally.* it only with immediate family members.

Sexual violence against women, and child abuse usually rise noticeably and rapidly in the wake of a natural disaster, and child trafficking rears its ugly head. Suppliers tend to capitalise on the suffering by raising prices, and corruption increases.

Within weeks, the urge to procreate overwhelms young men and women alike who, in some visceral way, appear to be seeking to celebrate life when all around them has been death and destruction. The result is a baby boom 10 to 12 months after the event [see *Disaster Misperception # 65*].

Even well-educated and comparatively wealthy people fail to take the simplest of measures to mitigate the risk of disaster despite knowing that they live in hazard-prone areas of the world. Although things are improving now, only 17% of people living along the hurricane-prone Atlantic and Gulf coasts in the US had taken steps to storm-proof their homes in 2006. The same figure applies amongst Californians who fail to take any seismic risk reduction measure despite knowing they are living in an earthquake zone.

The problem is, people systematically misperceive probabilities and risks of natural hazard events: low probability events are consistently overestimated, and high probability events consistently underestimated. So, too, recent events have a greater impact on our behaviour than earlier ones. These biases don't appear to be related to the frequency of the event, either; people underestimate risks they have not experienced, and overestimate those they have. Those who have driven a car without incident, for example, have a lower perception of the risk of having an accident than those who recently had one. This sense of invulnerability that comes from a close encounter with a previous event is frequently cited as the reason for failing to evacuate when asked by the authorities to do so. Survivors with first-hand experience believe they are better equipped to deal with future events, only to find out too late that they are just as vulnerable as everybody else.

Low probability events are consistently overestimated, while high probability events are consistently underestimated.

We also notice trends which aren't real. People notice clusters of events but they don't pay attention to the long gaps in between. Nor do we remember for long the impact of the previous occurrence. This helps to explain much risk-related behaviour, including both public and private decisions to take precautions against hazard risk.

Emergency services practice a number of 'critical incident' plans based on worst-case scenarios. When faced with a real sudden-onset natural disaster situation where mass casualties are involved, none of them go to plan. This is for two main reasons. The first is that command and control is lost when the communications go down. In the case of the 'Great Japan Earthquake and Tsunami' in 2011 mobile phone communications went down for three whole days. In Haiti the year before, the same thing happened.

The second reason is that crowds don't behave as predicted. Despite the aftershocks and threat of collapsing buildings, neighbours won't evacuate because they begin trying to rescue people from their street, people they don't even know. And those that do flee, run or drive in directions other than those indicated by the emergency services.

Every year in Taiwan during the May-November rainy season, floods and landslides result in many casualties and huge economic losses despite the government's best efforts at heavy engineering to stabilise slopes, construct dykes and improve drainage systems. It is painfully obvious that these technical mitigation measures are not enough to prevent repeated cycles of loss. Why is this? A large part of the answer lies in the fact that the potential victims' perception of risk and therefore consequent behaviour has been neglected by the planners. The fact that there are significant differences between the experts' apparently objective assessments of risk and the peoples' intuitive and subjective judgment of what to do when faced with the same threat must come down to the way natural hazards are perceived and risks are communicated.

16   *Disaster data is heavily influenced by observer and reporting biases.*

All data prior to more less the late 1980's have to be viewed with a certain amount of pragmatic scepticism. Not because much, if not all, of it before then was subject to major reporting and observer biases[19] – which it was – but simply because critical mass in the systemic international observation, reporting, and collation of disaster data did not take place until then [see *Disaster Misperception # 6*].

The key lies in the word 'reported'. This word is only useful if it assumes that each and every disastrous event was observed and faithfully recorded in some central database somewhere. But, until recently, they weren't. As awareness of what was happening on the far side of the planet grew through the latter part of the last century with the use of sophisticated remote sensing technology such as sea-bed pressure sensors, seismographs, and satellite mounted sideways-scanning infra-red laser spectrometry, so the disaster statistics began to

---

[19] The major causes of bias in disaster studies are 'selection bias', where the things being measured are not representative in the population at large, and or 'information bias' where people recall the same event differently.

mount. At the same time, access to low-cost international air travel and affordable mobile communications technologies meant that more and more people were beginning to record more and more events. Not only that, but those events that would previously have gone unreported because they happened to too few people or in remote places began to be logged by government departments set up after a UN-sponsored inter-governmental conference in the Japanese city of Kyoto in the mid-1990's, and by a burgeoning number of national and international non-governmental organisations who had a vested interest in doing so in order to demonstrate, amongst other things, the need for additional funding.

The table below is instructive as it reflects objective information captured by satellite and is thus a rare example of where the numbers leave little room for subjective interpretation.

Using tropical cyclones as an example, the data not only show no decadal increase in the number of events, but a clear divergence between the numbers of 'actual' and 'observed' events ... which would seem to refute the notion that the existing data is not seriously skewed by observation.

Governments tend to manipulate disaster data.

Another part of the challenge lies in separating out the basic questions; questions which the academic literature and statistics supplied by reinsurance companies so often conflate, as the metrics and definitions used by each are needed for different purposes. One group seems to be almost entirely engaged in proving or disproving links with global climate change while the vested interests of the other needs to understand the nature of capital risk so they can set appropriate – for some observers, this means the highest possible – insurance premiums.

Tropical Cyclones reported & detected
by satellite from 1970 to 2009 (average per year) worldwide

Decade	1970-1979	1980-1989	1990-1999	2000-2009
Events	88	88	87	86
Countries affected	142	144	155	146
Disasters reported	22	37	51	63

Governments can skew the data, too. For largely political reasons, governments, institutions and other interested parties sometimes over- or under-report what they have observed. Authorities may not be willing to admit their failure to respond properly, for example, or may not want foreign agencies to enter sensitive areas. Both these scenarios were the case in Pakistan following the 2005 earthquake and resulted in initial under-reporting of what was going on. Interestingly, countries with non-free press and countries with higher 'bureaucratic quality' (a measure of effective governance) tend to report fewer disasters than more democratic countries or those with a freer press[xiii]. Political concerns may also lie behind governmental decisions to declare – or, as in the 2014 Ebola epidemic in Sierra Leone, delay declaring – a state of emergency. Nor do governments like reporting outbreaks of communicable diseases like SARS or Avian Influenza, as it tends to panic the people, deter inward investment and scare away the tourists. On the other hand, the additional resources that accompany international relief efforts sometimes encourages governments to overstate the case.

At the same time, data which focuses on particular themes or countries may often come from different sources. Thus, the figure for, say, numbers affected by disaster in a country may well vary between one database and another. Neither figure is wrong, nor is either figure right. The bottom line, therefore, is to use disaster data with caution as it represents a collection of guesstimates and educated extrapolations[xiv].

17 *Mega-events skew disaster data.*

Hazard events causing large-scale death and destruction like the earthquake in Haiti in 2010 have happened in the recent past and will happen again in the future. They are the infrequent but devastating geophysical mega-events that have the potential to unleash awesome destructive power. But, as with the 'white whale' in Herman Melville's novel *Moby Dick*, while we know they are there, a sighting is rare and impossible to predict with any accuracy. Just one quarter of one percent (0.28%) of all the world's natural disasters since 1975 caused over three quarters (78%) of all deaths[xv].

Just 0.25 % of all the world's natural disasters result in over 75% of all disaster deaths.

These are the so-called 'mega-disasters'; rare but by far the deadliest.

And it only takes one extreme event to remind us of the devastation that natural disasters can wreak in the blink of an eye. Trends and patterns in disaster statistics are greatly affected by such single, extreme events which can cause excessive and disproportionate human or economic loss.

18 *Population growth is not the main driver of disaster risk.*

Population growth is one of the principal drivers of disaster risk around the world. After all, logic would suggest more people would mean more people potentially in harm's way, wouldn't it? Well, not necessarily, as there are three other 'drivers' which have some bearing on the matter, and these are: Ecological change (including climate change), Urbanisation, and Poverty.

Current projections by the UN predict a continued increase in population but a steady decline in the population growth *rate*, with the global population expected to reach somewhere around 10.5 billion by the year 2050 and transition to a rapid decline thereafter. The graph below shows the options, with the middle of the three confidence lines now thought to be the most likely.

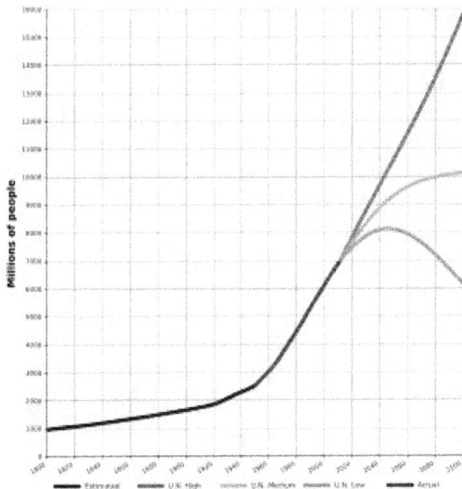

What this means is that the planet's population is no longer "exploding." In fact, the rate of population growth has been slowing since the 1960's, and has now fallen below replacement level across half the world[20]. Today's women are having half as many babies as their mothers, with global fertility rates having fallen from 4.7 babies per woman of child-bearing age in the 1970s to 2.6 this decade[xvi]. This is what the world's most famous statistician, Hans Rosling, is talking about in his TED-talks when he refers to us as having already attained "peak child."

Nevertheless, we still need to slow population growth rates don't we? And surely any effort made to reduce early childhood death will only result in the world's population rising more rapidly, won't it?

We have already reached 'peak child'.

Whatever you think of the morality of this position, and counter-intuitive as it may seem, the reverse is true. Poorer, less educated people tend to have more children. But it is wrong to assume that helping more children to survive to reproductive age is bound to increase the population in developing countries. Poor parents have large families so that at least two of their children survive to take care of them in old age. It's a kind of insurance scheme and pension plan rolled into one. As parents grow more confident that their children will make it to adulthood, they have fewer children. The evidence from Kerala in India suggests that this can happen within a single generation i.e 20 years or so. Furthermore, if reducing poverty makes it possible for families to send their children – especially their daughters – to school, further evidence indicates that their children will go on to have smaller families themselves.

19   *Globally, the number of people vulnerable to disaster is decreasing.*

As we have just seen, another principal driver of disaster risk is urbanisation. Cities have absorbed almost two-thirds of the planet's population since 1950, a time when only one third of the world's people lived in urban areas, and when New York and London were the planet's

---

[20] To maintain a stable population, the fertility rate must be around 2.1. Note that the decline in fertility rates is less marked among the least developed countries, where rates have fallen only from 6.3 to 4.4

only cities with populations of over 10 million. Now, there are 24 such cities, of which 19 lie on seismic fault lines, in the path of tropical storms, or in flood plains. By 2025 three out of every five people on the planet will be living in cities, according to the UN, of which some 630 million will live in 37 mega-cities[21].

Given this rising urbanisation, it is likely that disasters will become increasingly urban phenomena. Growing cities often mean that people are living on increasingly marginal land[22] and in informal settlements with poor housing conditions, making them more susceptible to the effects of natural hazards[23]. Despite 227 million people clawing their way out of poverty during the decade 2000-2010, the number of people living in these informal settlements – otherwise known as "slum-dwellers" – grew by 60 million over the same period.

In the meantime – and as explained in *Disaster Misperception # 18* – the planet's population is growing, and more people on the planet means more people potentially in harm's way.

But poverty, vulnerability and disasters are linked. Usually it is the poorest who are the worst affected and suffer most. Their poverty makes them more vulnerable, and their capacity to cope with disaster and recover from the effects are constrained by their lack of resources.

Happily, though, there has lately been extraordinary progress in lifting people out of extreme poverty. According to Homi Khara of the Brookings institution and Andrew Rogerson of the UK's Overseas Development Institute, the number of those suffering absolute poverty has fallen from almost 2 billion in 1990 to around 500 million now, and is likely to decline to around 200 million by 2025. "Roughly speaking, one billion people have been lifted out of poverty since 1990 in China, India, Vietnam, Indonesia, and even now in sub-Saharan Africa. In the last decade we've had the most rapid reduction in poverty in history," they state.

The number of poor people in the world is steadily declining.

---

[21] A 'mega-city' has in excess of 20 million inhabitants.
[22] Evidence from Pune in India shows that poor households prefer to have easier access to jobs even though they know they live in behind river embankments prone to collapse, or under unstable hillsides subject to landslide. This pattern is repeated around the world from Caracas to Chennai; property prices reflect the hazard risks to which they are exposed, so are cheaper to rent or buy.
[23] Even though 227 million people no longer met the criteria for defining 'slum-dwellers' in 2010, according to the UN, their numbers had nevertheless increased from 776.7 million 10 years earlier to 827.6 million.

Meanwhile, the number of poor people – defined as those who struggle to survive on two dollars a day or less – is not falling in fragile, low-income countries, and remains at around 500 million. But this too is set to reduce. Which means that, overall, and despite continuing population growth in China and India, the number of poor people in the world is steadily declining.

This is fantastic news, and testament, in part, to decades of economic growth and development. However, if these figures are correct, this still leaves roughly one billion people vulnerable to the ravages of natural disaster. But *are* these poor forgotten masses still as exposed and as vulnerable to such events as they were before? The traditional discourse from the aid agencies is that they are. In fact, even more so, as climate change, migration to urban slums in marginal land, population growth, and ecological degradation combines to make them so. This assertion is open to challenge, not least because most of the governments of the 36 countries considered most at risk from these "drivers of the apocalypse" have taken, and are taking, extraordinary measures to protect their people from hazards such as floods, storm surges, landslides, and earthquakes. How else is one to interpret the decline in frequency of disaster over the past decade?

20 *Natural Disasters can be prevented.*

Too many people die unnecessarily from impacts of natural hazards that could be avoided. And it's not as if the world lacks the knowledge to reduce the death toll. A combination of better land use, better construction practices, and improved civic education would dramatically reduce risk across the full range of disasters. Why, then, are these mitigation measures not adopted systematically and wholesale?

It is a deliberate choice not to prevent natural disasters.

The main reason is that the protection afforded is perceived to provide lower or more uncertain returns on investment than alternative expenditures in physical wellbeing. In other words, since the vast majority of people affected by disasters do not die, it may be easier, quicker, cheaper, and more politically expedient to prevent other causes of avoidable death when budgets are not sufficient to cover everything.

Regarding the probability of a destructive natural hazard event striking a particular area, even risk-prone regions very rarely have to contend with a major natural disaster because the major impact is concentrated in a tiny proportion of the territory at risk. This suggests that the majority of disaster-prone areas have experienced very few deaths regardless of the mitigation measures undertaken. It is not that mitigation worked, in other words, but that disasters did not occur. In turn, this says something about the likely costs and benefits of mitigation, as, in many cases, such measures will go unrewarded by saving lives in a disaster.

But prevention measures differ in costs and effectiveness. What people do or don't do affects others, too. Those living behind an embankment may be protected from floods, but the redirected waters could lead to greater damage elsewhere, and even those who thought they were safe behind the embankment would experience greater damage if there were a breach. Embankments such as those that line parts of the Bangladesh *sunderbans* or levées that line the banks of the Mississippi lower the risk of moderate damage to many, but increase the – albeit lowered – risk of catastrophic damage to a few.

The October 2005 earthquake and the July-August 2010 floods in Pakistan demonstrated that years of development efforts can be wiped out more or less overnight by disasters. Moreover, it is the most vulnerable, those already with the least access to services and resources that bear the greatest impact of disasters. If *disaster risk reduction* is not systematically integrated into plans, programmes and practices, this pattern is likely to continue with greater intensity and frequency due to increased exposure, poor development practices, environmental degradation and climate change. Disasters, in other words, will continue to seek out the most vulnerable, and ensure that they remain so.

Disasters are not only tragedies but also opportunities to do things differently and introduce new practices. Done properly, recovery efforts avoid creating new risks or exacerbating existing ones, and provide an important opportunity to build back better and enhance resilience. Frameworks have to include at least the following components if they are to be successful:

- raise risk awareness
- carry out hazard mapping and cross-referencing the analysis with vulnerabilities and capacities
- develop knowledge through education, training, research and providing hazard risk information

- commit government and local authorities to institutional frameworks, including organisational, policy, legislation, and community action

These components are not easy to do, and give rise to strategic and conceptual challenges which, for example, make a clear distinction between hazards and risk, require the adoption of a multi-hazard approach, and expand the emergency focus from preparedness and response to include prevention and mitigation.

And it is here, in this last challenge, that more can be done. According to the World Bank, this does not always require more spending, but requires spending differently. Eight aspects are generally thought to produce higher returns on investment:

Improving weather forecasting with faster sharing of weather-related information between countries and better use of information technology.

Establishing Early Warning Systems for areas exposed to higher risk, including improving communications and rehearsal of evacuation drills at the community level.

Ensuring that certain critical infrastructure remains functional after the hazard event. Super-storm Sandy showed that communication networks need their own independent power supply, for example. Typhoon Yolanda showed that retrofitting of hospitals is required to enable them to become command and control centres in addition to their role as a health facility.

Protecting environmental buffers such as coastal mangroves, sand dunes, and coral reefs.

Supporting free markets so that where property and land values reflect hazard risk correctly, people can make informed choices about where to live and what prevention measures to undertake based on where risk has been discounted and therefore prices are lower.

Securing land and property rights as security in land tenure and title allows people to invest in prevention measures. But this does not imply giving title in floodplains on which people have encroached, often illegally.

Making hazard risk information more widely available as prospective dwellers must be made aware of the risks of living in buildings close to active seismic fault lines, on soils liable to liquefaction, under unstable slopes, in floodplains, or in coastal areas liable to tsunami or storm surge. Governments would be advised to map geophysical hazards such as these, disclose them, and consult the public when deciding which zones are unsuitable for living in. This requires investment in remote sensing technology, geophysical surveys, hazard monitoring stations, early warning systems, and communications infrastructure so that the resulting information can be shared as a public good.

Implementing better building practices as many people die needlessly when buildings and other infrastructure collapse during earthquakes, severe storms, and landslides. Building resilient structures is not necessarily more expensive than building one's liable to collapse, but does require all involved to be well-informed about the physical properties of building materials as well as the penalties for not complying with building codes. Constant monitoring of construction workers is also needed.So, if we know what to do, why are there still so many avoidable tragedies? The fact that 'risk reduction' programmes are extremely complex in nature and complicated to put into practice has a lot to do with it. There are also few votes in spending money on preparing for something that may not happen. And, unless remote villagers and urban slum dwellers understand what might befall them, getting them to change their behaviour is extremely difficult. But it can, and, in the most 'at risk' places, must be done.

21   *Natural disasters don't always deepen poverty.*

The predominant view of the aid world is that natural disasters are an enormous barrier to economic and social development. It is certainly true that poor people lose a disproportionate amount of those assets on which their survival depends when disaster strikes, and very often the impact of several small adversities is all that is required to drive the poor from a state of vulnerability to one of total destitution.

Conventional development theory goes further by suggesting that "Disasters cause poverty while poverty causes disasters". This same theory also posits that the struggle by less developed countries to service their foreign debt limits the amount of revenue available to develop public services such as disaster warning systems or response planning departments[xvii].

However, while it is true that a drought or flood can destroy a year or two's income for a poor rural farmer in the blink of an eye, the inevitability of this situation is not as straightforward as it appears. Part of this somewhat counter-intuitive reasoning is connected to the way in which new technologies are absorbed. A country whose capital stock is reduced by a natural hazard event has an incentive to replace the lost infrastructure with newer technologies than that which was destroyed. Economists call this *Schumpeterian Creative Destructionism*.

The logic argues that older equipment and buildings are more exposed to damage when the natural hazard strikes and that replacing it by applying 'leapfrog technologies' has permanent consequences on the growth rate of the economy as a whole and therefore on the poorest in society who benefit later from the trickle down such growth brings.

If Mr. Schumpeter had ever visited a village in southern Bangladesh, he would have found that his basic premise seems to hold true at the individual household level. Having survived the ravages of cyclone *Sidr* in 2007, one villager made it very clear that, despite his house having been flattened and his livestock drowned and scattered to the four winds, the aid that followed meant that he now not only had a new house but also a functioning pit latrine for the very first time.

Nevertheless, at the macro level, developing countries are usually especially hard hit, not only because of direct damages, but also because of the indirect and secondary economic disruptions to the flow of goods and services following disaster. Take the example of Thailand, a country no stranger to floods. Rarely has a single flood event wrought as much economic havoc as the October 2011 event which cost $40 billion. This made it the most expensive disaster in the country's history and set back industrial production by 2.5%. Developed countries are not immune to the economic knock-on effects, either. Intel, the California-based semiconductor maker, announced in December 2011 that its revenues would fall by $1 billion because the floods had sharply cut the world's supply of disc drives, while Japan's industrial output reduced by 2.6% in November 2011 due to disruption to its electronics and automotive supply chains.

As if these effects were not bad enough, the possibility of further disasters in the same area can be a disincentive to external investors, especially if they think that underlying hazard risk has not been reduced and the country is not taking proper measures to prevent the next. The long-term impact of investor uncertainty can even equal or surpass the cost of the disaster itself[xviii].

Ground-Related

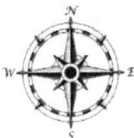

22   *The height of a building can determine its propensity to collapse in an earthquake.*

Louise Amantillo, a young and promising overseas student, excited to be in her first year of training as a nurse in Christchurch, New Zealand, was just preparing to leave for lectures when, without warning, her six-floor dormitory building collapsed in the devastating earthquake of 22nd February 2011. She managed to send a text message to her mother in the Philippines saying, "Mummy, I got buried".

About 40 minutes later came a brief call from under the rubble asking her family for help. "Her voice was shaking, like she was really scared," said her mother later.

After another harrowing hour, during which Louise sent six increasingly frenzied texts about the dark, the continued shaking, and choking dust, came one final message: "Please make it quick".

Buildings between five and eight floors in height collapse more than any other in an earthquake.

All structures have natural frequencies or periods of vibration. If a structure has a period of vibration similar to the seismic wave, it will resonate. And the longer it resonates, the more likely it is to fail. Resonance is affected by the height of the building as well as its design and the type of building materials used. The collapse of a single building in Christchurch, New Zealand – tragically, the one in which Louise was living – resulted in nearly two thirds of the total death toll city-wide. The building concerned may have been poorly designed and poorly constructed, as the report into its collapse maintains, but the fact that it was six floors high was surely a major contributor to why over 120 of Louise's friends and colleagues died.

Not far away, another, more modern six-floor building made predominantly of steel and glass remained intact, though, suffering only one broken pane of glass. This suggests that height alone is not the only risk factor. But statistics tell their own tale: buildings between five and eight floors in height collapse more than any other when an earthquake strikes. Higher buildings absorb the horizontal and vertical harmonics whereas shorter buildings, being more rigid, resist these same forces through brute torsional strength. That said, it should be recognised that risk of collapse can also be multiplied by age, as buildings of these heights are likely to have been built a while ago using older materials and older technologies.

Seismic waves cause the ground to move from side to side as well as up and down. This causes different parts of the building to move in different directions. To minimise the destructive potential of such movements, entire buildings can be isolated from the ground using foundations which have giant ball-bearings, shock absorbing pistons, or other such energy dampers built into them. The 'skyscrapers' you now see being built in seismic zones all over South-East Asia incorporate such technology.

Building height is a risk factor for injury in earthquakes.

Building height is also a major risk factor for severe injury in earthquakes. In the 1988 Armenian earthquake, people inside buildings with five or more floors were four times more likely to be injured than those with fewer. And in the 1990 Philippines earthquake, people inside buildings with seven or more floors were 35 times more likely to be injured[xix].

In a high-rise building, escape from the upper floors is unlikely before the building collapses, and if it collapses completely, as many as 70% of its occupants are likely to be trapped inside. On the other hand, in a low-rise building that takes perhaps 20 to 30 seconds to collapse, more than three-quarters of the building's occupants may be able to escape before it falls.

23 It's not only collapsing buildings that kill people in an earthquake.

It's slightly pedantic to suggest that people don't die from earthquakes but from the falling rocks and masonry that an earthquake produces. It's like saying guns don't kill people either, just people with itchy trigger fingers. But it's not just the rocks and rubble; there are other risks associated with collapsing buildings, such as fire from ruptured gas mains, or from accidentally touching downed high-voltage power cables that can be equally deadly.

Because earthquakes frequently affect densely populated urban areas with poor building quality, they often result in high death rates and mass casualties with many traumatic injuries. Those that survive the multiple blunt trauma, penetrating wounds and crush injuries that are typically seen in these events often require intensive medical and surgical care just at the moment when local medical response capacity has itself been almost totally smashed.

Many of these patients have subsequent complications that lead to additional death and suffering later. A surprisingly large number of patients also require acute care for non-surgical problems such as myocardial infarction, exacerbation of chronic diseases such as diabetes or hypertension, anxiety, and other mental health problems such as depression.

While images of collapsed structures in earthquakes around the world get most attention from the media, most buildings do not collapse at all, and, if they do, the collapse is only partial. Very few buildings collapse completely in earthquake-prone areas of developed countries, where strict building codes are applied.

Secondary effects can be just as deadly as the disaster itself.

Through most of the past century, by far the greatest proportion of earthquake victims died in the collapse of un-reinforced brick, stone or adobe buildings, or in insufficiently reinforced concrete buildings, as it is these older and less well built types that tend to collapse very rapidly even at low intensities of ground shaking.

Multi-floor stone, brick, and adobe structures in many areas of high seismic risk around the world – Turkey, Iran, Pakistan, China, South America, and the Caribbean – not only have walls prone to collapse, but very heavy timber-beamed roofs. It was these heavy timber beams that contributed most to the high death toll during the Pakistan earthquake of 2005, although it should also be noted that just as many people were killed in landslides as from building collapse.

Deaths from the 1999 Marmara earthquake in Turkey were blamed on poorly constructed reinforced concrete frames which had been made using concrete mixed with unwashed beach sand, the salt from which is highly corrosive to steel reinforcing bars. This sub-standard construction also took place directly above a known fault line. Similarly, over 6,000 schools were constructed in Gujarat, India using seismically weak pre-cast construction technology. Three quarters of these schools collapsed during the 2001 Bhuj earthquake despite having been built only a few years earlier. Both experiences illustrate that, while well-constructed reinforced concrete buildings are less likely to collapse in earthquakes than un-reinforced masonry ones, when such shoddily built buildings do collapse, they are more likely to kill more occupants.

Earthquakes with epicentres almost directly under urban areas can see levels of building damage and destruction reach 80%. This was the case in Bam, Iran in 2003, although clearly much depends on the age and design of the buildings, as well as the extent to which building codes were complied with. One of the most recent examples of this is the 2010 earthquake that took place in Haiti where most of the construction consisted of unreinforced concrete. If there were ever any building codes in Port-au-Prince, they were certainly not applied. The consequent destruction when the magnitude 7.0 quake hit on January 12 was massive and resulted in an estimated 270,000 deaths. This is in contrast to the magnitude 8.8 earthquake which hit a similarly urban area of Chile – a country where earthquake resistant building codes are rigorously enforced – only a few weeks later, and where the death toll was less than 800.

24 New York is at higher risk of an earthquake-related disaster than San Francisco.

The ground we stand on is thin and fragile. The Earth's crust is the same thickness, relatively speaking, as the membrane beneath the shell of an egg, and, being riddled with tectonic cracks, bits of it are continually moving over, under, or along one another.

The planet experiences about three earthquakes every minute.

In March 2011, a magnitude 9.0 mega-quake, the seventh largest ever recorded, rocked Japan, triggering a tsunami that killed an estimated 27,000 people. Continental USA was hit later that year in August 2011 with a magnitude 5.8 quake which shook New York City and put a crack in the Washington Monument.

While these events seem to suggest an ominous future, earthquakes have always been quite common. The planet experiences roughly three earthquakes every minute. That's about 4,000 every day. In any given year, about 30,000 of these are powerful enough to be considered as potentially catastrophic. Happily for most of us, only 30 or so[24] turn out to be so, as the rest occur undersea or in sparsely populated parts of the world.

Louise from Disaster Misperception # 22 probably didn't realise that Christchurch, the capital of New Zealand, was built above a seismic

---

[24] The frequency of earthquake disasters around the world has actually decreased over the past 10 years. Thirty such geophysical disasters were registered in 2011, six less than the decadal average of 36.

fault line and was as much at risk from earthquake as her own capital, Manila, or Nepal's capital, Kathmandu.

We generally think of the San Andreas Fault off California's coast or the Pacific Ring of Fire – the active faults of the Western Pacific – as being the riskiest zones for earthquakes. But the Northern Anatolian fault[25] that runs through Northern Turkey is actually much more dangerous. Given that the last earthquake in Tehran was in 1830, the entire 7.5 million population is exposed, as are the residents of Romania's capital, Bucharest, Uzbekistan's capital, Tashkent, Albania's capital, Tirana, and Istanbul which lies just 20 km to the North of the fault itself. Apart from having been built atop such a risky fault line, these cities have two other things in common: The first is that early warning systems are rudimentary; and the second is that compliance with building regulations have been shakily followed at best. This means that their combined populations of over 26 million people are living on borrowed time.

Across the other side of the world, its location on the San Andreas fault makes the US city of Los Angeles one of the most prone to earthquakes, yet it too has little in the way of sophisticated early warning systems. Unlike their Japanese counterparts – who are engaged, have a plan, and are in regular receipt of hazard alerts – this leaves its 14.7 million inhabitants at risk, with most people having little more than a bottle of water and a torch to fall back on.

Further North, the Canadian city of Vancouver is another disaster waiting to happen. When the Cascadia subduction zone slips, it will be hit with a massive earthquake and most likely be followed by a monster tsunami.

The arrangement of natural and physical features substantially affects the impact of an earthquake. Violent ground shaking in urban areas constructed on alluvial soils or landfill, for example, tends to result in the ground losing its structural integrity and act like a liquid[26], thereby exacerbating the effect of seismic oscillations. This can produce significant death and destruction at specific locations further from the epicentre than magnitude alone would imply. Parts of Mexico City are

---

[25] The North Anatolian Fault is an active right-lateral strike-slip fault in northern Turkey which runs along the boundary between the Eurasian Plate and the Anatolian Plate.

[26] Liquefaction is a phenomenon where soil loses strength and stiffness in response to an applied stress, causing it to behave like a liquid. Entire buildings then begin to sink as if into mud. Buried tanks and drains, on the other hand, may float in the liquefied soil due to their buoyancy.

at extreme risk because of this, as is nearly the whole of Indonesia's capital, Jakarta. Nearly half of Jakarta lies below sea level, in a flat basin with soft soil, near a fault line. This means earthquakes can be particularly dangerous to its 17.7 million inhabitants. Add to that Jakarta's risk of flooding and it becomes, along with Manila in the Philippines, one of the most potentially dangerous cities on the planet in which to live.

25   *Earthquakes are predictable.*

Earthquakes are entirely predictable in the sense that our eventual demise is entirely predictable. But they *are* also predictable in a more pragmatic sense:

Tectonic plates and fault lines grind against each other at about the same speed as our fingernails grow. Because we know where these fault lines are, and can measure where the strain is building[27], it is possible to predict where and approximately when major earthquakes are likely to occur. Typically, seismic hazard maps such as those available for the Kathmandu valley of Nepal show these predicted forces with 10% probability of being exceeded in 50 years based on this data, the local geology, and the history of past events.

Although the Nepal earthquakes of 2015 were anomalous in the sense that they occurred in largely unforeseen areas, this mapping can be extremely accurate. Were a sizeable earthquake to strike Dhaka in Bangladesh, for example, a 2 metre wide crack is predicted to appear one third of the way down the airport's main runway, rendering it useless for in-coming relief flights. With a fault line running the length of 151st Street in New York City, a significant jolt along the Ramapo fault could easily result in major damage in the local area[28]. In fact, a 2008 study by Columbia University concluded that, owing to the hardness of the rock on which most of Manhattan is built, the likely shallowness of any seismic event, the age of the infrastructure, and the

---

[27] Borehole tensor strain metres sunk to a depth of 200 metres measure strain in three directions in active seismic areas such as Japan, the US, Iceland, Nepal and Italy using a differential capacitance displacement transducer.

[28] Earthquake frequency in the North-Eastern United States is 50 to 200 times lower than in California, but the earthquakes that do occur in the North-Eastern US are typically felt over a much broader region than earthquakes of the same magnitude in the Western US.

population density in the New York area, even a relatively minor 5.0 event would be "extremely attention-getting".

26 The destructive power of an earthquake is determined by its intensity, not its magnitude.

Magnitude and intensity are the two measures used to gauge the strength of an earthquake, both measures being frequently confused.

The magnitude of an earthquake is a measure of actual energy release at the subterranean source as estimated by seismographic observations from multiple locations. This is measured by an open-ended scale called the *Richter Scale* where each whole number represents an increase of about 30 times more energy released than the number before it. With the scale being logarithmic, this means that an 8.0 earthquake releases 810,000 times more energy than a 4.0 earthquake … being the smallest you are likely to feel. A 5.6 magnitude earthquake is the level at which significant damage to poorly constructed buildings can be expected.

Intensity, on the other hand, is more subjective and measures the severity of shaking at a particular surface location. This is most commonly measured using the 12-point *Modified Mercali Scale*. Intensity is usually strongest at the epicentre – the spot on the Earth's surface directly above the actual site of the earthquake – and, depending on local rock formation and shape of the ground, reduces the further from the epicentre one is.

Intensity is more important than magnitude as it is this that determines levels of death and destruction. Related to intensity is the depth at which the earthquake occurred and the frequency of the pulses generated. The lesser the depth, the greater the frequency and therefore the greater the likelihood of significant damage on the surface.

27 The intensity of an earthquake is unrelated to the numbers that will die.

In his book *Outliers*, Malcolm Gladwell discusses what it takes to be a great basketball player. He suggests, all things being equal, that the taller the player, the better he or she will be. But only to a certain tallness, as there comes a point where any increase in height no longer results in any improvement in performance as the height advantage is offset by a reduction in speed and/or flexibility. In other words, there is a point at which tallness does not help a basketball player get any better; in fact it makes him or her worse.

This concept of *diminishing returns* also applies to natural disasters. Take an earthquake: If a building were to collapse in a 6.8 magnitude quake, it really doesn't matter much if the quake is a thousand times more powerful at 7.1; the building will still fall down, and the same number of people unlucky enough to be inside it at the time will still get killed or injured. It's the same with a windstorm: Once the wind is strong enough to blow off the roof, it really doesn't matter much if wind speed is any faster, as the roof has already gone. It's the same with skin being punctured by storm debris; once there is enough momentum for gravel or straw to penetrate exposed skin [see *Disaster Misperception # 54*], an increase in windspeed will increase the momentum imparted, but this is unlikely to result in any rise in rates of septicaemia later.

The most deadly earthquakes are not necessarily the strongest.

These examples show that the law of diminishing returns applies to intensity. It's the same, too, for duration and size. The longer a hazard event lasts and/or the more people there are exposed because of its size, the more people will be affected.

Similarly, the most deadly earthquakes are not necessarily the strongest. The 2010 earthquake in Haiti, for example, released 500 times less energy than the quake that hit Chile a few weeks later, yet the Haitian quake wrought much more death and destruction. The factors which determine such differences in impact are complex, and go beyond intensity, magnitude and building type to include:

- **The weather**: Extremely hot or cold weather will affect survivability among those trapped. High rainfall saturates soil, thereby increasing the likelihood of liquefaction, landslides, avalanches, and moraine dam failure. Storm-water run-off can exacerbate local tsunami effects, especially at high tide. Sub-zero temperatures will increase the death rate among those trapped, and rapid temperature fluctuations will make rock faces more prone to collapse, especially along mountain ridges where wave propagation results in greater intensity than in the valley below. Bad weather can also delay the arrival of rescue teams and relief supplies);

- **Timing:** Typically, death and injury will be greater during the day when the majority of the population are in large buildings such as schools, factories, supermarkets, and office buildings, than at night). There may also be tourist inflows or population outflows at certain times of the year which doubles or halves the population potentially exposed).

Less obvious, but equally important, risk factors include whether or not:
- Seismic resistant construction policies exist, and whether mechanisms exist in practice to ensure their compliance;
- First aid is included in the school curriculum;
- Evacuation drills have been recently rehearsed;
- Street committees have been established;
- Basic medical supplies – including spinal boards – have been stockpiled and the drugs are regularly rotated.

Ultimately, however, the key predictor of death in an earthquake is, as with all types of natural disaster, human behaviour, as how individuals, households, and communities perceive risk before the event, and the extent to which they panic during the event, will play a large role in determining the number of casualties [see *Disaster Misperception # 15*].

28 *Animals often provide early warning of an impending earthquake.*

What we perceive as one extended jolt actually arrives in stages. Energy released by movement in the Earth's crust travels through the Earth in various different forms. The primary P-waves travel at about 450 kms per minute, but, being longitudinal, don't carry that much power. Their arrival is the sudden vertical thump that many animals and some humans experience at the onset of an earthquake. The secondary S-waves carry a slower moving but extremely powerful pulse of energy in both horizontal and vertical planes. It's the shaking from these that "bat entire skyscrapers around like they are canoes in the surf".

When an earthquake hit the Eastern seaboard of the US in the summer of 2011, keepers at the National Zoo in Washington DC later reported that the zoo's gorilla, *Mandara*, gave a yell, gathered up her baby, *Kibibi*, and swiftly climbed into the topmost branches of a tree a few seconds before the ground started shaking. At the nearby National Aquarium in Baltimore, dolphins paired up and began swimming rapidly around the tank about 10 seconds before the seismic waves could be felt by humans. According to some in the veterinary world, it is quite feasible that animals can detect vertical accelerations in seismic P-waves which humans cannot.

There is a sequence at the beginning of the film *The Impossible* starring Ewan McGregor which relates the true story of what happened to Maria Belon and her family in Thailand during the 2004 tsunami disaster, where screeching birds take to the sky *en masse* just before the tsunami hits. This detail was noted by many of the survivors. It was the same with aftershocks in Kathmandu through the Summer of 2015 where I witnessed flocks of ravens leaving treetops seconds before I could feel the tremor myself.

29   *Earthquakes are not instantaneous events.*

It's important to realise that earthquakes, while being sudden-onset hazard events, are usually not instantaneous. In many cases, a building's occupants have tens of seconds to react before shaking reaches maximum intensity.

In the Japan earthquake of March 2011, the initial P-waves preceded the more violent and destructive S-waves by nearly 80 seconds, allowing enough time for automated early warning systems to trigger the sending of bulk text messages to all mobile phones in the potential affected area warning people on lower floors of buildings to evacuate; for railroad officials to slow high-speed 'bullet' trains; for lifts/elevators to disgorge their passengers at the next floor; for traffic lights near bridges and tunnels to turn red; for air traffic controllers to divert aircraft on final approach to land; and for municipal gas and water valves to be closed.

Such a warning system would not be very effective near the epicentre of an earthquake because the time delay between the arrival of the first P-wave and the first S-wave would be too short. But, the greater the distance from the epicentre, the greater the delay between the two types of waves, and the more time people have to protect themselves. Every second counts in an earthquake.

30 Blunt trauma is often not the biggest cause of death in an earthquake-induced building collapse.

Depending on the type of building, its design, its height, and the quality of its construction, about three quarters of people inside a collapsed building die within the first quarter of an hour. In Kobe, Japan in 1995, nearly three-quarters (71%) of all victims died within 14 minutes of the earthquake. A further 11% died within the next six hours. If the building is a ferro-concrete high-rise and has totally collapsed, these combined figures can rise from 82% to above 95%.

Typically, about four-fifths of people in a collapsed building are dead within 15 minutes.

At least half of those inside at the time of the collapse – in other words those that were too slow or too far away from street-level exits to run outside – die instantly from what doctors call "blunt trauma", a fancy term for being squashed or hit on the head so hard that the brain stops functioning. Within a few minutes, most of the others in this group die from asphyxiation; they cannot breathe, either because of the weight of rubble lying on their chests, or because they have inhaled concrete or brick dust and their lungs are clogged. The remaining few die from haemorrhage and/or penetrating trauma ... either internal bleeding or blood loss resulting from deep gashes sustained by rubble or, more likely, broken glass.

Huge amounts of dust are generated when a building collapses – one only has to recall images of the 9/11 Twin Towers collapse in New York to understand quite how much – and concrete dust being injected under high pressure to clog air passages and set hard in lungs is a major cause of death for many building collapse victims who could otherwise be saved.

Evidence from earthquakes in Guatemala in 1976, Mexico City in 1985, and Armenia in 1988 suggests that suffocation from dust inhalation was a significant factor in the deaths of many people who displayed no apparent external or internal trauma. Given this information, it is difficult to understand why more attention isn't paid to educating people about the threat posed by dust.

31 *Landslides are triggered more by human activity than by geology.*

Watching the side of an entire hillside slide into the valley below – trees and buildings all remaining vertical – is a surreal experience and requires anybody witnessing such a scene to suspend disbelief. Landslides are mass movements of surface rock and/or soil down slopes under the influence of gravity. They occur on terrain where conditions of geology, soil, moisture, and the angle of slope interact, and are triggered for the most part by heavy rain, floods, volcanic activity, and earthquakes.

Most landslides are caused by human interference with soil stability.

Landslides are aggravated by human activity, including deforestation, cultivation, road-building, and construction, all of which destabilise already fragile slopes by imposing new strains in new places. The most destructive types are soil and rock slides, and mud and debris flows.

Slopes are particularly vulnerable to landslip where soil is shallow and tree roots that formally bound the colluvium[29] to the bedrock have been replaced by shallow rooting plants. This is becoming more and more common in South Asia and South America where forest is rapidly being replaced by rubber and coconut palm plantations, or other 'cash crops' used for bio-fuel production.

The causes of landslides are directly related to instabilities on sloping ground. There is usually more than one cause, but there will only be one trigger. In the majority of cases, the main trigger is heavy or prolonged rain. A single rainfall event in Sri Lanka in May 2003, for example, triggered hundreds of landslides, killing 266 people and rendering over 300,000 people temporarily homeless.

The second major trigger is seismic activity. Landslides occur during earthquakes as a result of two separate but interconnected processes: seismic shaking, and pore water pressure generation.

The passage of seismic waves through the rock and soil produces a complex set of vertical and horizontal acceleration that effectively act to change the gravitational load on the slope successively increasing and decreasing the normal load. Similarly, horizontal accelerations induce a

---

[29] Colluvium is a general name for loose, unconsolidated sediments that have been deposited at the base of slopes.

sheer force due to the inertia of the ground mass during these accelerations. These processes are complex, not least because the seismic waves interact with the terrain to produce *topographic amplification* which magnifies the ground accelerations in some places while reducing it in others.

The maximum acceleration is usually seen at the crest of the slope or along the ridge line, meaning that it is a characteristic of seismically triggered landslides that they extend to the top of the slope. Water then increases the pore water pressure[30] and reduces the shear strength of the material. The velocity of the flow is dependent on the ratio of water content in the flow itself: the higher the water content, the higher the velocity will be.

In the five weeks after the two devastating earthquakes of 2015, Nepal experienced more landslides than in the previous five years combined.

32   *The risk of being buried alive in a landslide is lower than with other forms of natural hazard.*

Compared to other natural hazards such as earthquakes and tropical cyclones, the risk of being buried alive in a landslide is relatively low ... although it has to be said that many, if not most, small landslides, rockfalls, lahars, and debris flows that kill less than five people are not reported outside the country in which they took place making objective comparison difficult.

Over half (55%) of the risk of being buried alive in a landslide is concentrated in just 10 countries which, together, account for over three quarters (80%) of total exposure. These countries include China, India, Nepal, Guatemala, Papua New Guinea, Indonesia, Ethiopia, and the Philippines.

Recent research by Durham University in the UK, has shown that the global impact of landslides is much greater than represented by 'official' data. In total, 2,620 non-seismic landslides were recorded worldwide during the seven-year period 2004 to 2010, causing a total of 32,322 recorded deaths[xx]. In terms of events, this is 20 times greater than that indicated by the official CRED database which had only 140 events reported to them over the same period. If true, this represents a four-

---

[30] 'Pore Water Pressure' is vital to calculating the stress state in the ground and refers to the pressure of groundwater held by capillary action in gaps between soil particles.

fold increase in the number of fatalities. Paradoxically, the average number of deaths per event consequently falls from 57 to 12 as a result.

The economic and social ability of a country to invest in preventive measures plays a crucial role in reducing landslide hazard risk. This is true of many disaster types, but especially so for landslides which are typically small-scale in nature. Thus, Italy, a country prone to potentially fatal landslides, does not show a particularly high occurrence of disasters, probably because of successful landslide mitigation programs such as risk identification through geophysical survey, slope stabilisation efforts, netting of roadside rock faces, and enhanced early warning[xxi].

Landslide risk can be significantly reduced by geo-engineering.

Slope stabilisation is a form of geo-engineering that involves three predominant stabilisation methods in rock or earth: altering the geometry of the hillside by carting some of it away; reducing water content in the soil by laying non-permeable mesh across the top of the slope, and/or through improving drainage systems; or by driving anchors and ground nails deep into the underlying rock.

33 *Volcanoes are one of the least deadly natural hazards on the planet.*

Snow-capped Mount Vesuvius looms large and apparently benign across the bay from the Italian city of Naples. Although currently dormant, it is the only 'active' volcano to have erupted in mainland Europe in the last one hundred years. Its most recent eruption occurred towards the end of the Second World War in March 1944, destroying several nearby villages. Most famously, it erupted in 79 AD, burying Pompeii and Herculaneum in ash, killing an estimated 10,000 to 25,000 people. Now overdue for another eruption, it is regarded as one of the world's most dangerous volcanoes. This is because Vesuvius' eruptions tend to be explosive, but it is also because 3 million people live nearby, 800,000 of whom reside in private houses that have crept relentlessly up its flanks[31].

A volcano is an opening, or rupture, in the planet's crust, which allows hot, molten rock, ash and gas to escape from deep below the

---

[31] Volcano risk is increasing due to rapid urbanisation and the high density of populations living on volcanic slopes. About 500 million people worldwide are exposed to volcano risk and more than 60 large cities are located near active volcanoes.

surface. There are more than 1,500 potentially active volcanoes in the world, of which at least 500 have erupted in the last 10,000 years, meaning they are considered to be active at the moment. Vesuvius is one of these. In addition, there are more than 1 million volcanic vents under the sea. About 50 to 60 volcanoes erupt every year worldwide, and, on any given day, an average of 20 are erupting somewhere on the planet.

Compared to other natural hazards, such as earthquakes, volcanic eruptions generally cause fewer deaths as eruptions are often predictable and people can be evacuated before being overwhelmed by the gases, falling rocks, lava, ash, and lahars they produce. Molten rock (lava) flows like a viscous liquid: the hotter it is, the faster it flows. Eruption temperature is in the region of 1,155°C and its rate of cooling will depend on the course it takes on its inevitable journey to the sea. In the open, lava flows at about 10 kph, but, if following a channel, it can reach speeds of up to 50 kph ... which is faster than a human can run[32].

Inhaled volcanic ash causes significant avoidable death.

A pyroclastic eruption, however, is an entirely different affair. Pyroclastic flows are airborne mixtures of steam, hot gases – mostly sulphur dioxide, carbon monoxide, and hydrogen chloride – ash, fine pumice, and rocks that move like dense clouds, and which can cause heavy destruction over wide areas. Travelling at over 160 kph, the dynamic pressure wave produced flattens trees for many miles around. Most flows erupt at over 1,000°C, but tend to cool rapidly at the periphery, meaning that people sheltering indoors fearing their last moments have come may actually survive.

The Mount St Helens lateral pyroclastic eruption of 1980 is one of the few to afford the opportunity of scientific investigation. Despite official warnings and establishment of areas of restricted access, 160 people were within a few miles of the volcano when it erupted. Lines of downed trees 18 miles from the crater marked the extent of the pressure wave that followed. Extraordinarily, and against all expectations, half of those exposed survived even though they were caught out in the open. Autopsies carried out on the 25 bodies retrieved showed that 17 deaths were caused by asphyxia due to inhalation of ash, five were the result of having been burned alive, and three were killed by blows to the head. Once again, as with the dust produced by earthquake-induced building

---

[32] The maximum speed attained by an Olympic 100 metre athlete is 37 kph

collapses, it is inhalation of fine airborne particles – in this case volcanic ash – that results in significant death, almost all of which could be prevented by the wearing of a simple dust mask.

Volcanoes eject volcanic material, gas, and ash well into the atmosphere, with many of the resulting clouds rising to 12,000 metres in altitude i.e above the cruising altitude of commercial jet aircraft.

Volcanic ash consists of tiny jagged pieces of rock and glass. Ash is hard, abrasive, mildly corrosive, conducts electricity when wet, and does not dissolve in water. Eruption of a volcano under the Eyjafjallajokull glacier in Icelandic in April 2010 sent ripple effects around the globe as the ash it produced halted international flights to and from Northern Europe for weeks[33].

Falling ash can turn daylight into complete darkness. Accompanied by rain and lightning, the gritty ash can lead to power outages, disrupt communications, and disorient people. Wet ash can collapse even the sturdiest of roofs, and structural collapse under accumulating ash which was then rained on was the major cause of death in the Mount Pinatubo eruption of 1991. It can bring down power lines, short-out transformers, and clog water pipes. "It gets into everything and there's nothing you can do to stop it," said Ana Adelardo, a mother from Montevideo in Uruguay who was struggling to cope with the ash fall-out from June 2011's volcanic eruption in Chile.

Being acidic, inhaling volcanic ash can cause all sorts of respiratory problems[34] into the bargain, which is another reason for taking dust masks more seriously as a disaster preparedness measure.

Wet volcanic ash can collapse the sturdiest of roofs.

Some of the largest and most destructive landslides known have been associated with volcanoes. These can occur either in association with the eruption of the volcano itself, or as a result of slope failure within the very weak deposits that are formed as a consequence of previous volcanic activity.

Essentially, there are two main types of volcanic landslide: lahars and debris flows, the largest of which are sometimes termed "flank

---

[33] Airborne volcanic ash poses a threat to jet engines and avionics systems requiring the 'grounding' of aircraft.

[34] Respiratory symptoms from the inhalation of volcanic ash depend on a number of factors, including: pressure at which it was inhaled; airborne concentration of total suspended particles; proportion of particles in the ash less than 10 μ in diameter; duration of exposure; presence of free crystalline silica; and concentration of volcanic gases or aerosols mixed in with the ash.

collapses". For example, a part of the side of Casita volcano in Nicaragua collapsed on 30th October 1998 during the heavy rains associated with the passage of hurricane *Mitch*. Debris from initial small failure eroded older deposits from the volcano and incorporated additional water and wet sediment from along its path, increasing in volume about ninefold as it gathered momentum. The lahar killed more than 2,000 people.

Debris flows commonly occur at the same time as an eruption, but occasionally they may be triggered by other factors such as a seismic shock or heavy rain. Due to their size – they often have a mass of 10,000,000 m³ or more; equivalent to 250 of the world's largest aircraft carriers – and because they can travel at speeds of up to 80 kph, they are massively destructive. The most famous debris flow occurred at Mount St Helens in 1980 where it travelled more than 65 kph and ended up covering an area of 62 km², killing 57 people.

34 *Sinkholes can swallow entire buildings without warning.*

It doesn't make for a restful night to think that a sinkhole could open up without warning below your house and swallow you whole while you sleep. Or that you turn up to work one morning, put your key in the lock to the unloading bay door, to find a whole three-storey building suddenly disappear beneath your feet. Yet this is exactly what happened to the owner of a garment factory that fell into a 1,000 foot deep hole in Guatemala City in May 2010.

Sinkholes are depressions that form slowly over time as a portion of the Earth's surface is eroded away by percolating water, the collapse of a subterranean cave, or the lowering of the water table. Usually, it is a natural process of erosion as slightly soluble, usually limestone, bedrock or sandy soils are scoured away by strong underground water flows. More commonly, sinkholes occur in urban areas due to breaks in water or sewage pipes. They can also be caused by the over-pumping and extraction of groundwater as water in the aquifers below ground actually helps keep the surface soil in place. Either way, as the rock dissolves, a cavern develops underground. The surface usually stays intact until there is not enough support from underneath, at which point a sudden and dramatic collapse occurs.

35 The majority of deadly avalanches occur in Europe.

One cold and grey January morning in 1954, an avalanche buried 118 people in the sleepy Austrian village of Blons. As rescue workers attempted to dig them out, a second unexpected avalanche descended. The final death toll amounted to over 200 people. Thousands of avalanches like this continue to occur every year, killing an average of 500 people worldwide.

Alpine countries in Europe are the most prone to avalanches. In the past 10 years, France has recorded more avalanche fatalities than any other country, followed by Austria, the United States, Switzerland, Italy, and Canada.

Avalanches cannot always be predicted, but they are linked to weather conditions that can be forecast in advance. Most accidents now occur because people ignore warnings. Around 95% of all avalanche incidents are due to slab avalanches with skiers involved. They occur when massive slabs of snow break loose from the mountainside to race downhill, reaching speeds of 130 kph within about five seconds and pushing a shockwave ahead of them powerful enough to flatten forests and destroy buildings. The Vin Diesel movie XXX has a great scene which depicts the speed and awesome destructive power of an avalanche. It is not unusual for an avalanche mass to exceed 2.5 million tons. Violent internal swirls within avalanches have been measured at 300 kph. According to the 'professional survival solutions' book Everything That Follows ... there is enough oxygen dissolved in avalanche snow to maintain life for 45 minutes or more. In statistical terms, the victim apparently has a 90% chance of survival if rescued within 15 minutes, dropping to less than 30% after 45 minutes.

Water-Related

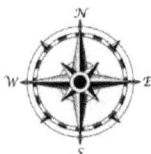

Drowning is not the main cause of death in a Tsunami.

The seventh largest earthquake ever recorded at 9.0 on the Richter Scale took place 140 kilometres off the North-East coast of Japan at lunchtime on 11th March 2011. In terms of 'unleashed energy' it was eight thousand times more powerful than the one that devastated the New Zealand town of Christchurch a few weeks before. The relatively shallow tectonic plate shift event occurred 10 kilometres under the sea-bed, causing it to rise by 4 metres over a matter of minutes. This displaced billions of tons of sea water above it which radiated a series of energy swells that, eighteen minutes later, surged onto the shoreline near the city of Sendai as a 10 metre high tsunami.

With only eight minutes between the warning sirens going off and its arrival, nothing that was not made of solid steel and concrete withstood the impact as the unrelenting wall of water , rocks, and debris pressed inland at speeds of up to 100 kilometres per hour obliterating everything in its path.

A later article put the event into tragic perspective:

"A ragged white line appeared on the horizon, and with unimaginable ferocity the line became visible as a wall of waves sweeping back inshore at immense speed and at great height. Just seconds later and these Pacific Ocean waters hit the Japanese seawalls, surmounted them with careless ease, and began to claw across the land beyond in what would become a dispassionate and detached orgy of utter destruction".xxii

Tsunami is the Japanese word for "harbour wave" and is the same word in singular and plural. They are often mistakenly referred to as "tidal waves", which they are not. First, they have nothing to do with the tide, which is the ebb and flow of the sea due to the effect of lunar gravitational pull. Second, they are not, strictly speaking, 'waves' – at least not in the sense that those of us who like playing with buckets and spades on the beach think of them – as they are generated by extreme energy pulses from the ocean floor or from impacts from above, not the wind.

A tsunami is the effect caused by anything that displaces a large mass of water. During a submarine event, an impulsive force displaces the water column above it, and it is this that generates a tsunami. With more than half of the 4,000 earthquakes that take place every day occurring underwater, energy releases are rarely enough to cause noticeable disturbance on the surface. But tsunami can also be caused by landslides taking place either above or below the water, submarine volcanoes, and asteroid impacts.

If you watch live You-tube footage of Japan's tsunami of 2010, what strikes you most is not so much the speed of the incoming water, but its relentless rise – a metre or so every minute – as it pushes inland. Before the water has time to recede, the next wave, often larger than the first, and arriving up to two hours later, increases the depth yet more.

Almost everybody caught in a tsunami dies from blunt trauma rather than drowning.

Most people caught in the swirling maelstrom of water, sand, rocks, coral, seashells and debris that is a tsunami do not survive. Not only is it not possible to swim in such turbulent water, but hundreds of thousands of tons of rocks and debris remains suspended and rotating in it as if in a giant washing machine. Most people unfortunate enough to be submerged in such currents die from blunt trauma before they have a chance to drown ... even though 'cause of death' is later certified as such by overworked doctors who see water-filled lungs as a sign of 'drowning'. There are some, though, like Ewan McGregor's family in the film *The Impossible*[35], who make it by clinging to tree-tops and pieces of wreckage. They are the lucky ones.

About one-fifth of all tsunami victims are never found. The bodies of roughly half of these will have been washed out to sea while the other half will have been pulverised beyond recognition. Later DNA testing of fragments might identify some of them. Of the 164,000 people who died in Indonesia in the 2004 tsunami, 37,000 simply disappeared. The same thing happened in Japan in March 2011 when, of the 26,000 who died, the bodies of 5,000 have never been found.

There are an average of two destructive tsunami per year in the Pacific basin. One swamped the Solomon Islands in February 2013, killing a dozen or so people and flattening up to five villages in low-lying atolls. But Pacific-wide tsunami – i.e those that reach the North and South American coastline – are a much rarer phenomenon, occurring every 10 – 12 years on average. Up until the mega-tsunami of December 2004, there were 94 destructive tsunami through the whole of the past century which resulted in a total of 51,000 deaths.

---

[35] This film is actually a true story of María Belón and her family.

Impact on-shore also depends on orientation of the shoreline to the event itself. The Japan impact was so 'energetic' because the fault displacement and the shoreline were parallel which did not allow for a glancing blow. The slope and morphology of the coastal slope also play their part, with wave energy morphing into higher waves where depth changes abruptly; the shallower the slope, the lower the wave height.

The waves we see at the beach are wind-generated, have a wavelength[36] of about 50 to 200 metres, and come ashore at roughly 30 kph. A tsunami, on the other hand, has a wavelength in excess of 340 kilometres, and, in very deep water, can travel at about 890 kph, the speed of a commercial airliner. This means it crosses from one side of the Pacific Ocean to the other in 12-18 hours, and with very little loss of energy. It slows on reaching shore, however, as its forward momentum translates into vertical height. But the total 'run up'[37] will be the same because the same amount of energy has to dissipate. This will, in turn, influence the speed with which the tsunami advances inland. In Aceh in 2004, this was roughly 30 kph i.e about one third the speed of the one in Japan.

The time between the triggering event and the tsunami's landfall is a key variable as it influences the effectiveness of tsunami early warning systems and the possibility for evacuation. Chile, India, Indonesia, Japan, Myanmar, Peru, Portugal, Pakistan, the Philippines and Sri Lanka all have particularly high levels of risk exposure given than a tsunami 6 metres or more in height could hit the shoreline in less than 20 minutes. But, as local topography and bathymetry attenuate and/or amplify the hazard, it is not inconceivable that those countries facing potential 'mega-thrust' tectonic shifts, particularly Indonesia, Japan, and the Philippines could face tsunami with heights of 16 metres or higher, with even less warning time[xxiii].

A mass of water 10 metres high, 100 metres wide and 100 metres long, weighs 100,000 tons. This is the weight of two hundred fully laden freight trains. A 30 metre wave packs 100 tons of force per square metre, which, according to Susan Casey, author of the book *The Wave*, is enough to tear the steel plate of a ship's hull in half. Not much can withstand these sorts of immutable forces, although well-constructed rounded concrete pillars will allow the 'force' to swirl around rather than 'through', which is why better made concrete buildings tend to

---

[36] Wavelength is the distance between two successive wave crests.
[37] 'Run-up' is the maximum vertical height above sea level reached by a tsunami, with 'run-up distance' being how far it ingresses inland.

remain when everything else is washed many miles inland. In Aceh, as in the Philippines town of Tacloban nearly ten years later, churches and mosques could still be seen standing proud, relatively unscathed amidst a sea of carnage because they were built with permanence in mind. This just goes to show that it is perfectly possible to engineer a survival solution.

37 Tsunami are not confined solely to the Pacific and Indian oceans

The Pacific is by far the most active tsunami zone, but tsunami are not unknown in the Caribbean and Mediterranean seas. A North Atlantic tsunami associated with the Lisbon earthquake of 1775 killed as many as 60,000 people in Portugal, Spain, and North Africa, and caused a tsunami 7 metres high in the Caribbean. The Caribbean has been hit by 37 verified tsunami since 1498, and a series of large tsunami were generated in the Sea of Marmara off Turkey after the Izmir earthquake of 1999. Emergency services in Cornwall in the South-West of England are taking the tsunami risk seriously enough to consider installing a sub-sea early warning system.

The highest recorded tsunami was 525 metres (1,600 ft).

Two of the largest tsunami ever recorded were generated, not by earthquakes or asteroids, but by landslides. The most recent took place in Lituya Bay, Alaska in 1958 and, judging by the height at which trees were smashed to matchwood, triggered a 525 metre wall of water, the highest 'wave' ever recorded. It was caused when an earthquake along the Fairweather Fault in Alaska loosened about 30 million cubic metres of rock above the North-Eastern shore of the bay which then plunged from a height of approximately 900 metres down into the waters of the sound.

The other, visible only through geological record, was caused by the collapse of an island off the west coast of Africa. This one wiped out most animal life in what was then North America and may have contributed to the Cretaceous-Tertiary extinction of dinosaurs 65 million years ago.

The most scary bit about those stories is that, despite the odds being no more than dying in a plane crash, exactly the same things could happen again. The Aleutian fault off the Alaskan coast is subject to almost the same stresses as the Asian fault that triggered such devastation in Japan in March 2011. Any tsunami triggered there would probably result in a tsunami tens of metres in height crashing into San Francisco less than two hours later.

More worrying still is that half the island of La Palma in the Canary Islands is supposedly poised to collapse into the Atlantic Ocean when the next major earthquake strikes there. And, with the island already spewing lava, this scenario suddenly doesn't seem so unrealistic[38]. Any tsunami triggered by the 150 trillion tons of rock which is predicted to fall into the ocean is likely to be at least 100 metres high when it reaches New York, Miami or anywhere else on the US East Coast six hours later.

But, having scared all East and West coasters in North and South America, it should quickly be pointed out that not only seismic events but also the tsunami that may or may not follow are incredibly hard to predict. One coastal area may see no damaging wave activity while in another, inundation can be quick and violent. The Japan tsunami of March 2011 saw a wall of water 10 metres high smash its way inland, but the same event only sent a 'wave' some centimetres high through the marinas of California eleven hours later.

✦

Most tsunami occur in open oceans, and are generated by sub-sea mega-thrust earthquakes. But inland tsunami are not unknown. Lake Tahoe in the US state of Nevada witnessed such an event 20,000 years ago that caused a wave over 30 metres in height. A 6th Century tsunami over 8 metres in height was also triggered in the usually placid waters of Lake Geneva in Switzerland by a landslide at the eastern end of the lake which took just over one hour to reach, and largely destroy, what was then the small Swiss town of Geneva forty miles away at the other end.

A tsunami today – and researchers at the University of Geneva[xxiv] suggest this is not unlikely – would be far more devastating. In the 6th Century, Geneva was a small market town. Today it is home to over 200,000 bankers, tax advisers, and UN officials, many of whom live in low lying areas near the lake shore.

---

[38] The Tsunami Society challenges the evidence and says that no such event is likely.

91

38 Teaching children to swim is not necessarily the best way to prevent them from drowning in a flood.

Teaching children to swim as a life-saving measure in the context of natural disasters has little impact on the numbers that drown. Despite its apparent potential for saving life within certain age groups, it is probable that the real benefit is to be gained from the resuscitation training associated with learning to swim, rather than learning to swim per se[39].

It takes less than half a minute for a child who has inhaled water to lose consciousness, and a small child can drown in just a few inches of water[40]. If, however, cardiopulmonary resuscitation (CPR) is correctly performed within a few minutes, it is highly likely that someone who appears lifeless can be brought round.

Most flood victims are small children who lack the strength to overcome turbulent and fast-moving flood waters.

Water hazards in developing countries are not swimming pools. For a start, surface water is likely to take the form of a river, lake, or pond. Hungry animals with sharp teeth lurk in the first two – crocodiles and hippopotamus' spring to mind – while a pond is likely to be the community's drinking water supply. All are likely to be contaminated with bugs, worms, and parasites, each one nastier than the one before. Not surprisingly, swimming is discouraged ... all of which makes what appears to be self-evident, much less so.

According to the International Life Saving Federation, 1.2 million people – or more than two people every minute – drown annually around the world. This means that as many people die from drowning in the developing world as from malaria. Half of them are children under five. According to the International Drowning Research Centre, an average of 18,000 children die every year in drowning accidents in

---

[39] This comment applies to flood disasters; the costs and benefits would be very different in a coastal urban environment.

[40] This goes some way to explaining why drowning is the second leading cause of preventable death in children in the US. According to the American Academy of Pediatrics, children aged 1-4 are less likely to drown if they have had formal swimming lessons.

Bangladesh, one of the most flood-prone parts of the world, and more than 6,000 a year in Vietnam.

Not enough is known about the circumstances of those deaths that are flood-related. However, it is quite likely that the majority of victims, being under five years of age, are too young to swim in turbulent and fast-moving flood waters where even strong adult swimmers couldn't survive for long. Many victims are also infants being cared for by younger siblings who have probably never been taught to swim themselves – especially if they are girls – or mothers unable to properly attend to all their children at once. Among older children, most deaths by drowning occur among teenage boys, probably because they are trying to salvage family assets.

39 Floods no longer cause more deaths than other types of natural disaster.

It used to be true that floods caused more deaths than any other type of disaster, but this is no longer the case.

Earthquakes (including tsunamis) killed more people than all other types of disaster put together, claiming nearly 750,000 lives between 1994 and 2013. Tsunamis are the most deadly sub-type of earthquake, with an average of 79 deaths for every 1,000 people affected, compared to four deaths per 1,000 for ground movements. This makes tsunamis almost twenty times more deadly than earthquakes[41].

Earthquakes kill more people than all other types of disaster put together.

The planet is covered with 1,385 million km³ of water. 97% is sea-water which means only 3% is drinkable without desalination. Of this 3%, two thirds is locked up in the form of glacial or polar ice. Most of the 1% that remains is in underground aquifers. This leaves a tiny fraction in the form of river or lake surface water and a tinier fraction still in the atmosphere. It's this last bit we're interested in because it's from this, less than 0.001% of the world's available freshwater, that the rain comes to cause riverine and flash flooding.

90% of the water vapour in the atmosphere got there as a result of evaporation, but only some of it has condensed to form clouds. If all this

---

[41] Though this does not take into account the long-term effects of drought.

water fell at once, it would reach a depth of 2.5 cms. This doesn't sound like it's enough to cause the metres of sustained floodwater witnessed recently in places like Pakistan and Australia which inundated areas the size of Belgium for weeks, but it is.

Floods are nature's most widespread hazard and affect more people than any other type of natural disaster. Some 1.5 billion people were affected in the last decade of the 20th Century, and now over 200 million people around the world live in zones at risk of flooding. Flooding is not only one of the most regular of natural disasters[xxv] but also causes the most damage. Water moving at 16 kph exerts the same pressure on a building per square metre as a 270 kph blast of wind. According to the Asian Development Bank, floods are the most common peril in the Asia-Pacific region, and "have become three times more frequent in the past thirty years".[42]

Water moving at 10 mph exerts the same pressure per m² on a building as a 170 mph blast of wind.

Flood risk depends most obviously on the volume of water – the size of the rainwater catchment area (watershed) – the ability of the ground to absorb the water running over it – both saturated ground and ground baked hard by drought cause high run-off rates – and the slope, which determines the speed with which the water flows. But the quality of shelter construction, including whether that shelter had previously been exposed to flood waters which may have weakened its walls, distance to high ground, and time of day all influence the numbers who drown. Of far greater significance, though, is the accuracy of weather forecasts, the reach of early warning systems, and enhanced mitigation measures such as building of embankments and dredging, and it is these three factors which have contributed most to reductions in death tolls around the world.

You would think that the risk of dying in a flood would be dependent on the ability to swim. To an extent, this is true as the majority of those who drown in riverine floods are girls under the age of three, followed by their mothers, their elder brothers – who are probably over-optimistic about their swimming abilities – and, lastly, their fathers, who stay too late in an effort to save the family home and livestock [see *Disaster Misperception # 36*].

---

[42] Subject to the comments about 'observation bias' made in *Disaster Misperception # 16*.

Public health and social problems in a community will be dramatically amplified by a flood. New diseases seldom emerge during floods. Rather, displacement for weeks on overcrowded embankments exacerbates the effects of poor sanitation, unsafe water, and lack of shelter, food, and health care. This is why more people, most of them children, die later from indirect causes, many of them, rather counter-intuitively, connected with dehydration.

40 *Snake-bite is a major cause of avoidable death in floods in Asia.*

An increased incidence of snake bite has been reported from countries such as Malaysia, Pakistan, and Bangladesh following floods. This is because both snakes and humans converge to take refuge on limited areas of high ground. During the 2007 monsoon flood disaster in Bangladesh, snake bite was the second most common cause of avoidable death after drowning, eclipsing mortality from diarrhoeal and respiratory diseases[xxvi].

An accurate measure of the global burden of death and injury due to snake bite poisoning remains elusive and the true impact is very likely to be underestimated. But South Asia is by far the most affected region. India has the highest number of deaths due to snake bites in the world with 35,000–50,000 people dying per year according to World Health Organisation, and in Pakistan, 40,000 bites are reported annually, which result in up to 8,200 fatalities. In Nepal, more than 20,000 cases of envenoming occur each year[43].

Snake bite results in acute renal failure and/or paralysis of the inter-costal muscles used for breathing, at which point victims usually die of respiratory failure if they are not adequately ventilated. Snake bite victims need to be immobilised to minimise venom absorption and transported as quickly as possible to a medical centre where they can be clinically evaluated, and where anti-venoms are available[44]. The time taken to get to the health centre is actually the crucial determinant of

---

[43] A cobra injects approximately 60mg of venom in an average bite but as many as 50% of cobra bites inject no venom into the victim.

[44] One vial of anti-venom of Indian production costs around US$8–10, which is equivalent to several days of salary for poor farmers. Thus, many cannot afford to purchase the average 15-25 vials needed to reverse the poisoning. Treatment also requires four days of hospitalisation in intensive care, probably needing mechanical ventilation .

whether someone bitten by a snake will die or not as most victims die in transit owing to the fact that those accompanying them don't know how to give and sustain mouth-to-mouth 'artificial' resuscitation.

Unfortunately, in many cases the biting snake is not seen, and if it is, its description by the victim is often misleading. Even when the dead snake is brought to the health centre, misidentification is common. Consequently, many victims end up receiving ineffective anti-venom even if they do make it there alive.

Vital time is often lost when victims go first to traditional healers, as the majority do[xxvii]. Popular traditional treatments include chanting, incisions, attempts to suck venom from the site of the bite, and the application of herbal medicine or snake stones. Victims in Sindh province of southern Pakistan ingest ghee, chillis and other substances to combat snakebite. None are of any proven use.

Most snake-bite victims die in transit for lack of CPR.

Over 90% of snakebite victims have tourniquets applied by anxious family members. Not only is this is not a good idea as tourniquets cannot be safely left on for long without risking severe local damage including ischemia, necrosis, and gangrene[xxviii], but they are usually applied too late.

In order to effectively treat snakebite, health centres should have a snakebite tray ready for immediate deployment when the victim arrives. If such a tray is made available in each hospital, including Basic Health Units (BHU) and Rural Health Centers (RHC), snakebite mortality will be dramatically reduced.

In practice, strategies to control snake populations and to prevent snake bites are non-existent in many South Asian countries. Many bites could be avoided by educating the population at risk. Sleeping on a cot rather than on the floor and under bed nets decreases the risk of nocturnal bites while rubbish, termite mounds, and firewood, which attract snakes, can be removed from the vicinity of human dwellings.

A complementary strategy is to decrease the risk of dying from envenoming snake bites. Many areas where snake bites occur are relatively inaccessible by road, especially during the rainy season, and transport to a health centre sometimes takes more than 24 hours. In Nepal, a programme for rapid transport of snake bite victims by motorcycle volunteers to a specialised treatment centre significantly reduced the risk of fatal outcome.

41 *Drowning is rarely the biggest single cause of death in a riverine flood.*

Emergency shelter, clothing, and blankets provide the thermal protection needed after a natural disaster, and are widely regarded as life-saving relief items without which survivors run a high risk of death from exposure.

Many deaths by drowning are in fact due to hypothermia. Immersion in water increases heat loss considerably. While dry clothing insulates, wet clothing does the opposite. And even imperceptible air currents over a naked human body have been shown to increase heat loss by 20-75%, even in tropical climates.

Many deaths apparently caused by drowning in a flood are in fact due to hypothermia.

In general, children are less able to tolerate environmental extremes for the reason that they are smaller and have a larger surface area relative to their body weight. Babies also lose heat more rapidly than older children. Given that these conditions are just as likely to be found after storm surges and floods in tropical and subtropical areas as they are in countries with cold climates, it should come as no surprise to find that the majority of flood victims are small children.

42 *GLOFs are a major hazard risk in mountainous areas.*

Two thirds of Himalayan glaciers are retreating at rates ranging from 10 – 60 metres per year[45]. When glaciers retreat, lakes commonly form behind the newly exposed 'moraine' banks of soil and rock carried along by the front edge of the ice wall. Rapid accumulation of water in these lakes could lead to a sudden breach of this moraine dam, causing a possibly catastrophic Glacial Lake Outburst Flood (GLOF). Such lakes have the potential to release up to 100 million cubic metres of water into vulnerable valleys below.

---

[45] And it's not just the Himalaya either; changing climatic conditions and warming temperatures are increasing the risk of natural hazards posed by melting glaciers in the mountain regions of Central Asia as well as the Andes and the European Alps.

Moraine dams are made up of small, fist-sized stones eroded smooth by glacial action and held together largely by frozen mud. These natural dams hold back a considerable volume of glacial melt-water which, when subject to the kind of energy shock of a tsunami-like wave triggered by a landslide or calving glacier, instantly shatters and melts, rendering the dam even more unstable than it was before.

Flood water from a catastrophic dam burst or over-topping event can sweep down a mountain valley at speeds of between 65-110 kph, and at an average height of 18 metres. Being more dense, GLOFs travel more slowly at 35-50 kph, theoretically allowing more time to evacuate. This means that those living 15 kilometres below a dam have about 20 minutes to reach ground higher than 18 metres above the valley floor. If unable to reach high ground in time, most victims are crushed by pieces of debris rather than drowned.

The world first became aware of GLOFs as potential hazards in 1985 when the lake at the foot of the 'Dig Tsho' glacier in Nepal suddenly burst the 60 metre high moraine dam which held it back to obliterate a large concrete hydro-electrical power plant 12 kms downstream. The lake held 6.75 million cubic metres (m^3) of water. This water took five hours to escape, forming a 6 metre high wave which travelled 40 kms down the valley at a speed of 35 kph. Typically, such flows dissipate within 10 – 60 kms of the dam site.

Typically, GLOF debris flows dissipate within 60 kms of the origin.

The speed of the advancing wall of water depends primarily on the overall friction of the valley according to something called the *Strickler Coefficient* and secondarily on the volume of water released. This friction has a strong influence on wave velocity and is a function of the valley's width, slope, and roughness, as well as the number and angle of bends, all of which serve either to accelerate or decelerate flow momentum. In addition, water flow is chaotic and three dimensional with intense turbulent mixing and vertical accelerations, possibly including fluid layer break up, splashing, water aeration and other such factors which make flow rates very hard to predict.

The advancing wave is not vertical, but takes 60-90 seconds to reach peak height with the level reducing thereafter depending on the total volume of water released upstream.

Records are incomplete but nevertheless show there have been 21 such events in Nepal alone since the 1960's, occurring with an average frequency of once every two to three years.

There are over 3,000 glaciers in Nepal of which 2,323 now have glacial lakes at their foot[46]. The whole Hindu-Kush Himalaya region which covers eight countries from Afghanistan to the South-Western borders of China and Tibet including Bhutan, India, China, Nepal, and Pakistan, has nearly 8,800 glacial lakes of which 203 are growing quickly and are considered potentially dangerous.

What makes GLOFs different to man-made dam-bursts is the amount of rock and debris suspended in the water. The three survivors of the 'Dig Tsho' event described the earth shaking and a growing rumble which turned to a roar as the wall of what appeared to be liquid rock swept round the bend up the valley and raced in slow-motion towards them. Lucky for them, they were working in the woods above the valley floor so saw the whole thing unfold beneath them.

Typically, such floods scour away the river banks as they thunder downstream. This, in turn, undermines and destabilises the slopes above causing landslides which add yet more trees, rock and mud to the mix. The total bulk density of rock suspended in what is now the semi-liquid slurry of a debris flow can reach 1.47 tonnes per m^3 (concrete weighs 2.4 tonnes for the same volume). To wash away the Namche hydro-electric plant, newly constructed of reinforced concrete, would have required a breaking stress in excess of 171 tons per square metre.

Over 3 million tons of rock and sediment was deposited, creating a life-less lunar landscape along 40 kms of what, five hours before, had been a quiet, green and forested valley. The Namche power plant was over 20m tall in some places. If any of it remained, it is now buried under this settled debris.

43   *Landslide Dam Bursts pose a significant secondary risk following an Earthquake.*

About one month after the earthquake that hit Nepal in April 2015, a massive landslide occurred which blocked the Kaligandaki river causing the waters to accumulate in a reservoir three kilometres long behind what was now a landslide dam over 150 metres in height. Water levels rose so fast, it took only 16 hours to reach the top. Top-down erosion caused the dam to suffer a catastrophic breach, sending a flood

---

[46] The other 700 or so are not melting, but are actually growing.

of more than 2 million m³ of water, rocks and mud racing downstream. Fortunately, swift government action had already evacuated villages at immediate risk, and widespread human casualties were prevented. Had the lake that formed upstream become much larger, with the river water retained for a few more days, the resulting flood would have caused catastrophic levels of destruction.

A similar type of dam of similar size blocked the Sunkoshi river nine months earlier. This one killed more than 150 people and caused fears of flooding as far away as the eastern Indian state of Bihar. In the event, the waters building up rapidly behind the dam didn't over-top but eroded the dam from underneath, this time resulting in a naturally controlled flow rather than catastrophic failure. Nevertheless, falling water levels behind the dam should not be taken as a good sign as the dam itself may be de-stabilising invisibly from within.

Falling water levels behind a landslide dam does not indicate reduced risk of catastrophic failure.

In the aftermath of the 8.0 magnitude Wenchuan earthquake in China in 2008, scientists recorded more than 12,000 landslides along the region's river valleys. As in Nepal, the earthquake and its numerous strong aftershocks triggered many large landslides that completely blocked fast-flowing rivers coursing through steeply sided valleys, resulting in the formation of more than 30 spontaneous lakes. One of these landslide dams blocked the Jian River, and more than 200,000 people living downstream, who were at immediate risk, were evacuated. This time the government constructed a sluiceway alongside the dam – an operation which exposes military engineers to considerable risk – to safely drain the lake and prevent large-scale devastation.

The sequence of events represents a classic cascading and inter-connected sequence of heavy rainfall, slope failure, valley blockage, lake formation, dam collapse, and catastrophic debris flow. Post-earthquake landslides like these move quite large volumes of sediment, including large boulders. Typically the riverbeds will aggrade – the bed level will rise as sediment is deposited – which will greatly increase the threat of downstream flooding later. The slug of sediment works its way downriver extending the effects of the earthquake well outside the area of original impact. In effect, this extends the effects of earthquakes in time and space.

In the Kaligandaki case, the height of the wave was never below 18 metres until it arrived at the flood plain where it instantly dispersed, but, in the narrower gorges, it reached some 87 metres in height.

44 Underwater gas eruptions can be lethal.

In 1989, a so-called *limnic eruption* at Lake Nyos in Cameroon triggered the sudden release of 1.6 million tons of carbon dioxide. This gas cloud rose through the water at nearly 100 kph forming a 91 metre fountain of water and foam at the surface of the lake and spawning a wave at least 24 metres high that knocked down all the trees lining the lake shore. The heavier-than-air gas spilled over the northern lip of the lake then rushed down two valleys at 20-50 kph in an invisible cloud 50 metres thick, displacing all the air and suffocating some 1,700 people as well as 3,500 livestock within 25 kilometres.

The normally blue waters of the lake turned a deep red due to iron-rich water rising to the surface and being oxidised by the air. The level of the lake also dropped by about a metre.

The disaster, however odd, wasn't unique. Two years earlier, Lake Monoun, 60 miles to the South-East, released a heavy cloud of toxic gas, killing 37 people. A third lake, Lake Kivu, on the Congo-Rwanda border in Central Africa, is also known to act as a reservoir of carbon dioxide and methane.

The science behind these disasters is fairly simple. Lake Nyos is a deep pool of water sitting in the throat of a dormant volcano. The real culprit is a pool of hot magma, lying almost 80 kilometres below the lake. The magma releases the carbon dioxide and other gases, which travel upward through the earth. The gases gets trapped in natural spring water, which eventually rises toward the surface and feed into the crater lake.

The carbon dioxide, instead of being released harmlessly into the atmosphere, collects in the cold water at the bottom of the lake. Over time, the lowest levels of the lake become more and more saturated with gas. And eventually, when they reach 100% saturation, the gas can bubble spontaneously out of the lake, creating a foaming column of carbonated water … exactly the same phenomenon experienced when you open a can of recently shaken cola. This eruption, or release, can be triggered even before saturation is reached by a landslide, earthquake, violent storm, or other disturbance of the waters.

Today, both Lake Nyos and Lake Monoun contain more gas than was released during the last disasters. At the very greatest depths, Lake Nyos is about 60% saturated with carbon dioxide, and the waters of Lake Monoun are 83% saturated. Recent scientific studies show that the gas concentrations in both lakes is increasing rapidly, and that another lethal gas release is inevitable.

Weather-Related

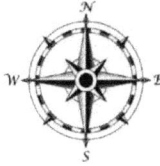

45 The frequency of disasters caused by extreme weather is not increasing.

Flooding caused the majority of disasters between 1994 and 2013, accounting for 43% of all recorded events and affecting nearly 2.5 billion people. Storms were the second most frequent type of disaster, killing more than 244,000 people. This makes storms the second most costly in terms of lives lost. Although there have been more floods year or year since 2000, there have correspondingly fewer storms, meaning that there has been no net increase in the number of weather-related disasters overall.

The Brookings institution is not alone in suggesting that ecological change is set to bring erratic changes of temperature, some of which will be extreme; more frequent heavy precipitation leading to an increase in landslides and flooding; more intense and longer lasting droughts over wider areas; and an increase in intense tropical cyclone activity in both the Pacific and the North Atlantic.

There is, however, no evidence as yet to suggest any of this is actually happening. In fact, there is quite a lot of evidence to the contrary, which suggests that the net impact of ecological change may be more beneficial for the planet and its human population than popularly supposed.

There is no evidence that the frequency of global tropical cyclone formation is increasing.

Globally, the number of disasters relating to tropical cyclones has been dropping, and the IPCC have stated that "it is likely that the global frequency of tropical cyclones will either decrease or remain essentially unchanged". Only in the North Atlantic has there been an increase in hurricane formation, but fewer have made landfall as warmer oceanic water is extending further towards Africa and therefore the storms are forming further East. At the time of writing, the US is undergoing the longest stretch in recorded history without a major hurricane, easily smashing the previous record of 2,300 days between events. The same thing is true for the Indian Ocean and South China Sea. A team from Korea[xxix] found that increasing sea surface temperature in the Western North Pacific has resulted in tropical cyclones – formation of which has significantly decreased over the last three decades – forming further to the West meaning that the proportion which make landfall has notably increased across East Asia.

They go on to say that, unlike in North-East Asia, cyclone landfall intensity for Vietnam, South China, and Taiwan has remained more or less the same over the last 30 years. These countries are closer to cyclone generation sites in the Western North Pacific. But the shift in where they form to the Northern part of the South China Sea means that these cyclones have a shorter lifetime and less time to intensify before hitting land in South-East Asia.

That having been said, the Philippines' Climate Change Commissioner, Nadarev Sano, has noticed changing patterns in typhoon occurrence in his country. While the frequency – about 20 typhoons a year – remains more or less the same, there are now five or six that are stronger, with wind speeds of about 220 kph, compared to the 2 or 3 strong storms previously. Recently, as with typhoons *Bhopa* and *Yolanda*, they have struck further South than usual, too. "And they bring a lot of rain," he said, projecting that the rainy season will be up to 60% wetter while the dry season will be 60% dryer.

Meanwhile, data from the US National Oceanic and Atmospheric Administration (NOAA) shows that 2013 set a record for the fewest tornadoes in US recorded history, with a mere 197 forming [see *Disaster Misperception # 53*].

There are those among the global warming activists, the NGO community, and their media allies that claim climate change – by which they mean 'global warming'[47]– is making extreme weather events more frequent and more ferocious[xxx]. Others, equally vehemently, claim the opposite and that extreme weather events are becoming less frequent and less ferocious as our planet gradually warms. As the IPCC points out in its latest report, there is no trend either way. The Earth is a big place with a dynamic climate. What there is, however, is a clear decline in the number that go on to become natural disasters.

As far as other types of natural hazard are concerned, a report from the Intergovernmental Panel on Climate Change, published in November 2011 was only prepared to say the following[48]:

---

[47] Extreme weather events are more common during cold periods as these are associated with larger temperature differentials between the equator and the Poles.

[48] In IPCC-speak, 'medium confidence means "it is likely that ..." while 'low confidence' means "it is unlikely that ...". The term 'statistically significant trends' means "has definitely increased ..."

In many, but not all, regions of the globe, there is medium confidence that the length or number of heatwaves has increased.

There have been statistically significant trends in the number of heavy precipitation events in some regions. It is likely that more of these regions have experienced increases than decreases, although there are strong regional and sub-regional variations.

There is medium confidence that some regions of the world have experienced more intense and longer droughts, but in some regions droughts have become less frequent, less intense, and of shorter duration.

There is low overall confidence that the magnitude and frequency of floods at regional scales has changed.

The graph below from NOAA appears to show a decline in hurricane frequency overall but an increase in those classified as severe. However, if you start the graph two decades ago in 1995, there will be a clear downward trend in both.

Global Hurricane Frequency -- Dr. Ryan N. Maue -- Updated September 30, 2012 --12 month running sums

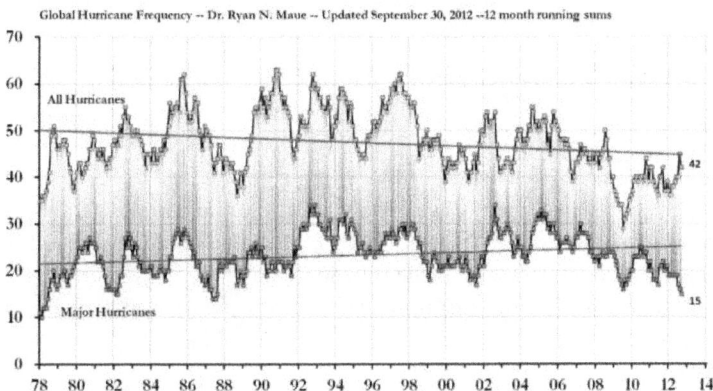

46 Droughts are becoming larger but not more frequent.

In a dried-out riverbed, under the thin shade of a wizened acacia tree, a young Turkana woman called Ajuma kneels beside a hand-dug hole in the parched ground. A baby sleeps strapped to her back, while her young son, his waist strung in colourful beads, scratches listlessly in the sand nearby. Ajuma uses the bottom half of a plastic Coca-Cola bottle to scoop the trickle of water burbling up through the sand and pours it carefully into her small yellow jerry can. Other mothers, draped in naked children with swollen bellies, wait their turn under the tree. The improvised well seems to be little more than dirty puddle, yet an entire community of 600 people depend upon it.She knows the dirty water is not safe to drink, but she also knows her family has no alternative. Climate change, war, and population growth has put increased pressure on dwindling resources. Droughts, which used to come every decade to this area of Sub-Saharan Africa, now occur every few years, she thinks.

Drought affects more people than any other form of natural disaster.

Slow-onset disasters such as this receive much less public attention than sudden-onset disasters such as earthquakes and landslides. The devastation caused by a cyclone or a volcano occurs quickly, sometimes instantly, in a way that arouses media attention and, with it, public sympathy. In contrast, drought develops over time, and images of farmers in dry or abandoned fields convey less urgency than pictures of people running from a tsunami or volcanic eruption.

Drought affects more people than any other form of natural disaster. In one of the few long-term analyses of the impact of natural disasters, it was found that over half of the 22 million deaths associated with natural hazards during the whole of the 20th century were due to drought, but that droughts accounted for only 7% of the estimated $1.2 trillion in economic losses caused by disasters[xxxi]. Since the beginning of the last century, then, more than 11 million people have died as a consequence of drought. In Africa, one third of the continent's population live in drought-affected areas, and in the Horn of Africa alone, drought affected 13 million people in 2011.

Drought is not peculiar to Africa, however. Half of the world's population will live in areas of high water scarcity by 2020. And drought is the single most common cause of food shortages, severely affecting food security in developing countries and jeopardising efforts to increase food production by 70% by 2050 in order to feed a predicted world population of 9 billion.

The bulk of scientific opinion maintains that regional drought and flooding from extreme climatic events are increasing in frequency and severity. This view is being challenged, however, with some in the scientific community suggesting that predictions of mega-droughts affecting Sahel areas of Africa and the Western United States may be wrong. "We could even be headed for wetter times", says Justin Sheffield of Princeton University.

The main measure of drought, the Palmer Drought Severity Index (PDSI), looks at the difference between precipitation and evaporation and uses satellite imagery to detect differences in such things as soil moisture content and leaf growth rates. But since evaporation rates are hard to determine, it uses temperature as a proxy on the assumption that evaporation rises as it gets hotter ... which it does, but not in the linear way you might assume, as wind speed and humidity also affect evaporation rates. When these variables are factored in, "little change in global drought incidence is found over the past 60 years"[xxxii].

The findings of Sheffield and his colleagues raise important questions, not least because a 'warming world' does not automatically imply a wetter world ... at least, not everywhere. As the IPCC itself has recently advised, it is probable that wetter areas will get wetter, and dry areas drier. The other question relates to the absorptive capacity of dry land when faced with more rapidly melting snow or sudden rainfall. The problem is that most of the rain falls in the wrong place. Not only that, but more of it is falling in shorter 'rainy seasons' which leaves soil baked hard by the summer sun unable to absorb as much as it could. This causes faster run-off, a phenomenon rendered more acute by urbanisation, resulting in the cycle of flood and drought we increasingly see today in equatorial zones of the world. There is also likely to be more rain at higher latitudes, and less in the middle latitudes where most of the world's food is grown.

Meanwhile, the drought that settled over more than half of the continental US in 2012 was the most widespread in half a century, while, at the same time, the UK experienced its wettest summer since records began. What was particularly striking about this dry spell was its breadth. In the US, nearly half of the nation's counties – 1,297 counties spread across 29 states – were designated as being under moderate or severe drought, the largest such area since December 1956. Yet much of the 1980's and 1990's were characterised by unusual wetness, according to the US National Weather Service.

47 Famine is not the inevitable result of prolonged drought.

Drought is predictable and does not happen overnight. It therefore follows that it should neither claim lives nor lead to famine; a situation which results when drought is coupled with policy failure or governance breakdown, or both. As with desertification, "drought is a silent and slow killer, and both have a way of creeping up on us, fooling us into underestimating their urgency", says Luc Gnacadja, Executive Secretary of the UN Convention to Combat Desertification.

While these problems exist across the Horn of Africa, the effects of the 2011 drought were most damaging in Somalia. Many observers attributed this to the country's weak governance, and drew a direct line between governance and famine which emphasised the state's role as a fundamental driver of disaster. At the time, the UN did not escape some of the blame. According to Edward Carr of the US Agency for International Development, when the UN first declared famine in Somalia, "attributing the famine solely to drought was a horrible abdication of responsibility for the human causes of this tragedy".

This is because he knows that famines are not only the result of natural occurrences. On the contrary, most are the shocking result of human error or, in the worst case, deliberate neglect. "A drought is made by God, a famine is made by man", is a well-known epithet in disaster management circles, and repeated by John Githongo, a former Kenyan government official. He is not alone in suggesting that drought is a unique form of natural disaster in that it brings in big money for corrupt elites. This is because, as he puts it, "it gives them the opportunity to import maize and other staples into the country, and make a killing off the backs of starving people". "There is a deliberate lack of preparedness on the part of the elites", he adds.

48 Death and destruction is not equal on both sides of a Hurricane's track.

Somewhere in the vastness of the Pacific Ocean a storm cloud forms. Then another. Slowly these vast pillows of condensed power merge and begin to grow. Imperceptibly at first, the emerging system begins to rotate. Within days, an immense white vortex of wind and rain begins its erratic but relentless westward journey towards the unsuspecting archipelago that is the southern Philippines. Satellites note the storm's rapid growth and plot its track, while weather-forecasters run the models to predict its likely landfall.

The government in Manila puts out an initial warning, alerting everyone who may be in harm's way to prepare. Civil Defence Units put their first responders on standby, while Mayors interrupt radio news bulletins to tell long-suffering coconut farmers and inshore fishermen to batten down the hatches as best they can. The storm, now sucking up energy from the warming waters of the ocean below at a rate greater than the entire world's electrical generating capacity, prepares to unleash itself on a poor and vulnerable island people.

The usually bright and sunny skies darken as the monster named 'Yolanda' approaches. The first drops of rain begin to fall as the wind backs and freshens. Policemen with megaphones instruct anyone who will listen to evacuate. Few do. Too late, women and children collect what little food and water they can, and scamper, plastic bags in hand, to their nearest school or church. Their husbands and eldest sons stay behind to protect and save what they can. For many, this is the last time they will see one another.

Angry seas, whipped by winds not much slower than a handgun's bullet, pound against an exposed coastline shorn of its mangroves. Thirty million palm trees whip themselves into a frenzy in the shrieking winds before toppling, their roots ripped from the rain-drenched ground. One by one, roofs peel back and over one million homes implode, to whirl away into a deafening black sky. And then the water comes. At first, a few ebbing waves, but then the full surge ascends and within minutes a maelstrom of water, twice a person's height, obliterates all in its path. Frightened humans huddle amidst the devastation unsure and uncertain.

Within hours, the winds miraculously slacken and the waters recede. Like most natural disasters before it, an all-too-familiar sequence of events follows: Survivors emerge dazed and bleeding into the silence to survey the wreckage of their former lives. Bodies lie unrecognised, twisted together in a giant tangle of devastation. Fear and chaos loom through the teeming rain as people run shouting to scrabble shoe-less through the rubble. Tetanus pierces unprotected feet. After two days of tears and anguish, the search begins in earnest for food and shelter.

Tropical cyclones[49] require ample heat and moisture to form, yet how they behave after that is still not fully understood. One pre-condition is that the surface sea temperature must be at least 27°C (80°F). Another is that the weather 'disturbance' sparking one off must be more than 555 kilometres – or five degrees of latitude – away from the equator as it is only such distances that allow the *Coriolis Effect*[50] to create the circulations that distinguish these killers from their cousins, the smaller and more frequent tropical storms. These circulating systems behave much like bathwater when going down the plug-hole in that rapid accelerations and centrifugal forces result in a swirling funnel of water with an 'eye' at its centre[51].

Unlike bath-water, these systems track across the planet's surface, and do so in unpredictable ways. In general, they travel in a westerly direction but may speed up, slow down, turn north, turn south, or even stop. But, all the while, they are building in strength. A large tropical cyclone circulates more than one million cubic miles of atmosphere every second and can pick up as much as 2 billion tons of water a day through evaporation and sea spray. The energy involved is massive and, in one day, is roughly equivalent to the United States' total electrical needs for an entire year.

The atmosphere holds up to 4% more water vapour than it did 40 years ago.

Evidence is beginning to show that warming oceans are increasing the energy available, and, with it, the magnitude of tropical cyclones. This stems from the simple observation that extra heat in the air and the oceans is increasing evaporation, which is resulting in the atmosphere holding 4% more water vapour than it did 40 years ago[xxxiii]. More vapour means more energy, and storms are driven by such energy. Severe thunderstorms develop when warm moist air near the surface is lifted upwards by an approaching cold front into the layer of cooler, drier air above, releasing this latent heat energy into the storm in the process.

---

[49] Tropical cyclones are known as 'typhoons' in the Pacific, and 'hurricanes' in the Atlantic.

[50] The Earth's rotation imparts an acceleration known as the' Coriolis Effect' which causes cyclonic storm systems to turn towards the poles. Tropical cyclones in the Northern Hemisphere usually turn north, and those in the Southern Hemisphere usually turn south.

[51] It's an urban myth that bathwater does the same thing when draining through a hole; the direction of swirl in draining bathwater is purely random.

Evaporation causes heat to be transferred from the water to the air. The higher the wind speed, the higher the rate of evaporation, and the more energy transferred. Because it is circulating, this energy cannot escape except back into the system which, as long as it is over the open ocean, means it is feeding in on itself. This what makes tropical cyclones so dangerous. Interestingly, this 'heat transfer effect' results in the water temperature in the tropical cyclone's wake being significantly colder than the water around it, making it less likely that a subsequent tropical cyclone can form. They typically weaken rapidly over land where they are cut off from their primary energy source, the ocean.

Numbers of tropical cyclones can vary substantially from one year to the next, but according to the Pew Centre, there are roughly 90 per year, approximately half (35-40) of which are tropical storms that do not reach hurricane strength[52]. Several metrics are used to categorise the magnitude of tropical cyclones, and are based on a combination of intensity (pressure gradient, rotational wind speed, translational forward wind speed), size[53] (its footprint), duration, storm surge height, and ability to inflict structural damage. The one most commonly used is the 'Saffir-Simpson Scale' which classifies North Atlantic and North Pacific tropical cyclones.

Roughly 90 tropical cyclones form per year, of which slightly more than half turn into full-blown hurricanes.

There are five categories, with the largest, Category-5, denoting sustained wind speeds in excess of 250 kph and gusts of up to 350 kph or more. At such speeds, cars are picked up and tossed around like plastic bags in the street on a breezy day, reinforced concrete beams can snap like matchsticks, and there will be widespread and complete failure of most types of roofing. For obvious reasons, these are sometimes referred to as "Super-Typhoons". *Yolanda* was one of these, and was reputed to be the strongest ever to make landfall. The storm surge and high winds she brought with her killed more than 6,500 people and destroyed the homes of over 5 million.

Size plays an important role in modulating damage caused by a storm. All else being equal, a larger storm will impact a larger area for a

---

[52] A full-blown tropical cyclone consists of sustained wind speeds in excess of 75 mph / 120 kph

[53] Tropical cyclones are typically between 100 - 4,000 kms in diameter, with an 'eye' of typically 30 - 65 kms.

longer period of time. In addition, a larger storm can generate a higher storm surge due to the combination of low pressure, steeper pressure gradient, and longer time over a larger expanse of water over which higher waves can be set up. Super-storm *Sandy* is a good example of this as it struck the eastern US in late 2012 having barely attained hurricane intensity, yet was one of the most damaging in US history because of its large size.

There are a number of other things to understand, too, about wind speeds and storms. The first, and an often misunderstood aspect of wind, is the potential for increased damage as wind speeds increase.

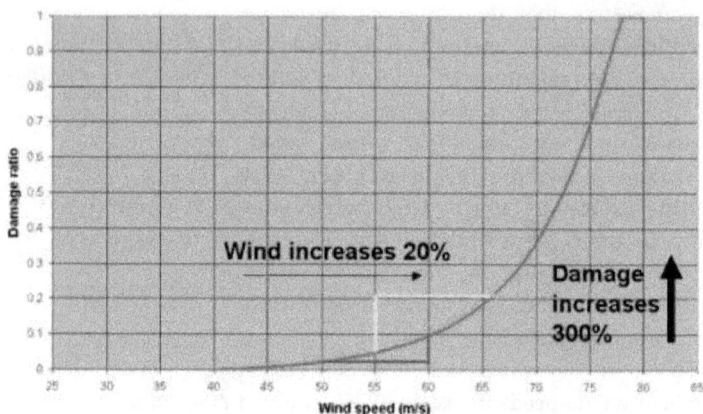

As this graphic from the Australian government shows, the force imparted to an object in the wind's path increases by roughly the square of the wind speed. A 240 kph wind is 20% stronger than a 200 kph wind, but the destructive power is 73% greater. Hurricane *Andrew's* sustained winds of 265 kph, for example, were 160% more powerful than hurricane *Katrina's* of 195 kph when it reached New Orleans.

A second aspect to note is that cyclonic wind speed declines in more or less linear fashion with distance from the centre. And the third, as all yachtsmen will tell you, is that wind speed is lower near the surface where it is slowed by the frictional effects of land, trees, and houses. The reduction in wind speed near the surface is quite different for different types of terrain. Over a city or rough terrain, wind speeds may be 40 – 50% below those experienced aloft, while over open water the reduction may be 25% or less. Yachtsmen will also know that wind in the lee of an island will generally be lower than on the windward side, but is likely to produce stronger gusts.

Finally, it must be remembered that all these winds and pressures are rotating. The storm is also moving across the planet's surface at anywhere between 15 and 75 kph.

All this talk of wind speed, pressure gradient, and rotation comes together for one highly significant reason: Tropical Cyclones are asymmetric. When one makes landfall in the northern hemisphere, windspeed over the ground and consequent death and destruction will be significantly higher – in fact, often up to twice as high[54] – right of the cyclone's track than to its left.

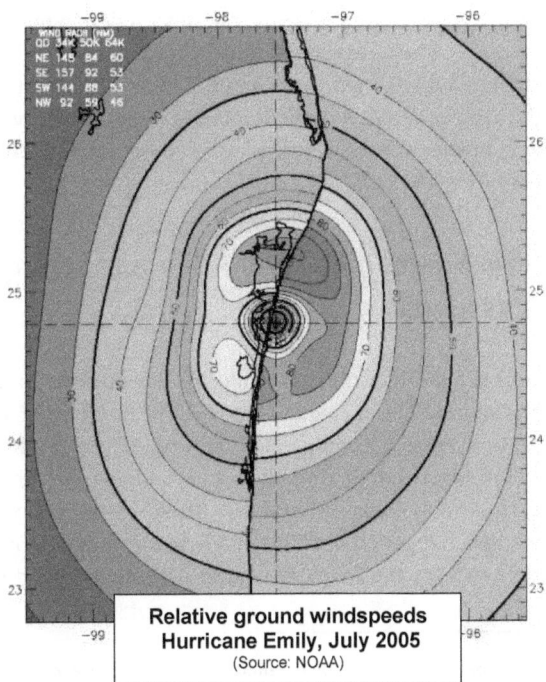

Relative ground windspeeds
Hurricane Emily, July 2005
(Source: NOAA)

The physics is quite logical when you stop to think about it. In the case of Typhoon *Yolanda* the air mass was rotating at 250 kph and moving

---

[54] Preliminary research carried out by the REACH project on behalf of the Red Cross (IFRC) and global shelter cluster in March 2014 during the Typhoon Haiyan response.

towards the coast at 50 kph. North of track – the path over which the eye of the storm passed – the combined wind speed over the ground was therefore 300 kph. South of track – less than 25 kms away – the combined wind speed over the ground was much lower at 200 kph. Typically, recorded maximum windspeeds occur about 12% of the time on the left, while maximum wind speeds occur about 61% of the time on the right in the northern hemisphere[xxxiv].

Death & destruction is up to twice as high to the right of a tropical cyclone's path (in the northern hemisphere) than to its left.

The result of the higher wind speed over the ground right of track is not just greater death and destruction, but a swathe of death and destruction which is almost twice as wide as that to the left[55]. Well-built timber framed houses will withstand winds of about 250 kph. Lightweight timber framed houses of the type typically found in developing countries will be severely damaged or destroyed[56] in winds of much more than 180 kph.

49   Storm Surges make landfall hours before peak winds arrive.

A *Storm Surge* is a swell or dome of water pushed ashore up to 250 kms ahead of the storm. The fact that it arrives in advance of the strong winds to cause extensive flooding is often forgotten by local authorities who are often surprised to find their evacuation plans thwarted by submerged roads and collapsed bridges. Although the police don't like to admit it, this happened in New York before super-storm *Sandy*[57] arrived. After striking the coast, the surge will move inland only to be

---

[55] The swathe of death and destruction is generally 5/8 North of track, and 3/8 South of track.

[56] Contrary to popular belief, few houses are blown over. Instead, they are pulled apart by winds moving around and over the building. This lowers the pressure on the outside and creates suction on the walls and roof, effectively causing the equivalent of an explosion.

[57] Of the more than 270 people killed across seven countries by super storm Sandy, over 70 died along the eastern seaboard of the US, with 650,000 homes either damaged or destroyed and 8.5 million people left without power in near freezing temperatures, some for weeks. Sandy was the largest tropical cyclone to impact the US since such measurements began being taken in 1988.

stopped when reaching high ground. Although the water will then begin to retreat, it will be retained by the high winds and persist until the wind speed slackens or reverses direction.

The right front quadrant of a storm contains the greatest volume of surge.

Near the eye of the storm, where the winds are strongest and the pressure lowest, this swell can be up to 8 metres in height. As we have seen, low atmospheric pressure plays its part although it is wind-driven waves that account for most of this rise. The slope of the seashore, the angle at which the storm hits the shoreline, and the tunneling effect of bays and estuaries also influence how much of the swell is carried ashore. Of even greater significance, though, is the height of the tide when the swell arrives.

As with the wind, which will be much stronger over the ground north of track as we have just seen, the right front quadrant of the storm will contain the greatest volume of surge, while the front left quadrant, with winds blowing away from land, will contain the least.

It used to be true that the deadliest part of any tropical cyclone was this surge of seawater. A 30-foot storm surge that hit Bangladesh in 1970 resulted in 300,000 deaths. But since then, storm surge deaths by drowning have decreased markedly in developing countries, while the majority of impact-phase deaths are now due to the high velocity winds. In developed countries, however, the situation is different.

Tropical cyclones have killed more than 25,000 people in the continental US over the course of the country's history, with the majority of those deaths attributable to storm surges rather than wind.

Most injury and loss of life is due to trauma induced by wind-blown projectiles and building collapse, the top three injuries being blunt trauma, lacerations, and puncture wounds. In the case of Typhoon *Yolanda*, an unusually high number of people drowned, most of them in the coastal town of Tacloban because they refused to evacuate. Further inland, however, many victims were sliced in half by flying corrugated iron sheeting, impaled by flying palm fronds, or had their heads taken off by coconuts hitting them almost horizontally with the speed of an 18th century cannonball[xxxv]. A falling coconut weighing 8 kgs can kill when it falls on someone's head even on a calm day. On windy days, rural Philippino children who would normally walk to school through a coconut plantation need no reminding to go the long way round to avoid this hazard.

It is not possible to stand upright when wind speed rises much above 190 kph. If the wind were perfectly level, you'd tumble along the surface, bouncing against the ground like so much tumbleweed in a corny cowboy movie. However, you could easily be lifted up and carried away by any updrafts. It's the same with a falling coconut.

50 Lightning strike is a significant form of natural disaster.

Somewhere between 6,000 and 25,000 people die around the world every year from lightning strikes[xxxvi], with serious and permanent injury being sustained by ten times more. This is more than from tropical cyclones or tornadoes combined.

The most common cause of death in a lightning strike is cardio-pulmonary arrest, with injuries including burns to the skin, damage to the nervous system including eyesight and hearing loss, and kidney failure. About 70% of these effects are permanent.

Approximately 100,000 storms occur per year, generating 25 million lightning strikes. That's about 100 bolts per second, with one person per minute being hit somewhere in the world. While standing under a tall tree is one of the most dangerous places to be in an electrical storm, over 80 villagers in what used to be called The North-West Frontier Province of Pakistan died after the corrugated iron-roofed house in which they had sought refuge was struck by lightning during the monsoon of July 2007.

One person per minute is hit by lightning somewhere in the world.

Lightning heats the air around it to temperatures five times hotter than the sun. This heat causes the surrounding air to rapidly expand, and it is this expansion which creates thunder. Bolts of lightning can reach over 8 kms (5 miles) in length, with each bolt discharging up to 1 billion volts of electricity[58] … enough to simultaneously boil all the electric kettles of Europe.

---

[58] This enormous electrical discharge is caused by an imbalance between positive and negative charges. During a storm, colliding particles of rain, ice, or snow in a cloud build up static electricity and increase this imbalance – negative charge collecting towards the base of the cloud while objects on the ground become positively charged – creating a 'potential difference' that nature seeks to remedy by passing a current between the two.

Wildland Fires are not increasing in frequency.

Wildfires are sometimes called 'forest fires' or 'brush fires', but they also take place in open tree-less expanses, which makes the term 'wildland fires' more correct. Such conflagrations are rapidly spreading, unwanted fires that rage through swathes of land containing combustible material threatening human lives, property and natural resources.

These fires are determined by four basic conditions coming together at the same time: vegetative resources to burn; environmental conditions that promote combustion, including moisture content; human influence such as undergrowth control and firebreak construction; and a spark, which can range from a carelessly tossed cigarette to a lightning strike.

Lightning activity doesn't accurately determine fire ignition potential, though, because fuel conditions must be considered in addition to the fact that most lightning is accompanied by significant rainfall. Nevertheless, although most global fire activity is directly attributable to people[xxxvii], these four factors determine why some parts of the world are fire-prone and others are fire-free.

Nature consumes the majority of accumulated forest biomass in one of two ways: it either rots or it burns, depending on the moisture available. As the planet warms, the balance shifts, and not always in ways we expect: for example, there appears to be an exponential relationship between fuel aridity and the area burned, with every degree that temperatures warm having a much bigger effect on the overall fire area than the previous degree did. The whole complex of life in arid and – were it not for the trees – barren landscapes, evolved to thrive in the presence of fire.

Wildland fires are the most prevalent hazard after drought.

In the past few years, however, we have been confronted by the new reality of the mega-fire. To some extent, the cause of these is as much to do with the absence of forestry management as it is connected to the climate. Reductions in fire suppression budgets, for example, have left more tinder on the ground to burn.

Climate change has undoubtedly played a part, especially when the effects of indirect phenomena such as more frequent lightning strikes, the growth and spread of beetle populations, and reduced snowpack are included. Wildland fires also release carbon dioxide, one of the main drivers of climate change, and reduce the number of trees available to absorb carbon dioxide, a double whammy for the atmosphere.

At the global level, wildland fires burn a total land area of between 3.5 and 4.5 million kms² annually, which is equivalent to the surface area of India and Pakistan together, or more than half of Australia[xxxviii]. In terms of surface area covered, this makes wildland fires the most prevalent hazard after drought[xxxix].

Recent examples of mega-fires include the 2009 'Black Saturday' conflagration in Australia which killed 173 people and incinerated many towns, and record-setting wildfires in Russia in 2010, where 62 people were killed and around 2.3 million hectares burned as a result of over 32,000 fires. The US experienced above average wildfire activity during 2011, where, across the country, 73,484 fires burned 8.7 million acres (3.5 million hectares), with an average of 119 acres (48.2 hectares) per fire. This equates to 2011 being the third most active wildfire season with respect to acres burned but the sixth least active in terms of number of fires[xl]. This means that, in the US anyway, a smaller number of fires are burning considerably larger amounts of land.

Climate change is expected to alter the geographic distribution of wildland fires, but exactly where, when, and how remains largely unknown. In contrast to expectations that climate change is resulting in more fires, regional increases in fire incidence seems to be counterbalanced by decreases at other locations, due to the interplay of temperature and precipitation. In other words, drier, more combustible zones are counterbalanced by wetter, less combustible ones elsewhere[59].

To see if this is true or not, global fire trends have been evaluated by looking at the aggregate number of night-time hot spots as seen from the GOES and MODIS Aqua/Terra satellite systems. Surprisingly, these satellites are seeing neither more nor less fires burning around the world, with the data furthermore showing that there has been no appreciable shift in the location, duration, or frequency of fires during the 14 year period 1997-2011[xli].

That said, while global average fire abundance decreased significantly since 1900 as technological advances in fire-fighting – particularly the use of helicopters, planes and flame retardants – became available, it is likely that global warming will reverse that

---

[59] Although there is a net balance at the moment, statistical models predict substantial invasion and retreat of fire across large portions of the globe in the medium-term.

steady decline by 2050, by which time the global climate will again become the primary driver of fire abundance worldwide. That said, the current pattern of longer fire seasons in certain parts of the world such as the Western United States is likely to continue as long as there is enough fuel to burn, but there will come a point – probably in the middle of the century – when there are not enough trees left to sustain such conflagrations.

Not only do wildfires threaten lives directly, but they have the potential to increase local air pollution, exacerbating lung diseases and causing breathing difficulties even in healthy individuals. Most deaths from fire disasters result from smoke and particle inhalation rather than from being burned alive. Most fire victims succumb to the asphyxiating effect of carbon monoxide long before the flames or heat affects them directly.

Smoke from wildland fires is a complex assortment of gases (mostly carbon monoxide, carbon dioxide, nitrogen dioxide and sulphur dioxide) and hundreds of different types of particles, the makeup of which depends on the meteorological and environmental factors present.

Satellites are seeing neither more nor less fires burning around the world.

Burn injuries requiring hospitalization are both serious and costly, requiring multiple surgical procedures and intensive care. They require more bed-days than any other form of injury and are one of the most difficult physiological and psychological injuries to treat. Apart from the pain endured by the victim, the film *The English Patient* gives some idea of how long burns victims take to recover.

Moist, forested areas are the most likely to face greater threats from wildfires as conditions grow drier and hotter. Surprisingly, some dry grassland areas may be less at risk, but not because they would be flourishing, but because drought is likely to prevent these grasses from growing at all, leaving these areas so barren that they are likely to lack even the fodder for wildfire.

Although drought is often blamed for the uncontrolled spread of mega-fires, Florida and Western Australia offer two examples where, despite the prolonged presence of severe drought, wildfire costs, losses, and damages are much lower than elsewhere. This might reflect more balanced prevention, mitigation, and suppression approaches ... or, as above, it might mean there is less combustible material to burn.

Additionally, a counterintuitive aspect of wildfires is that when the rains do come, mountain forest wildfires increase flash flood risk in lower-lying areas in the days and months following the fire due to loss of vegetation and the inability of burned soil to absorb moisture.

52 Heatwaves kill more people than freezing weather.

This is a slightly misleading statement as there is no definitive answer. It is fair to say, however, that heatwaves are the most insidious, most invisible, yet most lethal of disasters.

In any given year, heatwaves are quite capable of claiming more lives than all the world's storms, floods, and landslides put together. According to the Centre for Climatic Research at the University of Delaware in the US, an average of 1,500 American city-dwellers die each year because of the heat, while combined annual deaths from tornadoes, earthquakes and floods across the country are measured in the low hundreds.

In contrast to the sudden freeze which plunged New York into a new Ice Age in the film *Day after Tomorrow*, even Hollywood would find it hard to make a blockbuster movie about a heatwave. There's just not that much drama in watching a road melt. Heatwaves come on subtly, raising summer temperatures just that little bit higher than normal and then receding, leaving abandoned city folk to expire alone in their non-air-conditioned homes.

'Urban Heat Island Effect' can mean cities being 3°C hotter by day and up to 10°C hotter by night than nearby rural areas.

Heatwaves are not unknown in Europe, either. In 2003, a catastrophic heatwave produced the hottest summer weather in more than 500 years, killing an estimated 70,000 people. France was particularly hard hit. With temperatures soaring above 38°C (100°F) for seven consecutive days, 14,802 people died in Paris alone. Measured by mortality, it was the worst natural disaster ever in contemporary France. By comparison, Hurricane Katrina and the floods which devastated New Orleans and the Gulf Coast in 2005, exacted a death toll of 1,836. Seven years later, during the summer of 2010, another heatwave scorched Russia. With temperatures soaring to 42°C (108°F), it was estimated to have caused the death of 55,736 people.

Increased urban heat-island effects[60] and increasing numbers of susceptible people living in an ageing and urbanising world are likely to contribute to an increase in the number of people dying from heat-related causes. This is without the effects of climate change which pundits predict will see the frequency of future catastrophic heatwaves such as those experienced in Paris in 2003, Moscow in 2010, and Melbourne in 2013 increase too. The Australian Climate Council, a non-governmental body, suggests that heatwaves in Australia are getting hotter, becoming more frequent, are starting earlier and lasting longer[xlii].

But people freeze to death, too. Figures from the US show that 800 more people die every day through the three winter months of December, January, and February[61] than occurs on an average day during the rest of the year. Heart attacks and strokes are the major culprits. Additionally, cold weather makes the human respiratory system more susceptible to viruses, all of which makes it difficult to determine if it was really the cold that killed them.

The social dynamics of death from extremes of temperature are instructive. Victims tend to be the poor, the old, the less mobile, and those without shelter or air-conditioning ... the less visible and the homeless, in other words, as well as those with weakened immune systems.

It does not take a lot of extra heat to kill, nor, for that matter, a lot of extra cold. The body works in a very small temperature range. Even a healthy person who over-exerts in the heat can die of heatstroke, and, left exposed, humans die very quickly in extreme cold. But, unlike some other forms of natural disaster, extremes of hot and cold weather usually give a few days advance warning of their arrival; time enough for communities to mobilise and protect their most vulnerable members if they so choose. People can freeze to death within hours from

---

[60] A local urban effect generated by increased population density – their vehicles and air conditioners – shade-less streets; dark coloured buildings that absorb heat by day and radiate heat by night, thereby prolonging the daily heat burden; and reduced evapotranspiration owing to lack of vegetation.

[61] The winter months kill an average of 72,000 more US citizens than the spring-summer-autumn average.

hypothermia, but it's usually a couple of days before people start dying from heatstroke or hyperthermia[62] exacerbated by dehydration.

53 The frequency of large Tornadoes in the United States is decreasing, not increasing.

Jamal, aged 7, was lucky to suffer only minor injuries from the Tornado that demolished his family's single-storey home in March 2012. The Tornado sheared off the walls of his bedroom, picked him out of his bed and hurled him over a hundred metres onto the embankment of a nearby highway.

"I've never seen or heard anything like that," he said later, recalling the moment the 'twister' "sucked out the walls" of the house in the darkness, adding, "It was a terrible sound. I never want to go through that again".

Tornadoes are vertical funnels of rapidly spinning air. Winds frequently exceed 300kph and can wreak total destruction along the pathway more than 1 km wide and 80 kms long. It is the wind-shear more than then wind's velocity that indicates a tornado's destructive potential.

The US experiences an average of 1,284 tornadoes per year.

As parts of severe convective storms, tornadoes occur across every continent. However, some parts of the world are much more prone to their devastating winds than others. The United States is a major hotspot, experiencing about 1,284 tornadoes every year, and of which roughly 20 can be expected to be violent, and one might classify as an EF-5[63], meaning with estimated winds above 322 kph and almost complete destruction. These cause an average of 62 deaths and more than 1,500 injuries per year[64]. America suffers 75% of all the world's tornadoes, followed by Canada and Bangladesh. Strangely enough, relative to land area, the UK experiences more than all of these, although they tend to be smaller.

---

[62] Hyperthermia is a condition that occurs when core body temperature rises above 105°F or so. Other factors such as obesity, hypertension, and heart disease can contribute to such deaths by affecting the body's ability to regulate heat.

[63] Enhanced Fujita Scale, of which there are five categories representing likely damage, with 5 being the strongest.

[64] The decadal average for annual tornado-related fatality in the US is 62, according to US National Climatic Data Centre, with nearly 70% of all fatalities resulting from rare 'extremely violent' events which make up only 2% of the total.

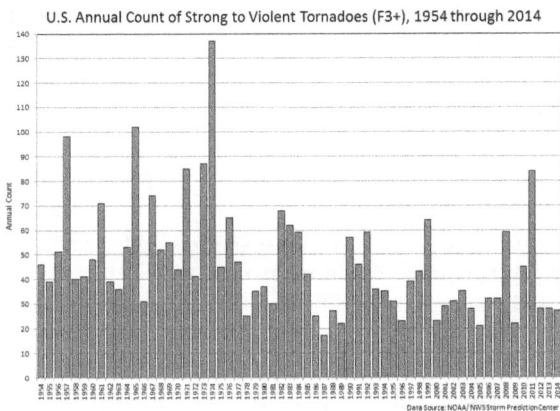

U.S. Annual Count of Strong to Violent Tornadoes (F3+), 1954 through 2014

Data Source: NOAA/ NWS Storm Prediction Center

With increased Doppler radar coverage, an increasing population, and greater attention to tornado reporting – not least by 'storm-chasers' seeking fame on Discovery Channel – there has been an increase in the number of tornado reports over the past several decades. This can create a misleading appearance of an increasing trend in tornado frequency. For the US, there has in fact been no increase in tornado frequency – or in the proportion of strongest tornadoes – over the past 55 years, with, if anything, a slight overall decline[xliii].

54 The number of Tornado-related deaths in the US is decreasing, not increasing.

Tornado-related deaths have declined dramatically over the past few decades due to higher risk awareness, better forecasting, improved mitigation measures in the form of building underground shelters, and enhanced early warning.

Tornadoes affect a limited area, and may cause serious death and destruction locally, but, in themselves, they are not comparable in scale to events like tropical cyclones. However, due to the higher number of events, the aggregate annual loss can be similar to when a major tropical cyclone makes landfall.

Puncture wounds from flying grass are a significant cause of post-tornado death.

While a large proportion of tornado-related deaths in the US occur in mobile homes, the leading cause of death worldwide is trauma to the head from flying debris or being crushed by collapsing structures. This is the same whether you live in Bangladesh or Birmingham, Alabama. Larger, low velocity flying objects also account for the high rate of head trauma, including decapitation. It is not unusual when the skull has been split open for the "cranial contents to be completely sucked out by the wind[xliv]." If this is not enough to make you reach for a motorcycle helmet when a tornado warning has been issued, nothing will.

Risk of being injured by a tornado appears to increase with age. This is presumed to be because of differences in house, car, and mobile home occupancy at the time a tornado strikes. Relative risk of death or serious injury in the US was calculated in 1980 as being 3:1,000 for people in brick-built homes; 23:1,000 for those in cars; and 85:1,000 for those living in mobile homes[xlv]. Since those days, the risks have declined as early warning and shelter has improved, but still remain more or less the same in relative terms. In other words, it is better to be in a car try to out run approaching tornado then in a mobile home, but being caught in the car is seven times more likely to get you killed than taking shelter underground.

A large proportion of heavily contaminated wounds are often found in tornado casualties, where clothing is often torn off by the force of the blast, leaving the skin exposed. It's the same with larger tropical cyclones. In most cases, wood splinters, soil, manure, and even tiny pieces of straw embed themselves deeply into open wounds caused by larger objects, but it is also possible for such debris to penetrate the skin. These types of puncture wounds are often so small they cannot be seen with the naked eye. When they infect with aerobic, gram-negative bacilli, as they easily do, they are difficult to treat and can become a significant cause of post-disaster mortality even in the most developed country. As with tropical cyclones, extensive deep abrasions due to the sand-blast effect of dirt striking exposed skin at high velocity is also common[xlvi]. It is estimated that between half to two-thirds of all those who survive require expensive and continuing anti-sepsis treatment. To give an idea of the forces involved, one patient hospitalised after the 1979 Wichita Falls tornado in the US was "coughing up grass four days after admission".

From a developing country perspective, this case study from Bangladesh, the second most tornado-prone country in the world, is instructive: On the evening of 20 March 2005, a tornado carved a path through the northern part of the country, destroying over 9,000 homes and impacting the lives of over 35,000 of the 655,000 people living in the area. According to a study by the Johns Hopkins School of Public Health who just happened to be in the area doing something else at the time, 10% of the population within the tornado-affected area were injured, and 56 deaths recorded.

The most common causes of death were head injuries, bleeding, or sepsis following wounds sustained. One fifth of all these deaths occurred 10 days or more later, and were attributable to post-traumatic infection, a situation exacerbated by inappropriate first aid, or by not seeking, or not being able to seek, appropriate healthcare. The elderly were almost 9 times more likely to die, and women 24% more likely to be injured than men, a statistic explained by the fact that mothers tend to shield their youngest children from the ravages of a passing storm.

55   *The power of Tropical Cyclones does not appear to be increasing overall.*

Tropical Cyclones are self-organised heat engines, driven by temperature, humidity and latent heat differentials. As a number of physicists have pointed out, the frequency and energy of Tropical Cyclones is therefore expected to diminish with a more uniformly warm planet, that is, with better heat distribution from the tropics to the poles (which is net global warming). This is because storm violence arises primarily from the difference in temperature between a warm reservoir, e.g. the ocean, and a cold reservoir e.g. the polar ice-caps.

The *Power Dissipation Index* (PDI) is an aggregate of storm intensity, size, frequency, and duration and provides a measure of total hurricane power over a hurricane season. At the moment, as global warming accelerates, the graphs overleaf show there is a strong upward trend in Atlantic PDI and a downward trend in the eastern North Pacific, with the effects of one cancelling out the other in global terms.

Observed Trends in Hurricane Power Dissipation

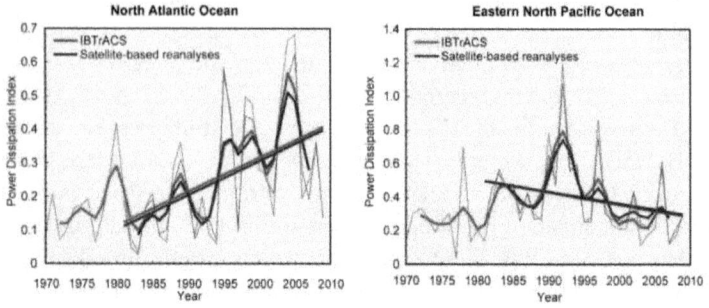

Health-Related

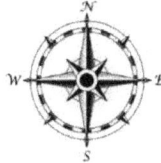

Epidemics of cholera and other communicable diseases are not inevitable in the immediate aftermath of a disaster.

Haiti's first cholera victim in 2010 had no name. Known in the village only as "Moun Fou" – Creole for 'Crazy Man' – this popular 28-year-old man was in the habit of walking naked down to the river to join the children for a bathe and a drink. His favourite place for this was a pool just above the old bridge, from where the children would jump on him, splashing and shrieking. Ducks paddled and pigs wallowed untroubled by the noise at the head of the pool, where chattering women in gaily-coloured dresses would chase them away from the newly washed clothes lying out on the rocks to dry in the bright morning sun. Unknown to them all, somewhere upstream a broken pipe was dribbling raw sewage directly into the water.

One evening, on 12th October, 2010 after playing with the children and drinking the river water, 'Moun Fou' developed severe diarrhoea. He died less than 24 hours later while staggering to the health centre. Two villagers who washed his body prior to his burial fell ill and also died. Less than one week later, 404 people were admitted in one night to the small hospital in St. Marc, over 30 kms away down on the coast. This is where the Artibonite River, in a tributary of which 'Moun Fou' and the children had been bathing, empties into the Caribbean. 44 of them died. As crowds began to gather at hospitals and health centres along the length of the river, it was clear that cholera had returned with a vengeance to Haiti for the first time in nearly a century.

The outbreak has since become one of the worst in modern history, having killed over 8,500 people, and making 700,000 more extremely ill. It has also been exported from Haiti to Mexico, the Dominican Republic, Cuba, Puerto Rico, and New York which is home to one of the largest communities of Haitians outside the Caribbean.

Long a matter of dispute, many observers assumed that a new and virulent strain of cholera had been introduced to a susceptible population who had not seen cholera in over three generations by UN peacekeepers from abroad.

Whatever the cause, it is clear that the outbreak had very little to do with the earthquake that wrought so much havoc in this already fragile country nine months earlier. In fact, a public health advisory written for the World Health Organisation and the Haitian Ministry of Health by the US Centres for Disease Control immediately after the earthquake expressly said, "Unless imported, an outbreak of cholera is very unlikely at this time, as epidemic cholera has not been reported from Haiti before".

Despite this advice, the first thing I did on arrival some three months after the earthquake was to convene a planning meeting with my Water, Sanitation, Health, Nutrition, Shelter and Education cluster colleagues to prepare for such an eventuality. We were as a result ready for an outbreak in one of the camps in Port-au-Prince – which happily never happened – but were caught completely off guard when the outbreak erupted up the coast a few months later.

✦

Epidemics[65] of typhus, plague, cholera, smallpox and other diseases have regularly accompanied war, displacement, and other aspects of violent social upheaval. Perhaps for this reason, and our general paranoia surrounding death and the proximity of dead bodies, it is still widely believed that populations affected by natural disaster face similar threats from disease. This is true even of doctors and disaster managers, who assume the risk of an outbreak to be very high in the chaos that follows a natural disaster, especially where specific diseases are endemic[66], have non-human hosts, or are likely to be exacerbated by overcrowding and poor sanitation.

The short-term risk for an epidemic after a natural disaster is very low, especially after an earthquake.

But, counter-intuitive as it may seem, there is an extremely low risk of a second wave of death[67] in the days and weeks following a natural disaster[xlvii], and many of the outbreaks that do occur, like the cholera outbreak in Haiti just described, are usually only indirectly related to the disaster itself. While it could be that the immediate humanitarian

---

[65] An 'epidemic' is when more cases of a communicable disease than would be expected in a defined community or geographic area over a given period of time occurs.

[66] Where a disease was already prevalent and regularly found among particular groups of people or in specified areas before the disaster occurred.

[67] Second-wave deaths related to such aspects as poor shelter and deteriorating environmental conditions do occur, though, and these are discussed elsewhere in this section.

response may be playing some sort of a role by providing safe water and improved sanitation, for example, years of evidence points to the fact that short-term risk for epidemics after a natural disaster is very low, especially after an earthquake[xlviii].

The risk of disease always remains, however, especially where pre-disaster measles immunisation coverage is low, and comes from those which are the common currency of poverty and low levels of public health activity throughout the developing world. These include the many types of diarrhoea, measles, whooping cough (pertussis), diphtheria, respiratory infections, meningitis, intestinal parasites, skin disease, and tuberculosis. Natural disasters also alter ecological conditions and therefore affect those diseases such as malaria, dengue and Japanese encephalitis which are transmitted by mosquitoes [see *Disaster Misperception # 58*], and those such as typhoid which are water-borne.

There are other specific 'risk factors', though: The sudden mass movement of populations, for example, can influence the transmission of disease by increasing population density – and thereby the opportunity to infect air[68], water and food – and/or by introducing a susceptible population to a new disease[69] to which they have not been exposed before and for which they have no immunity[70]. As we have just discussed, however, this is related to inadequate shelter and is more likely to be caused by foreigners arriving to help as it is by any movement of indigenous population groups within the country.

The Japanese tsunami of 2011, where mostly elderly evacuees lived on a diet of little more than rice noodles for months, also demonstrated that malnourishment can increase individual susceptibility to many communicable diseases.

Damage to water supply and sewage disposal systems also has the clear potential for increasing levels of disease after many types of natural disaster. Failures in piped systems force people to seek unsafe water from alternative surface or ground water sources, and/or cause cross-contamination with leaking sewage being sucked into broken water pipes. In rural areas, earthquakes can alter the water table and

---

[68] Climate will determine the organism and the way it spreads. For example, overcrowding in cold conditions will result in an increase in respiratory infections.

[69] Organisms do not come from nowhere. If an organism or vector is not present in the area and is not introduced, it poses no threat, regardless of conditions.

[70] The potential for outbreak is directly related to pre-existing vaccination coverage levels per type of disease.

often relocate springs, but, despite sometimes turning the water strange colours[71], this does not otherwise result in contamination of the water supply. This is not the same situation in floods, however, where unprotected wells often suffer ingress of decaying organic material, salt, or chemical pollutants requiring them to be drained and cleaned.

Of more importance than any of these is that potentially serious diseases are held in check by public health programmes which, if interrupted by disaster, might lead to an outbreak. Of most importance in this regard are vector control programmes where insecticide fogging or spraying ceases, leading to resurgence in the vector, or where routine immunisation programmes against the more common diseases such as measles, whooping cough, diptheria, and tuberculosis are disrupted, as is the supply of drugs for on-going therapies.

57 Mosquito-borne diseases such as Malaria, Zika and Dengue are not inevitable in coastal areas after salt-water inundation.

Malaria currently causes about half a million deaths in those aged five years and under around the world every year, making it the world's third biggest child killer. It is spread by the mosquito, and there are assertions that tsunamis and storm surges increase surface water availability, making it easier for mosquitoes to breed, thereby enhancing transmission. Certainly, water is an essential component of the mosquito's life cycle, but whether it is running or standing, clean or polluted, fresh or brackish, shaded or sunlit, permanent or intermittent, are the predominant factors determining which species of mosquito breed in it.

Transient, polluted salt water generated by a tsunami or storm-surge will not sustain most species involved in transmission[72] of dengue fever and malaria[xlix]. This explains why, after the Pacific tsunami of 2004, incidence of malaria in Aceh was nine times less than the average for

---

[71] Subterranean seismic activity often results in a temporary surge of minerals such as sulphur and metals such as iron oxide being released into the groundwater. Levels can be so high that the water turns yellow, black, or red.

[72] The range of conditions which occur after a disaster, and the wide variation in the breeding and biting habits of the many species of mosquitoes which transmit these diseases, are such as to make generalisations about transmission difficult.

that time of year. Even four months later, incidence was still only half of pre-tsunami levels[i].

Apart from inundation with salty sea-water, in a cyclonic storm-surge, tsunami or river flood disaster malaria and dengue require the presence of multiple risk factors apart from the event itself. These include:

Presence of the vector: Malaria and dengue are transmitted by *anopheles* and *aedes* mosquitoes respectively. Both have lifespans of between 23-28 days and neither can fly much more than 27 kms in their lifetime. This means these two diseases are highly localised.

Presence of the pathogen: Malaria is caused by the *plasmodium* parasite. Humans are not the only host. Disasters kill animals as well as humans thereby reducing the reservoir needed for completing the vector's life-cycle.

Polluted salt water generated by a tsunami or storm-surge will not sustain most species involved in transmission of dengue fever and malaria.

Breeding sites: Debris after a disaster can fill with rain-water providing ideal pools of stagnant water for mosquito larvae to thrive. Most *anopheline* mosquitoes, however, require not stagnant but slowly moving fresh water.

Exposure: Increased exposure to the vector may occur through loss of housing in the disaster.

Population migration: Populations moving from areas where malaria prevalence is low into areas where the disease is endemic are particularly susceptible as they have no resistance.

Access to health care: Diagnosis and treatment is difficult when clinics are partially destroyed and qualified health professionals in short supply. Rapid diagnostic test have revolutionised diagnosis with the result that false negatives[73] from time consuming and technically difficult blood-smear microscopy are now much reduced.

Disruption to control measures: Fogging and spraying with insecticides, intermittent at the best of times, will likely cease altogether in the post-disaster phase.

---

[73] A result that indicates a given condition is not present, when it is.

Distribution & logistical constraints: Bed-net distributions will be disrupted by poor road access. But, if incidence is lowered for months after the disaster, managers should question whether specific bed-net distribution programmes are the priority conventional response measures would have us believe.

Malaria was the biggest killer disease in cities like London and Stockholm only a few hundred years ago, and appears to be poised to make a comeback in Europe as ambient temperatures climb towards those more favourable for mosquito breeding. Southern Greece suffered its first outbreak for forty years in 2012, a situation exacerbated by lack of financial support for environmental control measures such as residual spraying of insecticide and emptying of stagnant water reservoirs.

In the past decade, much progress has been made in tackling malaria. The World Health Organisation estimates that death due to malaria has fallen by more than half since 2000, and the expanded use of artemisinin[74]-based combination (ACT) therapy has – along with bed-net distribution, improved surveillance, and insecticide spraying – played a major part in this. The continued efficacy of ACT is crucial for ensuring these gains are not reversed, and for the eventual elimination of malaria. These efforts might be in jeopardy, though, because of the emergence of artemisinin resistance in Cambodia, Burma, Thailand, and Vietnam; countries considered to be the cradle of now widespread resistance to previous front-line antimalarial drugs[li].

Many other diseases transmitted by arthropod vectors, including Leishmaniasis and Murine Typhus, are unlikely to present a hazard after natural disasters as they mostly occur in remote and sparsely populated areas, or have little tendency to epidemic spread.

Conjunctivitis, dysentery (shigella), and some parasitic diseases may be transmitted by domestic flies, the numbers of which explode temporarily after a natural disaster owing to an increase in the number of breeding sites available – a function of the rise in open defecation,

---

[74] Artemisinin is derived from the plant *Artemisia annua*, or Sweet Wormwood, and has been known, especially in ancient China, for its ability to swiftly reduce the number of Plasmodium parasites in the blood of patients with malaria.

presence of dead bodies and animal carcasses, and absence of garbage disposal.

The host for rabies is the dog. Post-exposure rabies prophylaxis is recommended in any and all cases of animal bite wounds, whether rabies is endemic or not.

58 Mass immunisation is not usually an immediate priority following a large-scale natural disaster.

Public health authorities are preoccupied with the possibility of disease outbreaks and how to control them following natural disasters. Their first concern is usually the organisation of immunisation programmes – notably, against typhoid and, nowadays with the introduction of new vaccines, cholera (see *Disaster Misperception # 57*) – and with the disposal of corpses and animal carcasses. To a certain extent, these concerns arise from a combination of inexperience, ignorance of disaster epidemiology, and pressure from politicians to be seen to be doing something.

With the exception of circumstances where Measles vaccination coverage rates are at 60% or less prior to the disaster, there are, however, more practical, effective, and efficient approaches to disease control after natural disasters than hurried mass immunisation whatever the short-term psychological benefits. The first focuses on reducing the disease hazard by appropriate public health interventions which focus on those areas which present the greatest risk such as water treatment, waste disposal, and vector control. The second approach is establishing a disease surveillance system – sentinel[75] at first, but comprehensive as soon as possible – capable of promptly identifying any outbreak that does occur, and then making sure that appropriate control measures are in place.

Epidemic prevention and control measures must therefore remain a priority during relief operations, and common endemic diseases such as diarrhoea, respiratory infection, measles, malaria and neonatal infection must not be neglected.

---

[75] A 'sentinel' disease surveillance system deliberately involves only a limited network of carefully selected reporting sites.

Public pressure for action, however, often focuses on the perceived need for mass vaccination, in particular against water-borne diseases such as cholera, Hepatitis-A, and typhoid; diseases which, along with tetanus, measles and malaria (which is not, yet, a vaccine-preventable disease) are most commonly associated with disaster. Donated vaccines are often available in large quantities and immunisation programmes provide a convenient, easily organised, and highly visible activity.

Special attention needs to be paid to neonatal tetanus after a disaster.

Because the possibility of food and water being contaminated with human excrement[76] often increases after a disaster, the risk of waterborne diseases may indeed be greater than usual. However, for the following reasons, mass vaccination against potential – as opposed to actual – outbreaks of communicable disease following a natural disaster is not usually necessary:

- If the organism is not present in the affected area, and has not been introduced after the disaster, the disease it causes poses no threat regardless of environmental conditions.
- The risk of typhoid fever or cholera is very small in comparison to other diseases.
- A mass vaccination campaign cannot provide protection against typhoid fever at the time of greatest risk from contaminated water for the simple reason that multiple doses are needed to confer the required level of immunity, a process which takes a few weeks.
- Given the sorts of supply-chain difficulties associated with a natural disaster response, especially those involving refrigeration, it is rarely possible to achieve more than partial coverage.
- Being vaccinated can provide a false sense of security which means that people fail to take the more elementary precautions of washing hands with soap and disinfecting the domestic water supply at point of use
- Personnel are diverted from more useful (and cost-effective) activities

Natural disasters lead to population displacement, which means over-crowded temporary settlements spring up in whatever large buildings

---

[76] Faecal coliforms such as E-coli.

remain standing. These provide ideal circumstances for disease outbreaks. Settlements for survivors of natural disasters, however, are different to the refugee camps created to cope with complex emergencies such as the one Syria and its bordering countries have been experiencing. For natural disasters, the shock is short-term, and communities can cope with problems more easily; pre-disaster health and nutrition status are better than in complex emergencies; the settlements are usually much smaller, which limits the spread of pathogens; access to food, safe water, and sanitary facilities is usually better; and most people stay only a few weeks or months.

Disasters that cause mass displacement of populations with low vaccination coverage into over-crowded camps creates an extremely high risk of measles transmission. Measles immunisation (with combined Vitamin-A supplementation) is the single most cost-effective public health intervention among children in disaster settings in developing countries.

Depending on pre-disaster immunisation coverage levels, tetanus has the potential to be a major killer in natural disasters. This is because of the high probability that rescuers will sustain cuts and puncture wounds when scrabbling through the debris of damaged buildings [see *Disaster Misperception # 68*].

Vaccination against influenza is not recommended even though it is a highly contagious disease and has a shorter incubation period than measles. Surprisingly, there have been no reports of an influenza epidemic whose spread was aided by a preceding natural disaster.

Measles immunisation (and Vitamin-A supplementation) is the single most cost-effective public health intervention for children in disaster settings.

59   *Bubonic Plague still poses a major risk to the public's health.*

The 'Black Death' is considered to have been the deadliest pandemic in history. Starting in 1347 and lasting five years, this severe and incurable bacterial *bubonic* plague killed 30% - 50% of the population of Europe. Coming as it did at a time of war and food shortages, it has always been assumed that this extraordinary death rate was caused by the population being immuno-compromised, poorly nourished and never having been exposed to this particular pathogen before.

Pneumonic (lung) plague, however, is the one we should worry about as it is a deadly killer. And just in case you thought it had died out along with chivalry sometime in the sixteenth century, ask yourself why it is one of the six 'deadly diseases' currently being monitored by the World Health Organization.

Plague is a caused by the organism *Yersinia pestis* transmitted when people are bitten by a flea that carries the plague bacteria from an infected rodent, usually a rat. But pneumonic plague can be spread from human to human just by coughing. Anyone who breathes in the microscopic droplets is almost certain to catch the disease as the infective dose can be as low as only a single organism. By comparison, should you have travelled in an underground railway recently, Flu requires a full-blown sneeze and millions of virus's to infect anyone standing nearby.

The time between being infected and developing symptoms is typically 2 to 10 days for a virus, but may be as short as a few hours for pneumonic plague. People with the plague need immediate treatment. If treatment is not received within 24 hours of when the first symptoms occur, death may be unavoidable. Without treatment, about 50 - 90% of those with bubonic plague die. Almost all people with pneumonic plague die if not treated. Treatment reduces the death rate to 50%.

60 *Many of those extricated from a collapsed building go on to die hours later from completely preventable causes.*

Most earthquake survivors who have escaped from partially collapsed buildings have suffered some form of injury. Their lives are nearly as much in peril as those still entombed in the rubble. While the world watches footage of dramatic rescue efforts, the wounded face death due to shock and infections that can easily be avoided with adequate medical care. Estimates from the World Health Organisation during the Haiti earthquake response suggest that as many as 20,000 survivors died as a result of inadequate medical care. A newly orphaned 11-year-old girl called Emélie rescued two days after the earthquake, for instance, later died because the first aid station she was rushed to was "not equipped to deal with her injuries". There were, unfortunately, many more stories like hers.

Almost worse are the preventable deaths associated with crush injury[77] where up to half of all those smiling, happy people you see being pulled, blinking, dazed, and covered in dust from dark holes in the rubble, can be dead within hours[lii]. This is because the most devastating systemic effects can overcome the human body when limbs which have been subjected to crushing pressure for more than a few hours are suddenly released.

Crush injury -- which is easily treatable with dialysis -- is a leading cause of avoidable death in an earthquake.

In the Armenian earthquake of 1988, crush injury was the third most frequent injury sustained by those extricated from the rubble, and became the leading cause of death[liii]. Death can be averted, however, by applying two relatively simple measures: The first is to provide timely oxygen and intravenous rehydration during the rescue; the second is to provide renal dialysis as soon as possible once extricated. About half of patients with crush injury syndrome develop acute renal failure, and roughly half of those require dialysis[liv]. During the Kobe earthquake six years later, over half (54%) of those with crush injuries needed dialysis. With such treatment, most survivors ultimately recover completely; without it, they die.

Lessons have been learned since then, and dialysis machinery is one of the first things loaded onto relief flights by medical aid agencies. But, as the experience of Haiti in 2010 exposed yet again, national and international response remains inadequate when faced with earthquake-induced mass casualties. One of the world's largest medical NGO's, for example, had only three dialysis units[78] operational within the first week, enough to take care of about 2% of the number of patients who were likely to need it.

---

[77] Crush injury is a systemic manifestation of muscle crush injury – where long-lasting continuous pressure on a muscle group has caused extensive necrosis of the muscle tissue – which results in acute renal failure and/or hypovolaemic shock when toxins are suddenly released back into the bloodstream after extrication. Untreated, crush injury can be fatal.

[78] Dialysis is complicated wherever it is carried out, and even more so in a disaster zone where the large volumes of clean water, uninterrupted electricity, sterile environment, nephrologists, technicians, supplies, and specialised machinery required are hard to come by. In many cases, the much simpler form of haemostatic dialysis will be sufficient.

61 Dust inhalation is a major cause of death in an earthquake-induced building collapse.

Depending on the type of building, its design, its height, and the quality of its construction, about three quarters of people inside a collapsed building die within the first quarter of an hour. In Kobe, Japan in 1995, nearly three-quarters (71%) of all victims died within 14 minutes of the earthquake. A further 11% died within the next six hours. If the building is a ferro-concrete high-rise and has totally collapsed, these combined figures may rise from 82% to above 90%.

At least half of those inside at the time of the collapse – in other words those that were too slow or too far away from street-level exits to run outside – die instantly from what doctors call 'blunt trauma', a fancy term for being squashed or hit on the head so hard that the brain stops functioning. Within a few minutes, most of the others in this group die from asphyxiation; they cannot breathe, either because of the weight of rubble lying on their chests, or because they have inhaled concrete or brick dust and their lungs are clogged. The remaining few die from haemorrhage and/or penetrating trauma – either internal bleeding or blood loss resulting from deep gashes sustained by rubble or, more likely, broken glass.

Huge amounts of dust are generated when a building collapses – one only has to recall images of the 9/11 Twin Towers collapse in New York to understand quite how much – and concrete dust being injected under high pressure to clog air passages and set hard in lungs is a major cause of death for many building collapse victims who could otherwise be saved. Evidence from earthquakes in Guatemala in 1976, Mexico City in 1985, and Armenia in 1988 suggests that suffocation from dust inhalation was a significant factor in the deaths of many people who displayed no apparent external or internal trauma. Why then is so little attention paid to educating people about the threat posed by dust?

62 Paralysis during extrication from a collapsed building is not unusual.

A major complication when extricating earthquake survivors from under the rubble of a collapsed building is spinal-cord injury. Over 73,000 people died in the Pakistan earthquake of 2005. 128,309 sustained serious injuries of which 741 were to the spinal-cord. Nearly three quarters (71%) of patients admitted to hospital with such injuries developed some sort of neurological deficit resulting in complete or partial paraplegia or quadriplegia. Most patients reported that they were able to move their limbs while buried under the rubble but, during their move, one or more limbs became completely paralysed . By contrast, Japan's highly developed emergency preparedness and response system operating during the 1995 Hanshin earthquake resulted in only six partial paralyses from a total of 140 reported spinal fractures.

Extra time is needed to immobilise those with suspected spinal injuries before extrication.

Pre-hospital management of spinal injury is of critical importance is paralysis is not to result. One only has to see how much care is taken when carting off some hapless football player with a suspected neck injury to realise what is involved. The first to respond in Pakistan, as everywhere following such disasters, were untrained community members. Being unaware of the importance of spinal immobilisation to prevent secondary paralysis, they worked frantically to rescue as many people as the after-shocks and falling rubble would allow. People with severe injuries were "dragged and pulled out of the rubble to be carried in blankets and put into the back of open pickup trucks" which then jolted their way through the devastation to the heli-pad for medical evacuation by military helicopter. Similar practices can be seen in all earthquake responses. "What else could we do?" said Arshad Amin who, years later, remained traumatised by the events of those days.

63 *Dead bodies pose little risk to disaster survivors.*

As a species we are hard-wired to be afraid of snakes and dead bodies. While we are right to believe that some snakes can kill us with a single bite – a tarpin has enough venom to kill 350 people – or swallow us whole as an anaconda did to Owen Wilson in the dreadful film of the same name, the general paranoia surrounding death and the proximity of dead bodies is completely without foundation in this day and age. This was not the case in medieval times when dead bodies were riddled with all sorts of "pox and aigues", but public health has moved on since then.

With dead bodies and animal carcasses rotting by the roadside and floating, bloated in ponds after large-scale natural disasters, it's hardly surprising that rumours and fears about the health threat they pose abound. It is assumed that dead bodies combine with disruption to health, water purification, and sewage disposal systems to somehow put survivors at imminent risk of contracting previously unseen deadly diseases. Fear of such epidemics is often dramatically emphasised by the media, and has sometimes led to mass burial. However, mass casualties after natural disasters are unlikely to have epidemic-causing infections and the public risk of infection from dead bodies is almost negligible[lv].

In reality, corpses of people who were perfectly healthy when they died do not harbour dangerous pathogens, so pose no threat to the living in death. Most pathogens anyway tend to die within a few hours of their host dying. Dead bodies only pose health risks in a few situations that require specific precautions such as where cholera or haemorrhagic fevers such as Ebola are already endemic in the immediate environment. In such cases, especially where it is the local custom to touch the dead body before burial, extra care must be taken to wash hands afterwards. Otherwise, recovering and identifying the dead and then giving them a culturally appropriate burial is more important to families for psychological reasons than any consideration of sanitation.

Corpses of people who were healthy when they died do not harbour dangerous pathogens, so pose no threat to the living in death.

If they are not quickly dealt with, however, especially in hot climates, dead bodies do tend to become overwhelmingly smelly[79] and make psychological recovery more difficult. They can also contribute to a dramatic increase in the fly population, which increases the chances of diarrhoeal disease transmission.

---

[79] Within two to three days of death, depending mostly on the temperature, a decomposing body begins to emit characteristic gases such as cadaverine, putrescine, indole and skatole. These are produced as microbes break down the body's carbohydrates, proteins and fatty acids, and are what give off the horrible and distinctive smell so familiar to 'search & rescue' teams. But in themselves they are quite harmless.

How long it takes for a body to decompose depends on several factors: the temperature, humidity, whether the body is in water, buried, or exposed to insects or carnivores or not. It takes more or less two months to reduce a human body to bones when left exposed, and up to a year when buried or submerged.

64 'Baby Booms' 10-12 months after a natural disaster are to be expected.

Within weeks of a natural disaster, the urge to procreate overwhelms young male and female survivors who, in some visceral way, appear to be seeking to celebrate life when all around them has been death and destruction. The result is a baby boom 10 to 12 months after the event.

Health facilities will have been damaged along with much of the housing in a large-scale earthquake, tropical cyclone, flood, or tsunami. Doctors and nurses will not have been spared, either. The direct knock-on effect is that most of these babies will be born in sub-optimal conditions in tented camps or temporary houses built mostly with salvaged material on earthen floors. In such conditions, the rate at which new-born babies die from neo-natal tetanus increases dramatically unless the mother is lucky enough to have been vaccinated.

65 Ingestion of Cholera and other bugs into the lungs during a near-drowning incident poses a significant health risk.

As we have seen, most of those unfortunate enough to be caught up in the maelstrom of water that is a tsunami do not survive. Of those that do, most suffer deep lacerations from dislodged corrugated iron sheets, puncture wounds from impalement on exposed nails, and deep abrasion from the scouring effect of turbulent soil-sand-and-shell-laden seawater. These wounds often become seriously infected, having been grossly contaminated with deep-water organisms found in this seawater slurry and the sewage suspended in it. In the 2004 Indian Ocean tsunami over two thirds of such wounds were infected with multiple microbes in this way[lvi].

A significant percentage of those injured will end up having amputation of one or more limbs, although this is proportionately much less than in an earthquake for the simple reason that the awesome destructive power of a tsunami is limited for the most part to a narrow strip along the coast, the area of inland penetration being limited by the topography and number of trees and buildings in the way. Corpses of people who were healthy when they died do not harbour dangerous pathogens, so pose no threat to the living in death

A small percentage suffer from an unusual form of 'near-drowning' where ingestion under pressure of the same contaminated slurry into soft tissue of the lungs exposes organisms to new and unusual places where they give rise to rarely seen and difficult-to-treat infections. Most types of cholera *vibrio*, for example, live in brackish estuarine waters or in deeper waters further out to sea where they cause no harm to humans. Once exposed to deep cuts and lung tissue, however, they can become deadly[lvii]. *Vibrio vulnificus* is an estuarine bacterium that causes serious wound infection which can lead to septicaemia and death, especially in patients already suffering from other underlying ailments. Ingested into the lungs, its effects can be even more dramatic[lviii]. The same can be said for various types of non-TB-causing *mycobacteria*. 'Tsunami Lung'[80] is particularly difficult to treat[lix], and all three Finnish holidaymakers who survived being caught up in water of the Indian Ocean tsunami died from its complications weeks after arriving home.

'Tsunami Lung' is difficult to identify and extremely difficult to treat if left undiagnosed.

The effect is not limited to tropical countries either. On a bright summer's day in 2011, a light helicopter lifted off from Manhattan's 34th Street heliport carrying four excited adults on an intended aerial tour of New York City. Seconds after lift-off, it suffered a tail rotor malfunction and crashed into the East River. The pilot survived, as did the other front-seat passenger. Of the three passengers in the rear seats, one drowned on the spot. The other two were rescued but had suffered 'near-drowning' and had ingested contaminated sea-water into their lungs. One died 10 days later, and the other, the pilot's wife, Harriet,

---

[80] Tsunami Lung is not confined to inhalation of water-born bugs; it can also refer to lung diseases caused, for example, by certain types of silica dust in volcanic ash. One such disease boasts the longest word in the English language: pneumonoultramicroscopicsilicovolcanokoniosis. Not surprisingly, most doctors refer to it as 'volcano lung'.

died one month later. Officially, both died from "pulmonary complications caused by near-drowning". In fact, they most likely died from inhalation of unusual bugs, including cholera.

66 Most limb amputations following a natural disaster are unnecessary.

Earthquake and tsunami casualties suffer mainly from musculo-skeletal injuries, especially blunt trauma and fracture, due to collision with debris. After the Yogyakarta earthquake in Indonesia in 2006, just over 1,500 (4%) of the 36,299 people injured required hospitalisation. Almost 60% of all injuries were fractures requiring orthopaedic surgery.

The seven orthopaedic surgeons present at the time were quickly overwhelmed, so additional surgical teams were sent from elsewhere in Indonesia. Within 24 hours, fifteen surgical teams were at work. Each team worked non-stop for three days by which time the acute phase was considered over. This was just the beginning, however, as the patients needed follow-up procedures or a second operation for infected wounds. Infections were rampant since antibiotics, mandatory in the treatment of open fractures, were not available for such a large 'mass casualty' event. In addition, definitive fixation of fractures was not possible due to the lack of plates, screws and external fixators, all of which had to be imported from abroad.

This story is not unfamiliar even in the developed world. Similar problems with availability of skilled surgeons, surgical teams, post-operative care as well as supplies of basic consumables such as antibiotics and gauze pads were in evidence in New Orleans in the immediate aftermath of hurricane Katrina.

Amputation is particularly devastating for a disaster survivor in a developing country.

According to Dr Sanjay Gupta, CNN's Chief Medical Correspondent, who was in Haiti in January 2010, doctors didn't have the proper equipment and were using hacksaws sterilised with vodka to perform amputations. "There's hardly any anaesthesia, or post-operative care, or blood to transfuse someone," he reported at the time. In this, conditions don't appear very different to Nelson's day at the Battle of Trafalgar. In all, Haiti's health authorities later estimated that between 6,000 and 8,000 Haitians lost digits or limbs following the earthquake.

In both Pakistan after the 2005 earthquake and in Haiti after the 2010 earthquake, thousands of amputations were carried out that many orthopaedic and plastic surgeons now deem to have been unnecessary, even allowing for the degraded state of health services available to provide clinical and remedial aftercare.

The *Surgeon's Dilemma* puts surgeons in an ethical quandary as it asks them to make a decision about whether to amputate or not that goes beyond the medical. It refers to the balance between early amputation – less risk of infection, but greater disability – and repeated limb salvage procedures, which means operating on fewer individual patients and tying up medical and rehabilitation resources for longer periods of time. Surgeons have to make such decisions knowing that ortho-plastic surgery consumes disproportionate resources at a time when health care provision at all levels is scarce. corpses of people who were perfectly healthy when they died do not harbour dangerous pathogens, so pose no threat to the living in death

The benefits of limb salvage in the wake of natural disaster are still hotly debated, despite some evidence that improved quality of life after reconstructive surgery and a lower overall cost to the healthcare system is the net result. Arguments in support of saving the limb in wealthy countries are good. In poorer economies with less support infrastructure, these arguments become even stronger as the human, economic, and societal consequences of limb loss are, relatively speaking, worse because of the lack of rehabilitation facilities. Adult amputees are 40% more likely to have difficulty in providing food for the family; their children's future becomes even more uncertain; and they are likely to always remain dependent on others. Amputation in most developing countries spells ostracism and lifelong penury, not just for the victim but also the family, and the impact on human health from losing the use of one or more limbs is far deeper and longer-lasting than supposed.

With much of the health infrastructure destroyed in the earthquake, and mobile field hospitals arriving from outside taking between four and ten days to set up, there is little that can be done to treat the sorts of deep infections and gangrenes that have by then set in, at least not with the limited facilities available. The longer the delay, the more preparatory operations are needed before the limb can be fixated. After a week of infection, this may require as many as four such operations. The fixation itself requires at least two surgical operations, and usually two or three more interventions as the patient recovers. In disaster zones, the traditional view is that it is simply not feasible medically, logistically, or financially to do this. Hence the amputation, which is immediately 'life saving', quick to do, and requires little medical follow-up in comparison to what is required to salvage and rehabilitate a limb.

There are many other challenges when considering amputation, not least the surgical. But crushed bones and open wounds are often less hopeless cases than many surgeons assume. According to Waseem Saeed, a Plastic Surgeon also in Haiti in January 2010, "You shouldn't amputate every complex injury you see in an earthquake zone. It's not necessary", adding that "a poorly functioning arm is better than no arm at all".

He argues that emergency surgery in a disaster zone follows too closely the experience of battlefield surgery, and suggests that wounds requiring amputation in the latter scenario may not need such drastic intervention in the former, even though both types of injury look pretty similar at first. The key difference, he says, "is that high-energy bullet wounds cause wide but not always visible injury that make limb salvage much more difficult, and that this is not the case in natural disaster situations".

67 *Tetanus poses a significant threat following a natural disaster.*

Most of us will remember to have a tetanus toxoid 'booster' shot before venturing into the developing world, but have otherwise forgotten how serious a disease this is. Tetanus can easily become a major killer in natural disasters where vaccination coverage is low.

Tetanus is caused by a toxin released by the bacterium *Clostridium tetani* and is transmitted through even the most superficial of scratches contaminated by soil and dust. It is a fatal disease which kills between 300,000 and 500,000 people every year in the developing world, a large percentage of whom are newborn babies.

Tetanus was the biggest cause of avoidable death after the Yogyakarta earthquake.

The disease has a case-fatality-rate of over 50% in un-vaccinated patients who are left untreated, but which drops to 20% or less when fully configured intensive care units (ICUs) with respiratory ventilators are available. Respiratory failure is the principal cause of death.

Low DPT (Diptheria, Pertussis, Tetanus) vaccination coverage rates pose significant risks in areas hit by earthquakes and tsunamis given the number of cuts and puncture wounds sustained while frantically scrabbling through the rubble and debris to rescue people. In Aceh, where between 30-35 tetanus cases are reported annually, 96 cases occurred in the first four weeks after the 2004 tsunami, most of which were adult males. None received boosters, and all required intensive care treatment including ventilator support, but all those hospitalised survived. Despite relatively high tetanus vaccination coverage rates in Indonesia, Tetanus was still the biggest cause of avoidable death after the Yogyakarta earthquake of 2006 and increased infection rates were noticeable in Kathmandu following the earthquake of 2015 in Nepal.

68   *The threat from Influenza virus' has not been exaggerated.*

Influenza – the 'Flu' – will be the most likely cause of any future killer pandemic[81]. And epidemiologists agree that it is not a question of 'whether' but 'when' such a killer will strike. We're not talking about the kind of Flu that knocks us out for a few days every other winter, but a mutated strain against which we have no built-in immunity and for which there is no cure, only preventive vaccination.

That's why *Avian* and *Swine* Flu caused such a commotion a couple of years ago, with the UN scaring the wits out of the world by suggesting that up to 150 million people could die[lx]. But statistical regression models clearly demonstrate that they were right then and they are right now. The threat has not receded.

Two recent outbreaks – the 2009 H1N1 *Swine Flu* and the H5N1 *Bird Flu* that emerged in Asia a few years earlier – failed to become the global killers predicted by the UN even though millions were infected. Bird flu was much the more virulent of the two, killing about half of those infected, and the fear is now that there will be a global resurgence that combines the virulence of the H5N1 with the transmissibility of the H1N1. The *Spanish Flu* of 1918 was one such "doomsday strain", killing between 50 million and 100 million people; around 4%-7% of the world's population at the time and many times more than were killed in the First World War.

It is the ease and speed with which these viruses are able to mutate that has meant that there is no generic vaccine that is effective against

---

[81] A pandemic is an epidemic that spreads through human populations simultaneously in different parts of the world over the long term.

all strains. When a new strain emerges, it takes several months to develop a viable vaccine and several months more before it becomes commercially available.

It is easy to imagine the mass panic that would result if something similar to 'Spanish Flu' were to emerge again. Power-station workers, doctors, delivery drivers, water treatment engineers, and petrol station managers would either be sick or dead. Hospitals would close their doors. The lights would go out, the shops would be empty, and cities would grind to a halt. With people fleeing to remote rural areas, law and order would break down. This is the scenario so vividly – and, according to CDC in Atlanta, so accurately – portrayed in the film *Contagion*.

69   *Asbestos still poses a major risk where buildings have collapsed.*

Inhalation of concrete and brick dust has been mentioned as a significant cause of unnecessary death in earthquake-induced building collapses.

Just as serious is to realise that, in developing countries, this dust is likely to include asbestos fibres. Asbestos is a common building material in developing countries, and was used until the late 1980's for floors, roofs, foundations and as insulation around water and gas pipes. When one of these older buildings collapse, tiny asbestos fibres become airborne. When inhaled, the fibres remain in the lungs for long periods of time, and can go on to cause serious lung disease including Asbestosis, Lung Cancer, and Mesothelioma, all of which generally have a 20 to 50 year latency period between exposure and the presence of symptoms. This is a serious health concern for those rescuers not wearing dust masks[82], especially once heavy machinery starts being used to move debris.

Rubble must be damped down before rescue and salvage operations begin.

---

[82] Rescuers should always wear protective equipment, including dust masks … and not those disposable paper ones, either, but the serious industrial variety.

To prevent these killer fibres from becoming airborne, rubble has to be well damped down before rescue operations begin[83]. This is easier said than done when water supply networks are likely to have been seriously disrupted and water tables shifted.

70 Silent Pandemics pose a serious threat to public health.

There are plenty of already familiar diseases that constitute "silent pandemics". One of these is Tuberculosis, an infectious disease caused by a *mycobacterium* ... of which there are 7,160 different forms. In the days before antibiotics, tuberculosis was incurable and referred to as "the white plague".

In September 2011, the World Health Organization urged Western Europe to be alert against drug-resistant tuberculosis in the wake of an "alarming rise" in the number of cases reported in the region. More than 80,000 new cases of this disease are reported each year in Western Europe, London being the hardest hit capital city with 3,500 new cases diagnosed annually. More and more of them are of the more lethal and extensively drug-resistant strain called 'Extra Drug-Resistant Tuberculosis', or XDR-TB for short.

XDR-TB and its MDR-TB (Multi-Drug Resistant Tuberculosis) precursor do not respond to the cocktail of five standard antibiotics currently used for treatment, not only making this disease more complex and costly to treat but increasing the threat that TB will spread more widely, especially in poorer environments such as homeless centres and prisons where it thrives. Over 14% of newly diagnosed TB patients have the MDR form, a percentage which is rising rapidly. Half of these sufferers are expected to die even with treatment. Major obstacles to controlling the disease stem from the microbe's ability to evade and outwit current treatments, which typically require prolonged use by patients and are often ineffective.

About 1.5 million people of the 8-9 million who get infected every year, die from TB.

Rising immigration from infected areas, especially Eastern Europe and Russia, has contributed to this rise, but WHO warn against

---

[83] Dampening of rubble prior to its movement is also needed after storm surges and tsunami despite the heavy rain normally associated with the former.

complacency among native populations. "TB can infect anyone," said Dr Gozalov of WHO's regional office in Copenhagen. "Any one of us can be exposed and get infected," he said, going on to caution that, "a big proportion of those who do get infected – currently, this is running at 5% – can 'convert' and develop the more resistant version".

About 1.5 million people of the 8-9 million who get infected every year around the world, die from tuberculosis each year, and it is thought that as many as 2 billion people (one third of the human population of Earth) may be infected. As most cases of TB infection are 'latent' and therefore have yet to turn into a disease for the carrier, WHO estimates that there may be as many as 50 million people now infected with drug resistant tuberculosis.

⊕

Anyone who saw Dustin Hoffman play a manic and obnoxious doctor from the US Centres for Disease Control (CDC) in the film *Outbreak*, or Kate Winslett in the more recent and realistic film *Contagion* will understand why there is reason to be alarmed about the threat posed by emerging infectious diseases. Emerging and re-emerging infectious diseases are those that are resistant to all known antibiotic therapies and/or for which the population has little or no immunity.

According to the US Institute of Medicine, if the next major infectious disease is not from a previously unknown bug, the biggest threat comes from HIV-AIDs, Hepatitis-C, Tuberculosis (TB), and new, more lethal variants of Influenza. They also think that hospital acquired infections will also pose a growing threat as drug resistance increases and new strains of *Streptococcus* or *Staphylococcus* emerge. Already, there is only one antibiotic left that controls spread of the "super-bug" *Staphylococcus aureus,* and there are signs that even this is losing its effectiveness. TB, cholera, and malaria are not only beginning to make a comeback, but are doing so with more virulent and drug-resistant forms.

Less than 2% of viruses that exist in the wild are known about.

In reality, there are bugs out there which can kill up to 80% or more of all people they come into contact with, and for which there is no cure. Except for the most exotic – by which we normally mean 'deadly' – you will have heard of most of them: Influenza, AIDS, Ebola, and Bubonic

Plague, for example. They may well 'self-limit' – i.e die out on their own accord – but not before millions are dead or dying.

But you are unlikely to have heard of *Henipah*, a particularly nasty form of virus found originally in fruit bats. Fruit bats have evolved with this virus over millions of years, and because of this co-evolution, they experience little more from it than the fruit bat equivalent of a cold. But once the virus breaks out of the bats and into a species that hasn't evolved with it, a horror show can take place, as one did in rural Malaysia in 1999. It is probable that a bat dropped a piece of saliva-covered fruit into a forest piggery. The pigs became infected with the virus, and then amplified it. And then it jumped to humans. It was startling in its lethality. Out of 276 people infected, 106 died and many others suffered permanent and crippling neurological disorders. There is no cure or vaccine. Since then there have been twelve similar, though thankfully smaller, outbreaks in South Asia.

There are many more diseases with more familiar names such as Measles, Pertussis (Whooping Cough), Diptheria, Tuberculosis, Yellow Fever and others, which kill an awful lot of people around the world every year, but about which we hear little because we think that vaccination has incurred life-long immunity. Diptheria in particular is making a comeback in countries of the former Soviet Union where health infrastructure is crumbling and vaccination coverage is a shambles. In developed countries, the situation is not much better, with vaccination coverage rates one third of what they should be to ensure 'herd' immunity[84].

Politics and trade also play their part. Intellectual property rights are frequently flouted by manufacturers in developing countries who make generic copies of drugs that are under patent protection, not always with the permission of the patent-holder. Some of the drugs manufactured in this way contain no active ingredient, or contain half the prescribed dose ... which is worse in many ways, as it fails to cure and stimulates resistance at the same time [see *Disaster Misperception # 77*].

Nearly two-thirds of emerging infectious diseases that affect humans originate in animals, with more than two-thirds of those originating in wild animals. The scope of the challenge this presents is

---

[84] Herd immunity describes when the vaccination of a significant portion of the population provides a measure of protection for individuals who have not developed immunity. The greater the proportion of individuals who are resistant, the smaller the probability that a susceptible individual comes into contact with an infectious individual.

huge and complex, not least because it is estimated that only one percent of viruses that exist in wildlife are known. And, with modern air travel and a robust market in wildlife trafficking, the potential for a serious outbreak in a large population centre is growing all the time. Increased ease of travel – one million humans are in the air at any one time – has radically altered the speed at which microbes can meet and recombine, and rendered us hideously susceptible to what results. Today, an aggressive transmissible influenza with an incubation period of a few days could be on every continent within 36 hours.

In other words, outbreaks of potentially deadly diseases reflect what we are doing, either deliberately or unwittingly, rather than just being things that happen. In this – and as the Ebola epidemic so vividly demonstrated – epidemics are no different to any other form of so-called 'natural' disaster.

We live in a world that, at least from the point of view of a virus or a bacterium, has changed very little. Our world remains fraught with the risk of new pandemics as microbes that have never encountered each other before combine to form mutant stains which will cause diseases capable of spreading in ways neither of their 'parents' could ever do.

✦

The appearance of a virus capable of infecting 40% of the world's population, and killing unimaginable numbers of them is not as far-fetched scenario as you might think. This is what Laurie Garrett said about Bird Flu (Avian Influenza) when it was making headline news in the years after 2005:

> *"The havoc such a disease could wreak is commonly compared to the devastation of the 1918-19 Spanish Flu, which killed over 50 million people in 18 months. But avian flu is much more dangerous. Doom may loom. But note the 'may'. If the relentlessly evolving (H5N1) virus becomes capable of human-to-human transmission, develops powers of contagion typical of human influenzas, and maintains its extraordinary virulence, humanity could well face a pandemic unlike any ever witnessed.*
>
> *Or nothing could happen at all.*
>
> *Scientists cannot predict with any certainty what this virus will do. Evolution does not function on a knowable timetable, and influenza is one of the sloppiest, most mutation-prone pathogens in nature's storehouse".*

Meanwhile, a horse dies mysteriously in Canada, a chimpanzee in Central Africa, a few pigs in Australia, and whole flocks of chickens in Indonesia. People in regular contact with these animals fall sick, and most die. These real-life cases, and others involving bats and unknown numbers of even more exotic species, represent not just isolated events, but a trend in the transmission of new diseases from animals to humans.

International health experts call such diseases 'zoonotic', meaning animal infections that somehow cross over to infect people. About one third of the 15,000 or so diseases known to man – including the modern day scourges of malaria, HIV, and more recently, Ebola – are in this category. For the most part, these diseases are the result of infection by one of three types of pathogen or bug: viruses, bacteria, and fungi. The most troublesome are viruses, mostly because of their abundance, their ability to adapt quickly, and the fact that they don't respond to antibiotics. In the 1995 film *Outbreak*, a sweet little Capuchin monkey carrying a "deadly virus" that was going to cause "the greatest medical crisis in the world" caused anxiety in millions of cinema-goers. The film gave zoonotic infections the Hollywood treatment but stripped of the hyperbole, it contained elements of reality. Zoonoses are a major threat to human health, and it is considered "highly likely" that the next pandemic will originate from an animal, as Ebola did.

Within the viral camp, there are two main sub-groups, the DNA and RNA[85] viruses, with the RNA viruses being particularly worrisome. HIV-AIDS is caused by a zoonotic RNA virus. So was the Spanish Flu Laurie Garrett referred to above. And so are Ebola, Marburg, Lassa, West Nile, Dengue, Rabies, Yellow Fever, SARS, and all those other spooky names which strike the fear of God into anyone who has seen blood oozing from Kevin Spacey's eyes after being infected by some unidentified bug in the movie *Outbreak*.

There are an awful lot of RNA viruses. They exist in the oceans, in rivers, in the soil, in forests, and in urban jungles. According to Professor Eddie Holmes of Penn State University, one of the world's leading virologists, it's possible that every species on the planet, bacterium, fungus, plant, and animal, supports at least one RNA virus,

---

[85] DNA stands for 'deoxyribonucleic acid', a self-replicating material which is present in nearly all living organisms as the main constituent of chromosomes. It is the carrier of genetic information. RNA stands for 'ribonucleic acid' and its principal role is to act as a messenger carrying instructions from DNA for controlling the synthesis of proteins.

though, as he puts it, "we don't know for sure because we've only just started looking."

It is only fairly recently that marine biologists have come to realise that the open ocean is teeming with viruses of a surprisingly wide range of types. Not all of these viral particles are infectious, as ultra-violet radiation inactivates most of them in the photic zone. However, the energy surge that is a tsunami cascades water from great depths and unleashes it into a completely alien environment that includes oxygen and sunlight. In this environment, viruses not usually encountered collide with wounded or drowning humans to cause illnesses not usually seen[lxi].

We do know, however, that influenza viruses – which are RNA viruses – can be lethal and that there are three types, rather unimaginatively called A, B, and C. The A-type viruses cause the most severe epidemics in humans, and only this type is further classified into sub-types on the basis of the two main surface proteins, one called Hemagglutinin (H), the other, Neuraminidase (N). There are 16 known H sub-types, and 9 known N sub-types, which means that at least 144 combinations, or strains, are possible. So far, only three (H1N1, H1N2, and H3N2) are in general circulation among people.

In the mid 1900's, scientists from the Rockefeller Foundation and other institutions conceived the ambitious goal of eradicating some infectious diseases entirely. They tried hard with Yellow Fever, spending millions of dollars over many years, and failed. They tried hard with Malaria, and failed. They tried again with Smallpox, and succeeded. Why? The differences between these three diseases are many and complex, but probably the most crucial one is that Smallpox resided neither in a reservoir host, nor in a vector such as a mosquito or tick. Its ecology was simple. It existed in humans and humans only, and was therefore much easier to eradicate. The campaign to eradicate Polio, which is still ongoing, begun in 1998 by WHO, is a realistic effort for the same reason: Polio isn't zoonotic. Eradicating a zoonotic disease, whether a directly transmitted one like Ebola, or an insect-vectored one such as Yellow Fever is much more complicated, because to exterminate the pathogen you either have to exterminate the species in which it resides or interrupt transmission in some other way.

Antibiotic resistance poses a major risk to society.

Superbugs are becoming increasingly resistant to antibiotics. This is because the more we use antibiotics, the more the bugs adapt to resist them. Bacteria that survive antibiotic attack emerge stronger, with an ability to repel new drugs[86], and misuse of antibiotics by patients, doctors and veterinarians is speeding things up further.

Patients often fail to complete their treatment because they feel better halfway through the course, making it less likely that their infections are completely cleared. This leaves some bacteria alive with greater resistance, and as these bacteria breed – which they do every twenty minutes, or so – resistance gradually spreads. Over-prescription of antibiotics by doctors "in case of secondary infection" results in patients taking them for illnesses for which they are ineffective, and farmers feed them to animals not to cure illness, but to promote growth, all of which increases the pool of resistant bacteria even more.

In the US, where as much as four-fifths of all antibiotics produced are fed to animals, at least 2 million Americans are thought to suffer antibiotic-resistant infections each year, leading directly to some 23,000 deaths and scores more from complications arising in other illnesses.

Antibiotic resistance is as much a strategic risk to society as climate change or terrorism.

The pipeline of new drugs is running dry. Most of the antibiotics in use today are derived, not from exotic plants hidden away in the rainforests of the world, but from microbes in the soil, most of which are themselves bacteria. Unfortunately, only seven new antibiotics have been created in the past 20 years, and no new class of antibiotics has been discovered since 1987. Partly, this is because research has failed to make the breakthroughs, but is also because pharmaceutical companies have had little incentive to seek new treatments as long as the old ones still work. Joint public-private efforts to reverse this lack of investment in the ultimate common good – our survival – will take decades to bear fruit. In the meantime,

---

[86] The conventional wisdom is that susceptible bugs perish, leaving behind a few individuals whose drug resistance is passed on as they multiply. As a result, some diseases which were previously treatable no longer are.

antibiotics are failing more often, and previously curable illnesses are beginning to become incurable.

According to the UK's Chief Medical Officer, "antibiotic resistance is as much a strategic risk to society as climate change or terrorism"[lxii]. She goes on to say that a concerted effort is required by all countries if this emerging crisis is to be halted – by changing the prescribing habits of general medical practitioners, for example – and suggests that antibiotics need to be viewed as a precious resource to be nurtured, like water or the ozone layer, and not continue to be seen as an inexhaustible supply. It seems that, without a concerted international response, the days of popping a few pills to cure a fairly typical infection are likely to become a distant memory. If so, the number of healthy years you can expect to live will shorten, perhaps by ten years or more.

The fight against drug-resistant infections received a setback in late 2015 when it was announced that certain bacteria were resistant to *Colistin*, one of the super-antibiotics of last resort. Even more alarming is that the gene providing the resistance could migrate from one strain of bacteria to another, meaning other types of infections could also become untreatable. The announcement prompted public health experts at the G20 meeting in Paris in December 2015 to renew their warnings that the world risks slipping into a deadly, post-antibiotic era.

It may be that the scientific community is petrified by its impotence in the face of these microscopic bugs. Certainly HG Wells was, as, in his prescient 1930's book *War of The Worlds*, his Earth-destroying *Triffids* were eventually overcome, not by the ingenuity of man, but by a common virus. This was then, and is now, a fight to the death between bugs and drugs, and it's not clear who the winner will be.

72   *Plagues of locusts still devastate parts of the world.*

A plague of locusts is another form of 'biohazard' which can cause a natural disaster. "Smaller than a bean but more dangerous than an elephant", according to one tribal chief in Mali, these infestations have been feared and revered since biblical times. They still wreak havoc today, and not just in Africa but in places like Kyrgyzstan in Central Asia. Egypt suffered a locust invasion in November 2004, when millions of the desert insects swept into Cairo and the Nile Delta. One local NGO reported at the time that over one-third of Egypt's crops had been damaged as a result of the invasion .

Locusts are solitary insects with lifestyles much like grasshoppers and crickets. But locusts have an additional stage in their life cycle called the 'gregarious phase'. When environmental conditions produce a bloom in green plants and promote breeding, each adult can produce up to sixteen offspring which then congregate into thick, mobile, ravenous swarms. These swarms devastate crops and cause major agricultural damage and attendant human misery, famine and starvation. Found in Africa, the Middle East, and Asia, they inhabit some 60 countries and can cover one-fifth of Earth's land surface. Desert locust plagues can threaten the economic livelihood of one-tenth of the world's humans.

A desert locust swarm can be 1,200 kms^2 (460 miles^2) in size and pack between 40 and 80 million insects into each square kilometre. Each locust can eat its own weight in plants each day, so a swarm of such size would eat 192,000 tons of plants every day. Swarms rarely settle, and can cover distances of up to 500 kms in a day with a following wind. Swarms have been known to fly from northwest Africa to Great Britain and across the Atlantic to the Caribbean.

Space-Related

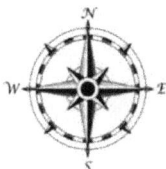

73

The threat posed by extra-terrestrial activity is not the stuff of science fiction.

Sceptics continue to think that the threat from space is pure science fiction. It isn't. The meteoric events of February 2013, when an undetected asteroid weighing 7,000 tons entered the Earth's atmosphere at 38,000 mph just missing the Russian city of Chelyabinsk, proved once and for all that we are not immune from extra-terrestrial risk.

This apocalyptic scenario, adapted from *The New Scientist*, is not as far-fetched as it might at first appear, and is the premise behind the rather predictable Hollywood movie *Knowing*, starring Nicolas Cage and many others in the genre.

> *It is late, and the skies of Manhattan are filled with undulating curtains of colourful light. Few New Yorkers have seen the aurora this far south but their fascination is short-lived. Within seconds, the street lights stretching down 5ᵗʰ Avenue flicker and dim to become unusually bright for a fleeting moment before going out. A series of muffled bangs reverberate beneath the now dark and bewildered streets as electrical transformers explode unseen. In a space of 60 seconds, the entire eastern half of the US is without power. Within eight minutes, so is half the world. Years of dark and cold begin as entire countries struggle to recover from the same fateful event - a violent storm, 150 million kilometres away on the surface of the sun ...*

✦

The sun's core – a seething 27,000,000°F plasma[87] spheroid six times as dense as gold – fuses 700 million tons of protons into helium nuclei every second, releasing the energy of ten billion hydrogen bombs in the process and bathing the Earth in more energy in an hour than civilisation uses in a year. Coronal Mass Ejections (CMEs), gigantic magnetic eruptions that belch billions of tons of heated plasma into space at just below the speed of light, are the consequence of this energy

---

[87] Neither solid, liquid, nor gas, the sun is made up of plasma, the fourth state of matter, which forms when atoms are stripped back to naked protons and electrons.

release, the effects of which can be felt on Earth as little as seventeen hours later.

When aimed at the Earth, these frequent but unpredictable proton streams produce powerful magnetic distortions in the ionosphere capable of knocking out our electrical power grids in much the same way that electro-magnetic pulses emanating from airburst detonation of nuclear devices can.

Three warning events in the past 25 years have demonstrated the danger that solar activity can pose to electrical power and distribution systems on Earth: In March 1989, a solar storm one third the intensity of the 1859 *Carrington Event* – the largest CME ever recorded – crippled the electrical grid in Quebec, Canada. According to NASA's Heliophysics Division, ten major solar flares over a two-week period in 2003, permanently disabled two Earth-orbiting satellites. And in August 2011, an X-class solar flare, the most powerful in NOAA's classification system, overloaded a sensor at the US Solar Dynamics Observatory in Boulder, Colorado.

It is difficult to predict the effect another *Carrington Event* would have now on an increasingly wired and electricity-dependent world, but, for sure, more transformers than the utility companies have stockpiled at the moment would melt, leaving many millions of people without heat, light, safe water, sewage treatment, air conditioning, fuel, mobile phones, perishable food, and temperature-sensitive medical supplies during the months and years it would take to manufacture and install new ones.

Most power grids have no built-in protection against the onslaught of a powerful geomagnetic storm. Even though most earth-based power grids would only be threatened by the rarest and most extreme of these solar storms, the damage could be widespread and catastrophic even though it will only affect the side of the planet facing the incoming pulse at the time. Australia, China, and the US are at higher risk because transmission lines are longer and capacity to replace melted transformers weaker.

Since large transformers are grounded to the Earth, such storms can induce currents that can cause them to overheat, catch fire, or explode. According to John Kappenman, a space consultant, "a solar storm like the one that took place in May 1921 would today turn out the lights over half of North America. One on the order of the 1859 Carrington Event could take out the entire grid, sending hundreds of millions of people back to a pre-electric way of life". NASA's Director of Planetary Sciences made an even more horrifying prediction when, in 2011 he said, "Large areas of the US, Europe and Asia could be without electricity for months or years, as power companies struggle to purchase and replace damaged hardware".

A recent National Academy of Sciences report estimates that such a solar storm could wreak the economic disruption of twenty Katrina-class hurricanes, costing one to two trillion dollars in the first year alone, and taking a decade to recover. And that's just in the US.

A solar storm could send hundreds of millions of people back to a pre-electric way of life for months, if not years.

Space weather is where terrestrial weather was when TVs were only able to show black and white images. Firstly, as Karel Schrijver of Lockheed Martin's Solar and Astrophysics Laboratory at Palo Alto, California, laments, "we cannot predict what the sun will do more than a few days ahead of time". Secondly, he goes on, "we cannot predict until then whether or not the Earth will be in the path of what happens". And thirdly, because the impact of a storm depends in part on how its magnetic field aligns with that of the Earth, the storm's intensity cannot be known with any certainty until it reaches the ACE satellite[88] some twenty minutes before it slams into the Earth's atmosphere.

The likelihood of Earth being hit by the efflux of a major solar storm has not changed – current evidence suggests that such an event probably occurs once in several centuries – but the damage one might inflict grows in proportion to our increasing dependence on space-based communications and navigation technologies. Meanwhile, the sun is shooting off a few small-scale CME's every day, of which approximately 20 per year are directed towards Earth. The last major event, which occurred in July 2012, was luckily pointed the wrong way. But, if it were not, utility companies would have only a few minutes to decide whether or not to deliberately cause continent-wide blackouts which might take days to restore, even if their instructions were enacted in time.

---

[88] The Advanced Composition Explorer spacecraft launched in 1997 monitors solar wind, while SOHO, the Solar and Heliospheric Observatory, carries a dozen detectors that record everything from high speed solar wind proton flows to low speed solar oscillations.

Since it formed over 4.5 billion years ago, Earth has been hit many times by asteroids whose orbits bring them into the inner solar system. Within the vast emptiness of space, billions of rocks, from star dust to those measuring many miles across, zip around the inner solar system, and collisions with the Earth's atmosphere are frequent. Most frazzle almost immediately. Larger ones, ranging from the size of peas to baseballs, are those we see streaking across the night sky as "shooting stars", but most of those never reach the ground. Objects the size of basketballs collide with our atmosphere every day or so, and car-sized ones hit every month or two. About 80 tons of such material falls to Earth from outer space every day.

About 80 tons of cosmic material falls to Earth from outer space every day.

As the meteoric events of 15th February 2013 in Chelyabinsk, Russia prove, these objects – collectively known as Near Earth Objects (NEOs) – still pose a danger to Earth today. We didn't see it coming, and, depending on the size of the impacting object, it is feasible that such a collision would be what NASA calls a "life extinguishing event". There is no doubt that sometime in the future, Earth will suffer another cosmic impact of this sort, but larger; the only question is when?

Asteroids are orbiting rocks of varying metallic composition that become meteors when they enter the Earth's atmosphere. Meteorites are the metallic remains which make it to the planet's surface. The bright streak seen over Chelyabinsk was the stony material burning off. As the pressure of entering the Earth's atmosphere built, it exploded at an altitude of 12-15 miles above the surface releasing an energy equivalent at least twenty times the size of the atomic bomb dropped on Hiroshima in World War 2.

NASA has catalogued 1,100 NEOs of 700 metres in width or wider, which it thinks is more than 95% of all those out there but less than 5% of the smaller ones. That the asteroid which was to become the Chelyabinsk meteor could approach Earth undetected and injure 1,316 people, almost all from flying glass, proves the point. Only a few years ago, a telescope in Spain discovered NEO 2012 DA14, an asteroid measuring 45 metres in width which passed Earth closer than many of our communications satellites. Purely coincidentally, this happened on the very same day as the Chelyabinsk meteor. Had 2012 DA14 collided with Earth, it would have released the energy equivalent of 2.5 million tons of TNT, or nearly ten times the energy of the Chelyabinsk meteor.

The shock wave from the Chelyabinsk meteor was violent enough to blow out windows over a wide area. Interestingly, the glass front to a Skoda car showroom remained intact while a beer bottle just a block away shattered in the hand of the man holding it. This is explained by the low frequencies of such sonic booms, which, like tsunami 'energy waves' and earthquake compression waves, are modulated and propagated by the surroundings with which they come into contact, to amplify in some places while suppressing in others just metres away. This is exactly the same physics used in noise-cancelling headsets.

Although those with the potential to end civilization have been mostly catalogued, a real concern remains that alterations in gravitational fields, the effect of solar flares, or even tiny impacts from meteorites can deflect any one of these into Earth's path at any moment[89], and that there is no way to predict what happens should any of these things happen.

Given these orbital uncertainties, another issue is how probable an impact must be before we decide to take action. The world economies cannot afford to protect against all low-probability hazards, and a 1-in-1,000 chance of a collision, for example, will probably be ignored. According to some scientists, they already are.

There is a lump of rock 575 metres wide sitting somewhere out there in space between Mars and Jupiter called RQ36. Discovered only in 1999, it is scheduled to pass close to us in 2186, with NASA once saying that it had a one in 1,800 chance of actually hitting us "causing", as they put it, "devastation from which it is unlikely our species could recover". Since this level of chance is ten times more likely than dying in a plane crash – for those that fly, the chance of dying in a plane crash is approximately 1 in 438,000 – an $800 million space probe, will blast off in 2016 as part of real-life effort to "take samples" which it is hoped will have the added benefit of deflecting it. That sort of money would not be spent if the threat were not real.

Whatever the chance of Earth being struck by a 300 metre or larger NEO in the next century, such an impact would deliver a withering 1,000-megaton explosion and cause perhaps 100,000 deaths. If the

---

[89] Asteroids are rocks and debris which are the leftovers of the construction of our solar system nearly 5 billion years ago. Most are in a belt which orbits the sun between Mars and Jupiter. However, asteroids occasionally wander from the main belt beyond Mars because of chaotic instabilities caused by the oscillating gravitational influence of Jupiter. Impact by other smaller asteroids, meteorites, or even large particles of space dust can also knock these large rocks out of their safe orbit.

impact occurred in or near a densely populated region, the Eastern seaboard of the United States, for instance, or Western Europe or coastal Asia, the fatalities could easily rise into the tens of millions.

Astronomers have long known that at least five pairs of super-massive neutron stars capable of colliding and spawning concentrated, laser-like beams of radiation called *Gamma Ray Bursts* (GRBs) exist in our galaxy. The last such burst took place over 200 million years ago and apparently unleashed more energy than our Sun will emit during its entire lifetime.

GRBs can last as long as a month, and, should one hit Earth, the planet's ozone layer would be largely destroyed thereby opening the way for more types of killing radiation over a much longer period. Known as *Wolf-Rayet* stars, several are close enough to put our planet in harm's way. Most attention has focused on a star around 8,000 light years away, known as WR104 which is massive enough and close enough to affect Earth.

But there's a caveat: The rotation axis must be pointed directly at us as the emissions from a Gamma Ray Burst are strongly beamed. We must fall in that beam-line in order to receive the full effect. The good news is that the axis of WR104 is around 30-40° off, which should protect us from the worst effects. And that's presuming it even turns into a GRB, which is far from certain.

Operations

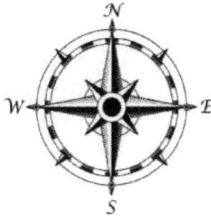

74

Urban Search & Rescue teams from around the world are not always needed in the event of mass urban destruction.

Leaving aside the moral arguments, it is suggested that mobilisation of Urban Search & Rescue (USAR) teams from anywhere other than a nearby country is neither efficient nor particularly effective and ties up financial, logistical, and management resources that could be better used doing something else.

Urban search and rescue efforts dominate the airwaves where there has been massive urban destruction and mass casualties. There is something compelling about the heady concoction of arc lights, cranes, smoke, dust, sniffer-dogs, and hi-tech infra-red gadgetry, not to mention the heroism of would-be rescuers wearing special helmets and bright orange uniforms covered in badges. And then the pure joy of pulling someone alive from the rubble makes for compulsive viewing. The Haitian earthquake was no different: Sixty-two international USAR teams, totaling more than 1,800 people and 82 dogs travelled to Haiti with their equipment in the days following the disaster, the first arriving on site a day-and-a-half after the event. Over the 10 days that followed, these teams were able to rescue 132 people from the rubble. In Nepal five years later, 72 USAR teams arrived from around the world and ended up making a total of 16 'live rescues'. The total cost was later estimated by the Humanitarian Coordinator to be "North of \$32 million" i.e \$2 million per life saved.

Each live rescue in the 2015 Nepal earthquake cost over \$2 million.

People trapped within the voids and spaces of a collapsed building can survive for many days in the post-collapse period. This "rescue window" provides an opportunity for USAR teams with proper capability and resources to rescue the victims trapped under such conditions.

Rapid rescue of trapped victims and early medical treatment of those with life-threatening injuries such as deep laceration, crush injury, or spinal-cord injury, makes a big difference to their chances of survival. Basically, nearly all those trapped will die if they are not rescued within six days and given appropriate medical treatment. The proportion of trapped people found alive declines exponentially as the duration of entrapment prolongs. Typically, more than 90% of victims who were trapped but survived either extricated themselves or were rescued within the first 24 hours, mostly by untrained volunteers.

This suggests that USAR teams arriving with a lifting equipment, dogs, infra-red heat sensors, ultra-sonic listening devices, and specialised paramedic training more than a couple of days after the event are unlikely to make much difference to the overall death toll. With the exception of trained personnel arriving from a neighbouring country, foreign assistance is more than likely to arrive after the affected community has already undertaken 99% of the rescue work. This is not to say, however, that people who were dead when extricated could not have been saved by a sophisticated team with sophisticated resources.

Apart from the equipment they bring with them, experienced USAR teams bring two things: specific knowledge of, and practice in, the extrication process; and an understanding of the characteristics of various types of construction. Buildings of the same type of construction collapse in much the same way, and common factors are present wherever the in the world the collapse takes place. Furthermore, all collapsed buildings contain voids where trapped people can be found, and USAR teams have experience in working out where these spaces are, and know how to access them quickly and safely ... without, for example, triggering fires in the debris while using acetylene cutting torches, as happened in the 2013 Dhaka factory collapse with tragic consequences.

Over 90% of those trapped extricate themselves or are rescued by untrained neighbours before USAR teams arrive.

An NGO, International Rescue Corps, estimates the cost for all aspects of deployment, including equipment, travel, food, accommodation, and administration, to be in the region of $232,000 per team[90]. In the case of Haiti, this equated to $145,000 per person rescued, although estimates from other countries put the figure as high as $214,000 (not including the figure given earlier from Nepal).

---

[90] These estimates do not include salaries – nearly all USAR team members are volunteers or salaried members of their countries' respective fire/civil defence services – or the costs of training and insurance. When teams have to travel much further afield, these costs can be considerably more.

Search and rescue attempts are usually wound up at the 10 to 12 day mark, but can be as early as the third day in small-scale events where it is easier to account for everybody. In sub-zero temperatures, it is highly unlikely that anyone, even if well clothed when trapped, will survive much beyond the third night.

Survival under the rubble produced by an earthquake depends on freedom from injuries, adequate space, access to fresh air, and availability of water. But, most of all, it relies on the mental resilience of the person trapped. Food is less crucial. The rescue of Evans Munsie 27 days after the Haiti earthquake is not the longest known example of survival in such extreme circumstances. On 10th December 2005, a 70-year-old lady called Naqsa Bibi was found in the kitchen of her collapsed house more than two months after the earthquake that hit Pakistan-controlled Kashmir. She had spent 63 days in a crouched position as the space was too small for her to stretch her arms and legs. Water trickling in from a stream and rotting food kept her alive. She emerged blinking and grateful, but apparently none the worse for her ordeal. After enquiring about her grandchildren – all of whom had survived – all she wanted to do was to get back to farming.

75 *Not all external aid is beneficial.*

The humanitarian impulse to give succour to those who suffer is a wonderful thing, and sets us as a species apart. But, if we're not careful, our humanitarian impulse can be distorted by the vagaries of human nature and the complexities of the modern world. Because of this, providing relief in time of natural disaster is not always the act of pure charity it purports to be, and can even sometimes have unintended and detrimental consequences. What this means in practice is that not all aid is good aid.

This is because donating involves more than giving away our time and expertise, getting rid of all those old things we no longer need, and chucking our loose change into the nearest collecting box. Bill Gates, the world's biggest philanthropist, said as much when pointing out that, "giving is simple; the key is to give effectively".

The earthquake that rocked Haiti in 2010 left a wide swath of destruction which left much of the government's infrastructure in ruins, almost all paper records destroyed, and many of their best bureaucrats dead or seriously injured. Into this void rushed many people willing to help on so many fronts: to rescue those trapped under buildings, bring supplies of food and water, save the lives of those who were injured, evacuate some for surgery or a better life, bury others, and counsel the grieving. All came eager to help. But, while much help was provided, the many myths that surround natural disasters reminded us once more that it is the behaviours and attitudes around these myths that make delivery of assistance more difficult and complicated than it need be. Good intentions are not enough.

At the individual level, 'resource mobilisation' translates into four forms of donation: Our knowledge; our time; our money; or our 'stuff', our surplus belongings. The first two involve volunteering, while the last refers to what the aid world refers to as "goods-in-kind". To be acceptable, they should each be appropriate to the specifics of the programme, and directly address needs in the field according to what is needed as opposed to what is desired or what is available. Too often, they are not.

✥

Disasters stimulate an atavistic, altruistic urge in all of us. Even if we are already paying a small amount every month to our favourite charity, images of death and destruction goad us into making one-off donations. Some go further by volunteering to go to the disaster zone, convinced that they can do their bit to alleviate the pain and suffering more directly. This is noble but frequently misdirected.

First, people unused to living 'rough' in a freezing or boiling bug-infested tent, not knowing where to find their next meal or how to purify their drinking water, find that getting through the day in one piece is a struggle. They can also be surprised to find that 18 hour days, seven days a week are considered 'normal' working hours. Even those with seemingly relevant qualifications are often puzzled to find themselves applying solutions which those who have been there before deem inappropriate. This is usually because they have little experience of working in developing countries, far less in disaster zones, and causes as much angst amongst the volunteers as it does within the professional humanitarian community who inevitably end up having to deal with the rapid turnover and frustration of staff that results. It also overloads already stretched resources.

✥

Instead of volunteering, we can donate our surplus 'stuff'. This is what governments do with agricultural surpluses – where the aid provided is more to do with what we have to give than it is to do with what those affected by disaster actually need – and it's what we can do as individuals. There are five considerations to bear in mind when deciding how your hard-earned donation is going to generate maximum 'bangs for bucks' and whether donating 'in-kind' is the kindest thing to do:

Appropriate Technology: In 1995, the European Union established a brand new radio station in Burundi called *Radio Umwizero* (Radio Hope). It was founded on the simple notion that most Burundians listened to the radio and lacked independent information on what was going on around them. Rwanda to the North, had just experienced the worst genocide in history, and Burundi was sadly not immune from the ethnic violence then spreading across its border. The first task was to get people listening. This was duly accomplished, first by distributing radio sets across the country, then by playing non-stop Bob Marley soundtracks with the words dubbed into *Kinyarwanda*, the local language – the first, and probably only, time the Bob Marley Trust has allowed such a change – and then by producing a daily soap opera that, with the script being written daily, aired up-to-the-minute local and national issues, many of which were related to health and hygiene. It was an instant hit, and became a model later to be replicated in Albania and elsewhere.

Soon, however, surveys discovered that listenership was tailing off badly. The team was perplexed. They knew the programmes were highly popular, so what was the problem? After digging a bit further, it quickly became clear that, with more people listening to more broadcasts, battery power was drying up. And batteries were in limited supply at the time, and expensive. It is thought that the development of wind-up radios was, in part, accelerated because of this experience.

The moral of this tale is that, however well-intentioned they are, complex and expensive projects like this can founder when they come up against the simplest of unforeseen challenges. It is the same with other types of high-tech machinery, too, especially medical equipment, which is often inappropriate because it cannot cope with the heat, dust, poor maintenance and erratic voltages found in developing countries. All across Sub-Saharan Africa, from Sierra Leone to South Sudan, you will find expensive high-tech equipment lying un-used in newly rehabilitated public health laboratories. Partly, this is because the technicians have not been trained in its use, but more frequently it's because the brand is unknown to the central procurement services of the Ministry, which means they have no spare parts or engineers trained in the specific maintenance schedules required.

Operational Support: Machines are complicated. Without rigorous maintenance they break down. As with the high-tech medical instruments just mentioned, this fact of life needs to be considered when donating machinery. This requires training as well as spare parts. Any donated hardware should have at least two years' worth of spare parts and tools supplied, as well as financial provision for training and running costs. In developing countries, neither the budgets nor the expertise can be assumed.

When visiting a cholera treatment clinic in Sierra Leone in 2012, I came across a brand new generator – a machine the size of a shipping container – sitting outside in the rain. Despite the lack of electricity in the hospital, it was silent. I went back inside to find out what the story was. It turned out that this machine had been donated by one of the international mining companies working nearby, but had arrived without connecting cables, tools, or even an operating manual. So I went to see the boss of the mining company concerned. He assured me that these parts would be arriving soon, and that he and his men would personally see to it that it was got up and running. At which point, I asked him whether his team would train the hospital maintenance crew, hand over the tools, and provide spare parts. He looked confused. And then, knowing that the hospital's budget could not possibly cover the costs of running a machine that would consume six gallons of diesel fuel every hour, I asked him if he was supplying fuel as well?

This story had a happy ending of sorts. An international NGO based in the town agreed to partner with the mining company and the hospital, which eventually got the power it needed. But, as is all too familiar to anyone who has worked in such resource-poor setting, only partially ... the hospital technician received his tools – which made him a powerful man in the community – but, when he proudly showed me the enormous operating manual a few months later, it was in French. And not many people can speak, let alone read, French in Sierra Leone. And the hospital had run out of fuel.

Quantity: Consumable supplies hardly ever come in the quantities needed; either too much or too little is the norm. In the case of former, the challenges of dealing with the surplus can more than negate the advantages of receiving the donation in the first place. One of the six UNICEF warehouses in Port-au-Prince, Haiti was completely full six months into the 2010 earthquake response with over two million ring-pull tins of breast-milk substitute which was not only not asked for – and contrary to international guidelines for this product – but was enough for Haiti's mothers for the next six years, by which time most of it would have long reached its expiry date.

Timing: For most programmes, timing is crucial. An item can be really needed at some stage, arrive in just the right quantity and be available at the right spot, but if it arrives too late it will be as useful as an ashtray on a motorbike. If it arrives too early, it will needlessly clog up storage space and waste the time of the limited number of fork-lift trucks available. It is hardly ever possible to time the receipt of goods-in-kind correctly.

Cost: Surely, goods-in-kind are, as the name implies, free? Well, no, actually they aren't. There are serious costs connected to receiving, handling, shipping, storing and distributing in-kind donations which often exceed the costs of buying the same item new elsewhere. This seems to come as something of a surprise to many donors, private individuals and corporations alike.

Think of the costs to your preferred charity of setting up the collection points, for bundling and preparation, for shipping, for cleaning and repair, and for maintenance in the field. Similar costs are, of course, connected to goods bought with donated money. But almost always these costs are much lower than for processing goods-in-kind. How can this be? Well, consider the following and the cost implications for each:

- Having to combine items from various locations instead of shipping it directly from one location (the supplier's);
- Economies of scale, where bulk procurement lowers the unit cost per item;
- Use of standardised items designed for cheap and simple transport, e.g. because they are lighter, can be nested or because a multiple fits exactly in a standard shipping container;
- Being able to easily consolidate shipments, leading to lower shipping costs;
- Not having to deal with reverse logistics and/or destruction of expired goods.

According to the UK retailer, Marks & Spencer, British shoppers throw away 10,000 items of old clothing every five minutes. The market for second-hand clothing is worth around $1 billion annually in the UK alone. In the US and other European countries, it is probably more. After large-scale natural disaster, this volume can easily double.

Most donors at this stage assume that their old clothes will be sent immediately to the disaster zone. In the case of smaller charities, they might be, but in the vast majority of cases, there aren't. Instead, the charities to whom you donate your clothes will either sell them in one of their High Street charity shops or, more likely, sell them on to commercial recyclers who, in turn, sort them by gender, age and season, grade them by type, condition, style, and material, and then sell them on to wholesalers in Eastern Europe, Asia, Africa, and Central America. At each step of the journey, profit is made. Very few of the NGOs to whom you made your original donation will still be involved after the first step.

And there can be downsides to donating old clothes in other ways. Importation of bulk second-hand clothing can undermine the local textile industry, for example. Thirty-one countries, including India, the Philippines, Ethiopia, and Nigeria, have banned imports of second-hand clothing in the hope of providing local garment manufacturers with better opportunities. The value chain often becomes opaque, too, with customs officials and middle-men taking a hidden percentage in the form of under-the-table payments, and import taxes being evaded. And, with more than one third of Sub-Saharan Africa dressed in Western second-hand clothes, indigenous culture is undermined.

Frequently, donated clothing is not sorted. This effectively renders them unusable as sorting out container loads of clothes and shoes that are dirty, un-sorted by age, climate, or gender is not only expensive in terms of the money spent in getting the stuff into the disaster zone in the first place, but places an intolerable burden amongst those at the receiving end who have to do it all for you. They often arrive dirty, too, and therefore containing spores and mites to which the beneficiary population has never before been exposed. This can accelerate the proliferation of communicable diseases, especially skin diseases such as scabies. And, unless baled and compressed, these blankets take up four times more volume on precious relief flights than those procured in bulk by the aid agencies.

It might sound ungracious, but mis-placed charity is often not appreciated by those being inadvertently patronised either. Beneficiaries may be poor, but not too poor to care about quality. During the earthquake response in Pakistan in 2005, people were often overheard saying something along the lines of, "we appreciate the thought, but somebody's un-wanted clothes from the other side of the world are not culturally appropriate here, and anyway, my family needs quilts more than clothes as we need these to insulate our tents". In fact, donated clothing piled up at the road-side to be eaten by stray goats and cows who then died agonizing deaths when their guts became clogged by un-digestible buttons and zippers.

76 *Drug donations too often result in a 'second phase' disaster.*

Large amounts of useless drugs and other consumable medical supplies are frequently sent to disaster zones. After the 1974 earthquake in Guatemala, 100 tonnes of unsorted medicines were airlifted to the country of which 90% were of no value because they were expired, had already been opened, or for which labels were written in foreign languages. In Armenia in 1988, only one third of the 500 tons of medical supplies sent were useable because of problems with identification and sorting; 11% were useless and 8% had expired. Ultimately over 20% had to be destroyed. Because the relief operations were conducted under the watchful eye of the media, medical relief efforts were pejoratively referred to as "the second disaster". Twenty-five years later, things have not improved that much.

Typically, at least one fifth of donated drugs have to be destroyed in situ.

Individually donated drugs are even worse, as not only are they usually time-expired when they arrive, and are therefore useless, but they have strange brand names so only a pharmacist with a copy of the 'pharmacopoeia' knows what they are good for. Worse, expired drugs contain toxins which have to be destroyed in specially constructed incinerators which, if the country had them at all, need to be specially rebuilt or constructed anew. Then there is the money spent on getting the drugs there in the first place, money which could have been better spent on something else.

Sadly, this also applies to bulk donations by manufacturers who all too often donate large quantities of their brands that are approaching their expiry dates. It's a win-win-win-win-win situation for them as they free up warehouse space needed for newer batches, transfer the cost (and safety considerations) of destruction to someone else, get a tax break, and are perceived to be 'doing good' by their employees and customers into the bargain.

Then there is the small matter of logistics. When working in Iraq after the war in 2003, I was tasked by the head office in Geneva to go to the airport in Amman, Jordan to officially receive a donation of intravenous fluids from the well-meaning government of a country in South-East Asia. Amidst much hand-shaking with ambassadors and bulb flashing from the world's press, we duly watched three jumbo jets off-load 180 tons of a product which comprised 98% water and saw it safely onto a fleet of lorries who were to spend the next five days transferring this stock to Baghdad; a journey not without risk to the brave drivers.

Two months later, I turned the key on a bulldozer and destroyed the whole lot by running over every single pallet. Why? Because, as with the rest of the city at the time, the refrigeration units at the warehouses where bulk medical supplies were stored lacked electricity, and these supplies – which when used are injected directly into the veins of patients – cannot be stored at temperatures exceeding 25°C. They had been exposed for weeks in direct sunlight at temperatures of 40°C or more. Some of the bags had turned green which meant the entire stock had to be destroyed.

There was no functioning public health laboratory where samples could be taken for testing, and with no surgeon willing to take the risk of injecting a patient with potentially contaminated supplies, there was no other option. At the time, it was estimated that the cost of this little exercise was in excess of $6 million. A mobile production unit complete with bottling plant and quality control laboratory which could have supplied the whole of Northern Iraq would have cost 10% of this, would have been up and running within days, and would have remained in operation through the months and years of transition as more sustainable structures were built.

So, drugs, consumables, and medical equipment that pour into disaster zones are often damaged, out of date, unusable, and constitute what a French NGO, Pharmaciens Sans Frontières, have referred to as "a second tsunami: a huge wave of drug donations that authorities are totally unable to handle".

The World Health Organisation has strict guidelines for donated drugs. They must comply with the WHO official list of approved medicine, be in use in the receiving country, be labeled in the appropriate language, and have an expiry date of at least one year from the date of importation. Sadly, these rules are often ignored, even by large corporate and government donors.

Here's just one example: 4,000 tons of drugs were received in Aceh Province, Indonesia after the 2004 tsunami for a population of 2 million people. According to a survey carried out by the same French NGO:

- 60% of the drugs were not on the national list of essential drugs
- 70% of the drugs were labelled in a foreign language (e.g Chinese, Hindi, Japanese)
- 25% of the drugs had an inadequate expiry date
- Some drugs arrived in excessive quantities. As an example, the quantity of Oral Rehydration Salt delivered was sufficient for 5-8 years' supply. At the projected rate of use this was three times their shelf-life
- 17% of the drugs (approx. 600 tons) had to be destroyed at an estimated cost of $3 million.

The survey concluded conclusively that it's wrong to claim that any drug is useful in an emergency situation. Instead, a crisis calls for a variety of different specific drugs relevant to the situation. This is important in order to avoid the risk of flooding the affected countries with tons of drugs that not only constitute a public health hazard because their distribution and control are poorly managed, but also constitute a destabilising factor in the local economy because of the costly destruction processes involved.

Politics and trade also play their part. Intellectual property rights, for example, are frequently flouted by manufacturers in developing countries who make illegal copies of drugs that are under patent protection. Some of the drugs manufactured in this way contain no active ingredient at all, or half the prescribed dose.

During humanitarian operations in Burundi in 1996, testing by a private laboratory discovered that up to one quarter of all drugs imported as part of humanitarian aid shipments contained no active ingredient. You get hints that these sorts of practices are widespread from Ralph Fiennes in the film *The Constant Gardener*.

These findings were confirmed in 2012 when it was found that fake and poorly made antibiotics are being widely used to treat TB. These sub-standard drugs are almost certainly making the disease more resistant, posing a grave health threat to communities around the world[lxiii] and make it more likely that the "white plague" will return. The study found that, of the thousands of samples collected at random from local pharmacies in 17 countries across Africa, Asia, South America, and Europe, nearly 10% failed to meet basic quality standards. The figure was over 20% in Africa. It appeared from the packaging that all these drugs had originated from legitimate manufacturers, yet those pills[91] that failed the test typically had too little, if any, of the active ingredient, the molecule that actually helps destroy the TB bacteria.

77   Field Hospitals do not always need to be deployed following large-scale natural disasters.

At 5.30 in the morning on 26th December 2003, an earthquake measuring 6.5 on the Richter scale struck the ancient city of Bam in Iran. Approximately 80% of all hospital capacity was lost. Within the first week, an estimated 1,800 aid workers arrived from 44 countries. A Ukrainian field hospital[92] was the first to arrive, and began to establish itself by the end of the third day. In total, 11 such temporary hospitals, of which 5 were military, were deployed, providing a total of 550

---

[91] Up to three-quarters of a pill is made of inert waste material, the most common being discarded Brewer's yeast. Shellac (the same varnish used on oil paintings) is used to mask unpleasant tastes.

[92] A field hospital is a portable, self-contained and self-sufficient tented or containerised facility comprising ten or more beds; at least one operating theatre (plus associated anaesthesia and resuscitation facilities); and basic laboratory and diagnostic facilities, including radiology (X-Ray). A field hospital is a highly complicated and complex affair that requires between 80 and 100 full-time staff, costs over $1 million to buy, and between $2,000 and $2,500 per bed per day to run. Including the beds and equipment, each field hospital weighs roughly 45 tons and takes three planes and ten trucks to transport.

hospital beds by the beginning of the second week. Most of these were erected next to one another.

The maximum occupancy rate at the 200-bed Red Crescent hospital during the two months of its deployment was 25%. During this time, 818 patients were admitted and 34 caesarean sections were performed. Surgical activities at the US mobile army surgical hospital (MASH) that arrived one week after the earthquake totalled 2 caesarean sections, one appendectomy, and four minor operations ... this with a staff of eighty. One report estimated the cost for all field hospitals deployed to Bam to be over $10 million.

Natural disasters are a significant cause of physical disability due to the 'double whammy' of increased injury and decreased access to disrupted health care services. Major disasters, especially in urban settings, result in mass casualties that quickly overwhelm those hospitals that remain even partially functional. The wounded require immediate emergency medical trauma care, and then continuing aftercare to cope with their post-surgical complications. The resources needed to deal with disaster-inflicted injuries continues for some time, too. Tsunami victims in Aceh in 2004 and earthquake victims in Haiti in 2010 required repeated operations and wound dressings, as well as anaesthesia and long hospitalisation. But the facilities and the staff to look after them no longer exist, if they ever did. The dispatch of transportable field hospitals from outside the affected area is a traditional first-line response in such circumstances.

It is often better to send mobile health teams than field hospitals to a disaster zone.

Yet field hospitals have been criticised for their disproportionately high cost, for not offering appropriate services, and for arriving too late to make a difference[lxiv]. With bed occupancy rates typically between 25% and 50%, there also appears to be over-supply. A study on the deployment of 43 Field Hospitals to earthquake disasters in Iran in 2003, Indonesia in 2004, and Pakistan in 2005 found that not one was operational quickly enough to provide life-saving emergency trauma care, and that only 15% followed the essential requirement for provision of follow-up trauma and medical care[lxv].

The main role for field hospitals is to substitute for nearby trauma care facilities that have been severely damaged. But these expensive assets inevitably end up providing primary and secondary care support to the collapsed healthcare system, a role normally undertaken by health centres, not hospitals. A distinction has to be made, therefore, between provision of mobile, light and flexible 'ortho-plastic' teams offering outpatient services in rural villages, and the establishment of static field hospitals in larger towns.

Contrary to popular belief, field hospitals are usually viewed by local health authorities as being "not very effective", either. In non-urban disasters, simple mobile primary health care teams are considered more efficient, and are better appreciated than large trauma care facilities. In Haiti in 2010, small mobile teams from places as far apart as Cuba and Israel saved far more lives than the best equipped hospital ships arriving much later.

Since substitution of national facilities tends to retard recovery efforts, a balance also needs to be found between evacuating the wounded from the affected area and bringing this level of external support, which, as has already been pointed out, takes at least a few days to be established. In contexts where affected areas are isolated or cut off, it may be better to send helicopters than field hospitals.

78 *Food aid should not always be the default response.*

Food aid is usually a key component of any disaster response. But critics say that it often arrives late, is the wrong commodity, in the wrong volume, and of the wrong quality, and is usually out of proportion to other elements of the response. They also say that food aid is not the life-saving 'magic bullet' that logic suggests it might be, and argue that it distorts availability and price in local markets, builds dependency, and slows recovery. It also kills people every time it is indiscriminately airdropped from the back of a cargo plane without a parachute, or chucked out of a hovering helicopter.

Relief supplies kill people on the ground every time it is indiscriminately air-dropped.

It might come as a surprise to those of a more idealistic bent, but there are powerful vested interests that skew humanitarian aid provision towards favoured countries, groups, and types of relief. Food aid has always been a prime example of the latter, as it is lobbied for by farming groups, agri-business, and the shipping industry, among others. These special interests continue to distort the food security situation in many countries. The US, for example, is the world's biggest donor of food aid, providing roughly half the world's supply[93]. But, according to NGOs like Oxfam[lxvi], its programmes – funded with taxpayer's money through humanitarian contribution and (hidden) farm subsidy at the same time – "deliver more to the pockets of agri-business and shipping companies than to the mouths of hungry people".

For years, the aid world has criticised what it perceives to have been the 'dumping' of food aid – mostly agricultural surpluses of wheat, yellow maize, and rapeseed oil from North America and Europe[94] resulting from subsidised farming which enriches northern farmers while simultaneously impoverishing farmers in the developing world – disparagingly referring to these food aid programmes as little more than "truck and chuck" logistics exercises.

In the meantime, it is worth considering that nearly one third – 6 million tonnes – of all food purchased in British supermarkets ends up being thrown away. A British NGO, appropriately named the 'Waste & Resources Action Programme', or WRAP, reckons that the figure is nearer 50% when the trimmings from commercial food processors and the raw material which never leaves the farm are added to the equation. In 2010, WFP distributed 5.7 million metric tons of food aid to 87.8 million people in 78 countries. This means that British households throw away more food in a year than the entire amount of food aid disbursed globally.

79 *Aid and Charity are not the same thing.*

Charities exist to make the world a better place. But the word *'charity'* is a mean, pinched Victorian word that conjures up images of a Dickensian poor-house of the type you see in the film *Oliver*; a word dripping with notions of the great and the good giving alms to the passive and down-trodden destitute who have no say in their own destiny.

---

[93] Traditionally, the US has been the biggest in-kind donor of food aid to the UN's World Food Programme (WFP), but this is changing as there is less and less surplus to donate as more and more US farmland is given over to growing cash-crops for alternative fuel production. This has forced the agency to broaden its business model.

[94] In 2010, 90% of global food aid was funded by 47 donor governments. The top five donors (USA, Japan, Canada, UK, and the EC) accounted for nearly three quarters (74%) of all food aid delivered. Of the food aid channelled directly through NGOs, 88% was provided by the US.

Many in the aid business feel that the word 'charity' no longer does justice the depth and breadth of what they do, even when responding to disasters. Not-for-profit and non-governmental organisations are fully-fledged businesses, they argue, struggling to differentiate themselves and survive in a highly competitive, mature and saturated aid sector which the OECD says is turning over $124 billion per year. While they are to be applauded in meeting humanitarian needs in conditions and places that most of us would fear to tread, they are in almost all respects similar to commercial enterprises.

Thirty-four members of Interaction, the NGO platform in the United States, manage budgets of over $100 million a year. The largest global international NGO, World Vision International, has 46,000 staff and a $2.57 billion global annual budget. CARE International, Save the Children, and at least eight others are not far behind; all of them being larger than UNICEF in terms of both annual turnover and staff[lxvii].

NGO private funding outstrips humanitarian financing from some of the world's largest government donors. According to Development Initiatives, an independent organisation, Médecins sans Frontières / Doctors without Borders, for example, channelled $495 million to disaster response in 2006, outspending the humanitarian budgets of 20 individual governments, including France, the Netherlands, Germany and Norway. In 2008, the aid budget of World Vision exceeded that of Italy. Plan International spent more than Greece, and Save the Children, more than Finland.

In the year 2011 to 2012, the 162,831 registered charities in the UK raised over $90 billion. According to a study by the fundraising website Charity Choice, roughly 85% of this goes to the 15 large and established NGOs such as Oxfam and Save the Children, who make up less than 5% of the sector, but who reap disproportionate benefits because of the collective clout of their dedicated marketing budgets. Worldwide, 11% of international NGOs generate 94% of the total revenue in the sector.

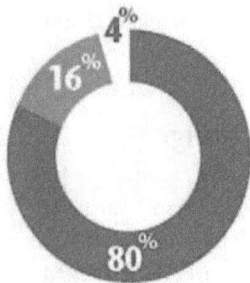

80% Programs
16% Fundraising
4% Administration

Not having shareholders, however, the only difference is one of 'non-distribution' which legally limits how much money those running the agencies can distribute amongst themselves. This puts NGOs at a comparative price advantage over their commercial, private-sector competitors.

Like all commercial enterprises, aid organisations have overheads. These are the regular day-to-day costs of maintaining the business such as heat, light, and administration, and do not include costs directly associated with implementing a specified relief programme in the field. When fundraising, policy research, and internal governance is added, between 75-80% remains available for what the NGO community calls 'programme' costs[95] (see the doughnut chart above published by MSF-Canada in March 2015), some of which are 'direct', such as procurement and distribution of relief commodities and promotion of the 'know how' associated with them; and some of which are 'indirect', such as in-country office rental and running costs, satellite and radio communications, salaries, benefits, vehicle hire, administration, information management, finance, human resources, training, legal costs, travel, food, accommodation, social security, insurance, assessment, monitoring, evaluating performance, and security.

Salaries and consultancy fees[96] constitute the largest of these operational costs, and can consume up to half the programme budget on their own[97]. Vehicle fleet management comes next, followed by insurance and security components which, given the operating environment in which aid agencies work nowadays, can consume one fifth of programme budgets.

One-third of charitable donations or less reach the intended beneficiary.

Financial disbursement can be direct from donor to beneficiary, but can also involve up to seven intermediate levels, each of which subtracts a percentage, typically between 2-7%, to cover overheads and administrative expenses. The diagram below shows the possible routes the money can take: first to an inter-governmental organisation such as the UN, thence to an international NGO, to a national NGO, to a community-based organisation, and then to a commercial sub-contractor or two, before being finally committed to goods or services.

---

[95] In general, institutional donors consider that at least 70% of the total budget for any given relief programme must be allocated to 'direct' programme costs (Source: DFID Discussion Note, 2012)

[96] An informal study conducted by the Shelter Cluster during the Yogyakarta earthquake of 2006 found that, six weeks into this major response, over half of those managing humanitarian operations on the ground, whether for donors, NGOs, or the UN, were not full-time staff of the aid agencies, but freelancers and consultants.

[97] According to a report by the Swedish Government in September 2013, staff salaries and benefits account for roughly half of ICRC's total annual budget.

FUNDING FLOWS

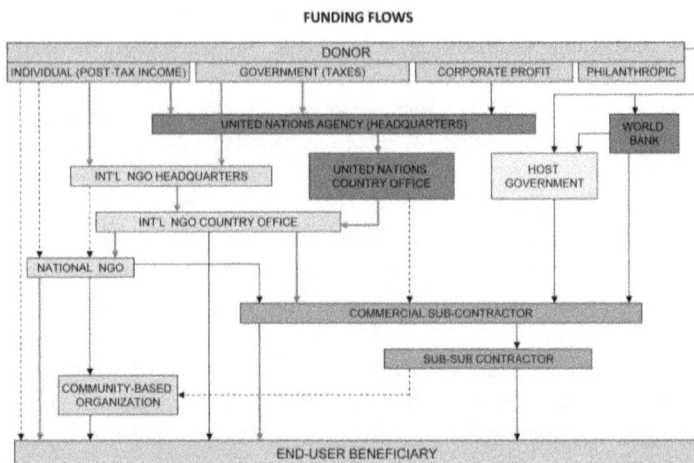

Although this might appear to be a rather expensive way of doing business, NGOs argue that allocating resources to local sub-contractors can make a lot of sense as they are likely to have better relationships with, and better understanding of, the communities they serve. But, in a field with limited regulation and where markets have either been disrupted or failed completely, the optimal allocation of resources can be difficult to achieve.

80 Cargo piling up at the airport does not necessarily indicate poor logistics management.

The world's oldest games rely on the world's most advanced logistics. So said an advertisement for UPS, one of the world's largest logistics companies, in advance of the 2012 London Olympics. The staging of an Olympic event requires the transportation, storage, and handling of over 30 million pieces of equipment, accommodation for officials, athletes, horses, and so on, all of whom are converging from all over the world for a series of competitions lasting 17 days. Such an enormously complex undertaking involves a vast and global supply chain, every link in which has to be choreographed with utmost precision for everything to go smoothly. This involves more than just putting things on planes. It means packing unwieldy items, real-time tracking of individual items, vehicles of every description at both ends, loading equipment, customs clearance formalities, and mountains of paperwork, most of it virtual.

Now imagine planning the same event but not knowing where or when it will take place, what sports are on the schedule, or even how many athletes will compete. The near impossibility of this task gives some insight into what humanitarian logisticians are up against when racing to a disaster half way around the world in a country whose airport and bridges have just been destroyed, whose phones and internet connections have gone down, and whose electricity supply cannot be relied upon.

Logistics can be one of the most expensive parts of a relief effort, especially when air operations are part of the equation, and encompasses a range of activities, including preparedness, planning, procurement, transport, warehousing, handling, tracking, tracing, and customs clearance.

Within days of the Asian tsunami in 2004, the sheer volume of arriving cargo-laden humanitarian flights overwhelmed unloading and ground handling capacity at the airport, leaving aid agencies struggling to sort through, store and distribute the piles of goods that mounted up alongside runways. Incoming relief flights were turned around in mid-air while warehouses bulked out, and agencies struggled to hire the trucks needed to distribute such volumes.

Despite the rapid mobilisation of air-traffic control systems and ground handling assets, this situation was repeated during the earthquake response in Haiti in 2010 and again in Nepal in 2015 despite the pre-positioning of a jointly Government and UN run 'forward logistics hub' at the airport which was opened only weeks before the earthquake struck. A certain amount of backlogging is only to be expected when responding to mega-disasters.

81 *Early warning systems are generally highly automated.*

In reality, almost all disasters are not just predictable but give at least enough warning to take some form of protective action. In Cuba, five successive hurricanes in 2008 left only seven people dead following the installation of extensive early warning systems, and developing countries facing repeated natural hazard events like Bangladesh and

Indonesia, have experienced significantly less death and destruction over the years by developing their own.

Early warning systems require high-tech hardware to collect the data, powerful software to collate and analyse it, and a competent human to interpret it.

Lead times vary enormously depending upon the category of hazard, from seconds for earthquakes, to minutes or hours for tsunami, to days or weeks for volcanic eruptions, floods, and tropical cyclones. Even a few minutes warning gives people time to flee from a tsunami or landslide, and seconds can be enough to allow people to take shelter from a tornado or earthquake. Of course, the longer the lead time and the more accurate the forecasting, the more time there will be to evacuate those at risk from specific areas most likely to bear the brunt, and the more people that will do so when prompted.

The challenge lies in the accuracy of the computer models used for prediction, the speed and trustworthiness of the technology, and our ability of humans to properly assess the threat and take effective action. Early warning systems are, after all, of little use if the people 'at risk' don't trust them enough to heed the warning.

An early warning system is an integrated system for monitoring, collecting, collating, analysing, interpreting, and communicating data which can then be used to make decisions early enough to protect the public. These procedures require high-tech hardware to collect the data, powerful software to collate and analyse it, and a competent human interface to interpret it. Each element has to be reliable and physically robust as false alarms erode trust in those it seeks to save, in turn leading to delays in taking mitigating action such as pre-positioning of equipment and supplies, protecting property, lowering of reservoir levels to accommodate incoming floodwaters, or evacuation.

As if the technology is not complicated enough, the prediction, detection, and monitoring of natural hazards requires an internationally coordinated effort, with many real-time actions that need to be synchronised across countries and time-zones, and therefore across languages and cultures. All aspects of early warning play out at a global scale, but, at the end of the day, are dictated largely by complex social and cultural circumstances which play out at the local level. This is a massive and highly complex undertaking which requires the rapid and systematic sharing of compatible datasets, instant access to high bandwidth communications systems, and use of common predictive models which simulate oceanographic and atmospheric physics at different spatial and time scales and resolutions. And then comes the hard part: it needs qualified human resources who are not just awake but functioning 24/7.

Warnings and alerts must carry the authority of government if they are to be believed. At some point, automated alerts triggered by computer algorithms need to be communicated to whoever is on call at the relevant disaster management agency. He or she will probably have to be woken up by a slightly panicked technician. This person, now only half awake, must then conduct a rapid risk analysis which, depending on the timescales involved, will probably involve calling colleagues, some of whom may be the other side of the world. This risk analysis is likely to be based as much on unknown demographics and uncertain behaviour patterns as it is on known scientific probabilities. The sequence then moves from the technical to the political, as the decision on whether to warn the public, initiate evacuations, and activate emergency response plans will usually be made by a politician, and a senior one at that.

All wait to be certain before alerting the next higher level, a process which can take ten minutes or more. The opening sequence of the film *Independence Day*, portrays this 'credulity gap' very well despite the fact that the computer-generated alert is of imminent invasion by aliens rather than swamping by tsunami.

To decide is to weigh their costs and benefits. False alarms are expensive, with much of the cost borne by the people, as real warnings at a later date are ignored. But false warnings have additional costs, as politicians perceived as being indecisive or wrong rarely get re-elected, and technicians feeding up what later turns out to be incorrect advice find themselves without jobs, all of which tends to delay the moment the 'panic button' is pressed.

Once the 'panic button' is pressed, however, effective emergency response is entirely dependent on how thorough the preparation has been, including pre-positioning of rescue equipment and essential relief supplies, training of first responders, establishment of rapid resource mobilisation procedures, and the setting up of emergency communications systems. Planning, however, is not enough. Periodic rehearsal at all levels, but especially among communities considered most at risk is required if mass casualties are to be avoided[98].

Arguably, the latter is the most important aspect of any early warning system, as, in order to allow effective measures to be taken for hazards with extremely short early warning times, people need to be aware of the potential risks facing them. They also need to react, and react correctly. This is achieved by regular evacuation exercises and information sessions as well as by the constant teaching of risk factors in schools.

In Tacloban, the Philippine city worst hit by typhoon *Yolanda* in November 2013, those living along the seashore were not aware of what a storm-surge was, let alone how deadly one could be. The authorities provided early warning over the radio while police officers and civil defence officials with bull-horns criss-crossed town urging residents to occupy higher ground or take refuge in designated evacuation centres. But it is not enough that people be warned of an approaching hazard and the need to evacuate; they need to be informed of the forecast wind speed and anticipated level of inundation, remembering that the surge of water can arrive hours ahead of the actual storm and that the threat it poses depends on the state of the tide when it makes its anticipated landfall. Over 7,300 people died; most of them because they failed to heed the warnings. Francisco Alvarez, a taxi driver now working part-time for the Red Cross, said afterwards, "I heard the warnings, and parked my taxi on the rising ground behind town just in case, as I couldn't risk losing my livelihood. But then I went home to the family. They told us there would be a 'tidal surge', but nobody took it very seriously. There isn't even a word in *Tagalog* for 'storm-surge'. We were lucky, and escaped the worst. But many of my friends did not," he added.

---

[98] Spontaneous fires, for example, in Peru and Chile after earthquakes are nowadays thankfully rare because householders know to turn off the gas taps in their homes before evacuating along known routes to pre-designated evacuation centres.

Technology

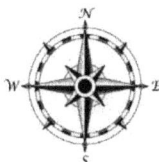

82 Mobile phones can help predict how many people are trapped under the rubble following an earthquake.

Mobile technology increases accuracy and compresses time. Nowhere is this more effectively employed than before, during, and after a natural disaster. Targeted messages can be sent to specific groups of people warning of impending calamity, for example, and then, after the event, data can be collected in real time allowing humanitarian action to be targeted at specific disaster-affected communities more quickly and more accurately than ever before by knowing who has been affected and where.

In Bangladesh, bulk messages are sent warning of the likely scale, location, and timing of floods, storm-surges, tropical cyclones, and tsunami, together with instructions about where to seek shelter. The latter part of the message is tailored to each locality. Syed Ashraf of the country's Disaster Management Bureau says that, "being localised, it is also much more accurate and gives advice relevant to the area which makes people trust it more". Follow-up messages are sent regularly advising on preparedness measures to take.

Mobile phones can now help determine with reasonable accuracy how many people are affected and where they are.

But it's not just about verbal or text communications. When delivering humanitarian aid to disaster-stricken areas, there is often a severe lack of basic information on the locations of the people in need of help, including the number of people who have left the disaster area. This seriously hampers efforts to deliver the right amount of supplies to the right places, even when sufficient resources are available. Using data supplied by mobile phone operators, it is now possible to determine with reasonable accuracy how many people are affected and where they are, even in remote areas with limited coverage. This technology was used successfully in the Pakistan floods of 2011.

Mobile phones can also be used to predict how many people have been killed, injured, or trapped in an earthquake. When referenced against previous movement patterns, lack of movement of individual mobile phones within a particular cell zone after an earthquake indicates how many people may have been in a particular building at the time. Absence of use and the rate of signal decay due to flat batteries provides a further indication of how many may be trapped and possibly still alive.

Mobile phone tracking can also be employed to reduce the chance of disease outbreaks. During the response to Haiti's cholera outbreak in late 2010 and Sierra Leone's in late 2012, it was possible to know which areas had received people from the affected zone, and therefore which areas were at potentially increased risk of a new outbreak[lxviii]. This, in turn, allowed for health messaging over public broadcast radio services to be targeted at particular areas alerting both the incomers and indigenous populations to the heightened risk and what to do to prevent the outbreak from spreading. There is no technical reason that such messaging could not have been targeted to the individuals concerned, although data protection concerns currently preclude this. Mobile technology has also revolutionised the way communicable diseases are monitored after disasters. Already, mobile phones have detected spreading pneumonias in Sri Lanka, and escalating diarrhoeal diseases in Tamil Nadu within a day of the disaster occurring.

The most basic tool, text messaging, is used to communicate with specific disaster-affected populations. Geo-SMS identifies phones in a specific area and sends out messages from relief agencies asking if help is required to those phones only. A reply triggers a menu of options they can choose from, such as: "Do you need: 1) First Aid, 2) Medications, 3) Transport, 4) Food, 5) Water, 6) Shelter (press the corresponding number)". This system is also used for sending early warning alerts. In the case of a tsunami, for example, it is pointless and potentially counter-productive to send such messages to mobile phone subscribers living on hillsides above low-lying zones where violent ingress of water could be expected. Yet, at the same time, it is important to alert those who may be involved in the aftermath, such as hospital staff.

Absence of timely and accurate data following a natural disaster is one of the greatest obstacles to overcoming public health challenges as people struggle to survive. Less than a decade ago, a woman in premature labour brought on by the stress of a disaster's aftermath would have had few options to access life-saving treatment if an emergency health clinic had not been set up nearby. But today, mobile telephone technology can help her obtain medical advice over the phone, alert a community midwife to her plight, or even ask a volunteer to get her to the nearest hospital.

Also, the time taken to record health information can be slow when health workers have only paper and pencil to record where suspected cholera cases live, which children have been vaccinated, or where vital supplies have been sent. Paper is cumbersome; it has to be carried, kept dry, and it has to be photocopied. And then the data has to be re-entered manually on some computer somewhere. All of this is inefficient, and takes time. Software such as *EpiSurveyor* which was developed by the UN and the Vodafone Technology Partnership as an open-source platform, is typical of the sort of technology that can be used to control supplies and monitor areas where outbreaks are suspected, as it is "much cheaper, faster, of better quality, and easier to do than pencil and paper".

And finally, there is mobile cash transfer. In October 2011, the UN's World Food Programme started using mobile telephones to facilitate cash transfers to 54,000 of the most food insecure people living in the Ivory Coast who lost their livelihoods during the political crisis earlier in the year, and who lacked the resources to buy their food in the local markets.

For the potential of mobile telephony to be unlocked in the ways described here, the service providers have to be involved. For reasons of data protection, they are unusually discreet in how they apply the algorithms needed, and with which national and/or international authorities they coordinate. Care also has to be taken in how apparently valid information is moderated, as the humanitarian sector is as prone to manipulation and hacking as anyone else. Dilemmas over the unprecedented level of information sharing facilitated by this technology have led to debates over how the humanitarian sector can most effectively harness the full potential of this technology while retaining a principled approach to disaster preparedness, response, and recovery.

83   *Coastal cholera outbreaks can be predicted from space.*

Cholera always seems to be a particular paranoia in the wake of natural disasters. This is hardly surprising given that, in its extreme manifestation, cholera is one of the most rapidly fatal illnesses known to mankind. Although perfectly treatable with aggressive rehydration and, in some cases with additional antibiotics, a healthy person may die within 2-3 hours if no treatment is provided.

Cholera is a particularly nasty form of water- and food-borne diarrhoeal disease[99] caused by a toxin emitted by the bacterium *Vibrio cholerae*. There are over 200 known strains, with almost all being non-virulent and therefore posing no threat to humans. A single serotype, designated O1, is responsible for epidemic cholera[100].

Most of these strains live and thrive at depth in the sea or in brackish estuarine coastal waters, but only above certain temperatures[101]. Since many major cholera epidemics start in such estuaries, remote sensing by satellite is now being employed to predict where and when these might happen. This magic is achieved by keeping a lookout for algal blooms which turn up as bright red blotches on images taken by infrared cameras in space[102]. These algal blooms appear when certain ecological conditions of sea temperature, salinity, nutrient concentration, and contamination with human faeces, coincide. Happily, these factors rarely converge[lxix].

Once an algal bloom is detected, it can be assumed that Cholera will begin to appear in coastal settlements in the contaminated area about two weeks later, and in the capital two weeks after that. In the intervening time, public health workers can be despatched to make sure that fishers and market traders take special care to wash their hands with soap before handling fish infected with the Cholera vibrio.

If ingested into the lungs under high pressure in near-drowning incidents during tsunami, rare and usually deadly forms of pneumonia collectively referred to as "tsunami lung" are the result[lxx]. As was so vividly portrayed in the tsunami survival movie *The Impossible* which had Naomi Watts' character coughing up all sorts of disgusting black

---

[99] Person-to-person transmission of cholera is rare without contamination of food or water. This is because the infectious dose – the number of bacteria that need to be ingested to cause disease – is high when compared with viruses. The infectious dose for cholera ranges from one million bacteria in certain foods to over one billion in contaminated water.

[100] However, there are three distinct O1 biotypes, and each biotype may display the classical or El Tor phenotype. The disease is caused by toxigenic Vibrio cholerae O-group 1 or O-group 139. Only these two toxigenic strains have caused widespread epidemics and are reportable to the World Health Organisation as "cholera".

[101] The 2004 Indian Ocean tsunami took place in the winter when the sea temperature was too cold for cholera transmission.

[102] The satellite is actually looking at chlorophyll content in the phytoplankton. Cholera bacteria attach themselves to copepods and other zooplankton which feed on this phytoplankton. Fish and various crustaceans then feed on the zooplankton. The satellites also monitor local surface sea temperature and salinity (local sea level will rise as the water warms and as fresh-water content increases due to rainwater run-off).

stuff, these pneumonias are complicated, difficult to diagnose, and, often being drug-resistant, difficult to treat. The expensive antibiotics needed for such treatment are not generally available in developing countries, either. Timely and appropriate treatment is essential as near-drowning-associated pneumonias cause high fatality rates in young, otherwise healthy persons.

✦

Other water-borne diseases could also theoretically be spread in flood situations, although in practice the risk is reduced by the enormous dilution of contamination by the volume of flood water. The risk of typhoid fever outbreaks from such contamination, for example, would seem to be small, as the typhoid bacterium does not multiply in water.

Leptospirosis is a bacterial disease spread by rodents, pigs, dogs, and cattle, but mostly by contamination of mud or water with rat pee[103]. Flooding facilitates spread of the organism because of the proliferation of rodents and their proximity to humans on shared high ground.

Hepatitis-A is endemic in most developing countries and most children are therefore exposed and develop immunity at an early age. As a result, the risk of outbreak is low. In areas where Hepatitis-E is endemic, outbreaks frequently follow heavy rains and floods. The illness is generally mild and self-limited, but for pregnant women case-fatality rates can reach 25%.

84 It is technically possible to provide early warning of a Landslide.

Early warning of imminent 'wet mass movement' landslides is perfectly feasible and can provide adequate time for evacuation.

Simple sound sensors using sand-filled aluminium tubes buried in the ground are increasingly being used to predict the likelihood of a landslide. As soil moves within the hillside it creates noise. The greater the movement, the louder the noise. This noise builds to a crescendo as the slope becomes increasingly unstable, warning of an impending catastrophic soil collapse.

---

[103] Rodents shed large amounts of *leptospires* in their urine, and transmission occurs through contact of the skin with water or mud contaminated with this urine.

A similar system, this time called 'Distributed Acoustic Sensing' (DAS) allows sunken fibre-optic cables buried along the top of a likely slope to be turned into a string of smart underground microphones which can also monitor areas at risk of potential landslide. The system works by sending sharply defined pulses of laser light down a fibre-optic cable. When the minute vibrations caused by soil particles rubbing against each other are transmitted through the ground, the light-scattering properties inside the cable change in tiny ways. This can be detected when the pulses are received further along the cable. Ultra-high-speed signal processing techniques originally developed for nuclear submarines can interpret more or less instantly what these sounds mean.

Simple and reliable technology exists that would allow timely evacuation of those living at the foot of landslide zones.

These "acoustic fingerprints" are then subjected to a series of algorithms which, depending when, where, and how frequently they occur, filter out the background clutter to alert us to anomalies. Each of these anomalies is then assigned a level of risk which, when a pre-set threshold is reached, sends an automatic text message to every registered person living at the foot of the slope. Given the way soil and water act on each other, ten minutes warning of impending slope failure is not unusual.

85   *Volcanic eruptions are predictable.*

The MODIS thermal alert system[104] enables scientists to detect volcanic "hotspots" anywhere in the world before they become visible to the naked eye using data provided by infra-red sensors aboard NASA's Terra and Aqua satellites. These heat sources may be active lava flows, lava domes, or lava lakes. This system achieves complete global coverage every two days.

While MODIS data is ideal for quickly providing researchers with information about new eruptions, other satellite-based technologies such as Synthetic Aperture Radar (SAR) are better suited to looking at the geologic changes that often precede an eruption. Surface changes

---

[104] NASA's Moderate Resolution Imaging Spectroradiometer project

are usually the key to predicting major volcanic eruptions. The technique operates on the premise that if the radar signal reflected back to the sensor differs between two images of the same object taken at two different times, then the object has moved or changed. Differences measured in millimetres can be measured from space in this way.

Deformation refers to surface changes on a volcano, such as subsidence, tilting, or bulge formation due to the movement of magma below the surface. A change, even of millimetres, may indicate that an eruption is about to occur. An example of visible deformation occurred in 1980 when a bulge appeared on the north flank of Mount St Helens prior to its 18th May eruption. Scientists estimated that just before the eruption, the bulge was growing at a rate of 1.5 metres per day.

From the earliest moments of a volcanic eruption, a global network of Volcanic Ash Advisory Centres begins monitoring the flow of ash through the atmosphere. Armed with satellite images and modelling data[105], the appropriate centre will issue 'dispersion advisories' which describe the current ash location and project where the ash plume will be in 6, 12, and 18 hours. There are nine such centres, each responsible for a defined geographic region. One of these, the US government's advisory centre in Alaska, issues over 1,000 advisories each year. This means volcanic ash is almost constantly in the atmosphere. But where? Computer models simulate the complex dispersion patterns to be expected and predict where the particles will fall. Not surprisingly, even the most sophisticated advection algorithms, stability modulations, dispersion equations, and chemical transformation data get this wrong. The UK paid the price for this in 2010, with air corridors closed to commercial air traffic for days on account of volcanic ash that wasn't there[106].

---

[105] The computer model for tracking where smoke, chemicals and volcanic ash travel and disperse with the winds is the 'Hybrid Single Particle Lagrangian Integrated Trajectory' (HYSPLIT) model.

[106] This is a good example of a natural hazard creating a technological event ... as disrupting the travel plans of hundreds of thousands of people could hardly constitute a disaster.

86 *Tsunami early warning systems not yet very effective.*

More than 90% of all tsunamis result from strong undersea earthquakes, with those most threatening to life onshore being caused by shallow and powerful mega-thrust events. But not every earthquake generates a tsunami. For this reason it must be determined at sea whether or not an earthquake has actually triggered the deadly 'energy swell' that comes ashore as what one survivor of the Japanese tsunami of March 2011 called, "a giant and endless wave."

Fast, accurate and reliable early warning of impending tsunami has only become possible in the past few years as the result of technological innovation in pressure sensing, seismology, satellite communications, and computer hardware, not to mention the software that links it all together and makes it work.

Tsunami early warning systems are among the most complex systems ever devised by man.

There is no single 'best practice' model for tsunami early warning systems. The Pacific Tsunami Warning System, for example, is not of much use for Indonesia's unique geological situation. Earthquakes in the Indian Ocean off the coast of Indonesia occur along a subduction zone, the Sunda Arc, which extends from the North-Western corner of Sumatra to Flores in the east of Indonesia. Should a tsunami occur here, the waves will reach the coast within 20 minutes, leaving very little time to warn those who live in coastal areas to evacuate.

Four things need to be known if a tsunami is to be predicted: The first is the type and extent of seismic shift, it's depth, it's epicentre[107], its deformation, its direction, and the vertical and horizontal accelerations involved. This will allow the likely energy release to be determined and therefore the level of expected hazard. The second is the depth of water below the epicentre as the mass of water involved needs to be known, as does how it changes given the shape of the sea bed. Thirdly, changes in underwater pressure need to be measured, both on the seabed and near the surface. A passing tsunami pressure wave is not only strong – making it easy to identify – but has a unique signature. Data from both sets of pressure sensors are relayed to buoys at the surface and passed on from there to a central warning centre via satellite. These buoys do

---

[107] The point on the surface immediately above where the event took place.

not only function as relay stations but also as independent detection instruments. Finally, and most importantly, GPS antennae mounted on the buoys are used to determine surface sea motion and sea levels in the open ocean, but their data needs to be triangulated with that simultaneously being sent by automated tidal gauges onshore.

The technology must not only be robust enough to withstand the rigours of life "on the ocean wave", but accurate enough to detect movements measured in centimetres. After all, tsunami, for all their ferocity once they near land, are pretty benign out in the open ocean with swells of three metres or less and wavelengths that can exceed 200 kilometres. To recognise a passing tsunami, normal sea motion 'clutter' such as wind-generated waves, bow-waves of passing ships, and even tide has to be suppressed.

These four different types of sensors then feed their data into a central computer which runs a series of simulations based on previous events in order to synthesise an overall picture of the situation. These simulations can predict wave heights and arrival times, but this is not enough to issue a warning as the model also needs to factor in information on the population potentially at risk, its density, its vulnerability profile, and the resilience of the infrastructure. Only then is a decision to issue a warning made. And it is made by a human being. And not just one.

This is one of those areas that Hollywood more or less gets right. Any number of disaster movies, from *Day After Tomorrow* to *Armageddon*, shows a sleepy lab technician being woken at 3 o'clock in the morning by an automated alarm going off. He or she then spends the next few minutes fumbling around trying to verify that it's not a false alarm, after which a series of ever-more senior people are woken up until, eventually, the President – and, being Hollywood, it's always the President of the United States – give the order to take action. It's not dissimilar in real life. The stakes are high. Too many false alarms don't just result in people taking no notice next time – thereby increasing their exposure – but tend to result in politicians not being re-elected. Nobody down the food-chain wants to be blamed for either, as they are likely to lose their jobs too.

Arguably the most important aspect of the entire early warning sequence is to make sure that only those in harm's way actually receive the warning. A fisherman tending his nets on the beach needs to know; a farmer harvesting bananas halfway up the hillside behind him does not. GPS-enabled phones with the correct 'app' installed – obligatory by law in many disaster-prone countries but not, curiously, in the most disaster-prone of them all, the US – can make this distinction, as the location and therefore the altitude of the owner is known. In order for the warning to be heeded, those in receipt of it need to trust it and know what action to take. The latter is achieved by regular evacuation exercises and information sessions as well as by the constant teaching of risk factors in schools.

Unfortunately, early warning systems installed after the 2004 tsunami have tended to focus on the technology while overlooking the institutional arrangements and local capacities to respond appropriately.

As ever with multi-million-dollar "technology fixes", the instruments have proved either too sophisticated or too fragile for the marine environment and rustic tropical Asian conditions. Human behaviour being what it is, fishing nets inadvertently pull up the pressure sensors, and pirates steal the solar panels from the buoys, which doesn't help. As a result, some of these systems are not yet in a state of readiness to swiftly and decisively handle a tsunami warning on a 24/7 basis.

Risk Management

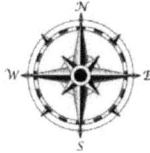

Humanitarian preparedness and response decisions should be based on objective assessment of risks, costs and benefits.

Economics – the study of optimal use of society's scarce resources which have alternative uses – plays a key role in determining which humanitarian programmes should be prioritised following a disaster and which preventive measures to take. Some programmes have been proven to be more cost-effective than others over time. This is not to suggest that, unless we can prove the economic value of an intervention it is socially worthless – human life should not be measured in terms of return on investment, after all – but it does recognise that cost-benefit decisions are applicable to at least some humanitarian activities. This is because, to consume something means to give up something else. In this sense, even a free lunch is not free because it consumes time that could have been spent doing something else. This is the economic reality of resource scarcity.

In other words, the axiom that underlies all analysis of costs and benefits when preparing for or responding to natural disaster is that society has limited resources and therefore cannot provide all the things those affected by disaster need, far less wish, to have. It also means that, if a finite amount of money is available, then spending it on one solution means there will be less to spend on the other.

When disaster managers are deciding which relief programmes to prioritise – to allocate resources for something indirect like disease surveillance, for example, as opposed to, say, something more directly 'life-saving' such as additional water treatment technology – they are not just assessing the costs and benefits of one intervention versus another in terms of its potential to avert additional death, but are, by definition, putting an intrinsic value on human life [see *Disaster Misperception # 98*].

Amongst competing ideas, logic would suggest that the proposal with the highest benefit to cost ratio would be preferred. But it's not always quite so straightforward.

Take the case of Bangladesh, where the government has invested heavily in cyclone preparedness measures including construction of raised shelters and embankments, mangrove re-planting, enhanced early warning systems, and community awareness programmes. That these measures were effective can be seen from the impact of three tropical cyclones over a number of years. In 1970 a cyclone affected 3.6

million people and killed 300,000. Twenty-seven years, and hundreds of millions of dollars later, cyclone Sidr affected 3 million people in much the same area of the coastal *sunderbans* as before but killed less than 1,000 people.

Efficiency of resource allocation is best served by 'cost-utility' analysis.

Cost-effectiveness is measured in terms of cost per unit of output – cost per litre of safe water, or cost per vaccination, for example – whereas cost-utility is a measurement of societal benefit – number of avoidable quality of life years averted, say – per dollar spent. Vaccinating all the children within a disaster-affected village for measles would be extremely effective in health terms, but the efficiency with which it was done would depend on such things as how well the cold-chain functioned and how many doses from multi-dose vials were wasted. If the village is particularly isolated and hard to reach, the cost-utility ratio will rise ... which doesn't mean the intervention shouldn't happen, just that the transaction costs will be higher.

Typically in developed countries, disaster risk reduction programmes – including retrofitting of buildings against seismic risk and structural flood defence measures – demonstrate an average cost-benefit ratio[108] of between 1.5 and 4.0. In other words, for every dollar invested in prevention, up to 4 are saved in terms of death and destruction averted[lxxi].

In developing countries, there is considerable evidence of higher returns on investment for programmes that emphasise planning and community preparedness, especially for floods and cyclones. A review of 21 studies on public and private investments as diverse as planting mangrove forests to protect against tsunami and storm surges, relocating schools away from high hazard-risk areas, strengthening the roots of banana trees to protect against windstorms, planning the village escape route, providing flat-bottomed boats for evacuation, protecting water pumps, making a platform for livestock, and identifying reliable individuals responsible for early warning, demonstrated ratios of between 3.0 and 20.0[lxxii].

Developing countries experience huge and disproportionate economic impact from natural disasters. During the ten years 1996-2005,

---

[108] Cost-Benefit Ratios refer to the net societal gain in dollars when compared to a 1 dollar investment in preventive action. The higher the ratio, therefore, the more cost-effective the action.

disasters caused $667 billion in direct material loss worldwide. These losses are twenty times greater in developing than developed countries. This disproportionate effect has many underlying causes. Lack of development itself contributes to disaster impacts because the quality of construction is often low, and building codes, land registration processes, and other regulatory processes are either lacking or corrupted. Other competing development priorities displace attention from the risks posed by natural hazard events.

It is sad but true that people in developing countries die for a range of easily preventable reasons all the time. Most of the time they die for reasons that are more easily and more cost-effectively prevented than those related to natural disaster[lxxiii]. The fact is that the vast majority of people don't die in disasters, and it may be easier and cheaper to prevent other causes of death than to apply the technical or engineering solutions employed in typical disaster risk management activities.

Over half-a-million children die from malaria every year, for example. That's about five times more than all age-groups who die from natural disasters. And highly cost-effective anti-malarial measures exist, including insecticide-treated bed nets that can be produced and distributed for around $8 - $10 each without the need for sophisticated engineering talent and advanced regulatory oversight. We can look at this another way: Whereas an average of 2,500 children die each year in school collapse, more than 10 million children under the age of five die each year from other causes before they even make it to the school gates.

✦

What can be done about this in practice? Take the real-life example of the Philippines after typhoon *Yolanda*, when, four months after the event, the government was trying to decide whether or not to build specially designed 'cyclone shelters'. Of the 634 schools, churches, community centres, and commercial buildings designated by the government as safe evacuation shelters on the island of Samar, less than sixty remained standing after the typhoon swept through this low-lying area. The buildings were neither strong enough, nor high enough, to withstand the enormous forces unleashed on them by the winds and the waves, and over 500 people died in and around them when they thought they were safe.

The government had no option but to consider building stronger infrastructure from scratch capable of withstanding such forces; rehabilitating buildings that were clearly not up to the task could only be an interim measure. They turned to Bangladesh for inspiration, where in 2007 cyclone *Sidr* killed over 3,000 people and made millions more homeless. The story of one village, Angul Kata, was particularly illuminating:

Despite the odds, all but two of the village's population of nearly 2,000 survived the disaster unscathed, a fact largely credited to the village's sole cyclone shelter, a simple three-storey building which also served as the village primary school.

Within 30 minutes of the cyclone striking, over 1,500 people had clambered up the central stairs of the school, which sits upon eight reinforced concrete pillars, to escape the five-metre-high storm-surge that followed. Seconds later, residents quickly closed its iron shutters to the 220 kph winds that raged outside. Had the shelter not existed, Bangladeshi authorities say the death toll could easily have been in the hundreds.

But if each of these shelters costs over $220,000 to build, is it worth it? To make such a life-and-death decision, the likelihood of a cyclone hitting the country first has to be figured out. Disaster epidemiology provides not just the historical data, but extrapolates using trend analysis, regressions, and climate change models to predict the frequency of future such events and where their track is most likely to fall. Such data also helps determine what magnitude of storm constitutes the threshold above which the hazard can be assumed to be life-threatening. This is not just a function of wind speed and likely storm-surge height, but the other factors of vulnerability we will come on to discuss.

Then the number of people potentially living within the cyclone's footprint during the planned design-life of the proposed shelter has to be calculated. This is not as straightforward as it appears when population statistics might be 10 years or more out of date, and current birth rates unknown. And then the cost of designing, managing, building, and maintaining each shelter has to be worked out. If the 'value' of the people who might be saved is greater than the cost of the project then the shelter gets built. This is where it gets a bit more tricky.

First of all, what value is assigned to the lives of people living in the affected area? There is also the opportunity cost of not spending the money on some other, perhaps more cost-effective, intervention, and for which there might be considerable political support. And, when all of that has been considered, the realisation that the available budget will not be enough to build the number of shelters needed, and that some areas will have to be prioritised over others, means that someone has to decide the criteria for that, and then implement the project in the full knowledge that not everyone can be protected.

88 *Donors don't always fund disasters based solely on assessed need.*

Despite numerous public commitments made to the principles of 'good humanitarian donorship' in places like Oslo and Paris, many governments will not engage if it is not in their country's best interests to do so. Usually, the only factor to overturn this geo-political self-interest is the profile given to a disaster by the media. The UN estimates that 18 million disaster victims are "forgotten and consigned to the shadows of unfashionable crises" because their plight does not attract sustained media coverage.

Experts have long argued that it makes more economic sense to pour money into helping local governments and communities minimise their exposure to disasters, than mopping up afterwards. The trouble with this evident logic is that, "funding for disaster risk reduction and disaster preparedness is not very sexy for donors", as Jouni Hemberg of the Finnish NGO, FinnChurchAid, put it. "For many donors, installing a city drainage system or devising a programme to help coastal villagers cope with rising sea levels just doesn't sound as appealing as distributing food rations to 100,000 earthquake survivors or vaccinating 20,000 children in a refugee camp".

Donor funding practices tend to make relief operations one third more costly.

Some donors continue to tie their aid to certain conditions, too. This means, for example, insisting on the use of NGOs, consultants, and commercial contractors from the home country or training health professionals abroad using overseas aid budgets, with every intention of luring them home with tax breaks and visa's once they are qualified.

American aid in particular is still delivered according to wildly outdated models which appear designed to help US foreign policy goals as much as the poor, disproportionately being allocated to geo-politically important countries such as Jordan and Pakistan. There is also a powerful political system supporting the way aid is delivered and allocated, with an absurd law still in place that requires much of the US government's emergency food aid destined for crisis-hit countries to come from American farms, be carried by American vessels, and be monitored by American government employees [see *Disaster Misperception # 79*].

Tying aid is inefficient and makes the overall aid effort 30% more costly, according to Karin Christiansen , director of the watchdog NGO Publish What You Fund, suggesting, "it acts like a hidden subsidy".

Governments are no different to you and me, in that they tend to discount low-probability future losses and seem reluctant to invest in managing disaster risk management. Governments often cite a lack of financial resources as a constraint, but the allocation of available public resources reflects political priorities ... reducing the threat of a disaster that may not happen is usually perceived as less of a priority than spending on education, defence and healthcare, which goes on every day.

The imperative to invest in managing and mitigating 'disaster risk' is likely to be greater in countries with effective institutions, and where a strong civil society can hold governments and other stakeholders to account for poor decisions. It is also more likely in countries that are continually affected by one type of disaster or another and where the risks are more evident to the vote-wielding public. In general, countries that experience more frequent major disasters are more likely to invest in risk reduction.

Predictable disasters, such as recurring tropical cyclones, stimulate more social demand for risk management, because a failure to reduce foreseeable risks will expose government negligence. In contrast, when confronted with low-probability events, governments are more able to evade their responsibilities and blame external forces such as God, nature and, more recently, climate change.

But there is something else going on. There is a strong political imperative for disaster relief, and politicians have always understood the power of symbolic and real responses to disasters. Saving lives and assisting disaster victims is a moral, humanitarian and political vote-winner that few would contest. As such, disaster relief can be a powerful tool for leaders, enhancing their political profile and facilitating patronage, both now and once they have left political office. In contrast, the incentives for reducing disaster risk, a public good, are far less obvious, and the benefits take longer to accrue than democratic election cycles allow.

89 *Humanitarian action is littered with unintended consequences.*

Humanitarian aid is sometimes viewed as a double-edged sword: while some form of help is probably warranted in the wake of disaster, the argument is sometimes made that the *Samaritan's Dilemma* – when succour cannot be denied even to those who are evil, culpable or negligent – is to inject a perverse incentive ... that is, an incentive *not* to do something or to knowingly do something wrong. The 2010 flood in Pakistan is a fairly recent example.

With meteorological warnings of record upland rainfall and Himalaya snow-melt unheeded, illegal de-forestation rampant, and flood mitigation schemes through dredging and levée building paid for but undone, the humanitarian community was expected to step, literally, into the breach. But should humanitarian aid – and the neutrality and impartiality of the agencies dispensing it – compensate for the corrupted inaction of others going back decades?

In fact, humanitarian aid can actually encourage carelessness when it comes to preparedness. This is because aid pouring into a country following a disaster can create a "bailout effect" similar to that seen during the financial crisis. Just as large financial institutions know that they are "too big to fail," and that government will bail them out in a crisis, so, too, can governments expect to be bailed out in the event of a natural disaster. Haiti's government was too poor to meet many of its basic disaster risk prevention obligations. Spending government revenue on disaster prevention wouldn't have been on the top of the priority list, in part due to the expectation that this was the class of expenditures that donors would deal with after the fact.

Zimbabwe offers another example. Cholera is endemic in Zimbabwe, but when an epidemic erupted in 2008, the government turned to the international community for help despite a decade of so-called 'development'. They had spent the money on other priorities in the full knowledge that this form of 'insurance policy' would be forthcoming at no cost, either financially or politically, to themselves.

In addition, inappropriate government policies, including subsidised insurance, create a *moral hazard*[109] whereby individuals are

---

[109] Moral hazard occurs when a party insulated from risk behaves differently than it would behave if it were fully exposed to the risk. It arises when an individual or

perversely encouraged to live in dangerous places because they don't bear all the financial risk of doing so. This, as the inhabitants of New York found out when super-storm *Sandy* hit them in October 2012, can also place relatively wealthy people at greater physical risk.

90   *Humans are not very good at calculating risk.*

Twenty years ago, Peter Bernstein wrote a thought-provoking book on probability theory called *Up Against the Gods*. In it, he argued that one of the key things to distinguish modern societies from their pre-modern forbears is how people perceive risk. Pre-modern cultures, he suggested, could not model risk in any systematic way because they lacked clocks and algorithms. Thus they viewed life fatalistically, as something shaped by capricious Gods, or natural elements. Modern societies, on the other hand, measure risk methodically and develop proactive strategies to mitigate and prevent risk accordingly.

But perhaps we're not always as 'modern' as we like to think? Take, for example, the tsunami that devastated North-East Japan in early 2011. Modern Japanese, even of the older generation, understood perfectly well what happened in scientific terms, and knew all about the finer details of mega-thrust events, water run-up, and the efficiency of early warning systems. But, for many in the fishing communities dotting the coastline, the explanation was very different: Sea Spirits had been angered and were punishing the people.

Risk is the way we measure uncertainty.

The Japanese are not alone in this respect. It's the same in the high mountains of the Himalaya, where the literal translation of the Kingdom of Bhutan is, "Land of the Thunder Dragon". If you are lucky enough to go there, you will quickly realise why, as the booms and crashes of rock-slides and calving glaciers mingle with the sound of thunder to reverberate like the roar of a dragon along the steep sided valleys, echoes amplifying in the thin blue sky. Being a Himalayan kingdom, much of Bhutan lies in a seismically active area, and, with tremors felt almost weekly, even the remotest village is well rehearsed in what to do if the walls come tumbling down. But, as Buddhists, they simply don't believe the scientific rationale for the cause of an

---

institution does not take full consequence of responsibility for its actions, and therefore has a tendency to act less carefully than it otherwise would.

earthquake, preferring to know only that any death and destruction must somehow have been deserved.

Most civilisations throughout history have used mythology and religion in similar fashion. The resulting oral traditions are cultural forms that organise our perceptions about the world. Although stories are used to acquire, synthesise, store, and share information relevant to survival, they are more than this; they enable us to make sense of probability and of the unpredictable, destructive natural forces in our landscape.

Today, we understand risk as a measure of uncertainty. If the weather forecast says there is a 100% chance of precipitation this afternoon, then there is no *risk* of rain. It *will* rain. If it says there is a 75% chance of precipitation this afternoon, then there is a one in four chance that it *might* rain. At this point, you decide whether to reach for the raincoat or not. In so doing, you are making a trade-off between one expected outcome – getting wet – and another – staying dry – with a whole host of complicating factors in between.

Even now, people who think of themselves as modern still find risk a difficult concept to grasp. This is for two main reasons: The first, being simply about the mathematics, is explained in Steven Levitt and Stephen Dubner's thought-provoking book *Freakonomics*, like this:

> "Consider the parents of an eight-year-old girl named, say, Molly. Her two best friends, Amy and Imani, each live nearby. Molly's parents know that Amy's parents keep a gun in their house, so they have forbidden her to play there. Instead, Molly spends a lot of time at Imani's house, which has a swimming pool in the backyard. Molly's parents feel good about having made such a smart choice to protect their daughter.
>
> But according to the data, their choice isn't smart at all. In a given year, there is one drowning of a child for every 11,000 residential pools in the United States. In a country with 6 million pools, this means that roughly 550 children under the age of 10 drown each year. Meanwhile, there is one child killed by a gun for every 1 million-plus guns. In a country with an estimated 200 million guns, this means that roughly 175 children under 10 die each year from guns. The likelihood of death by pool (being 1 in 11,000) versus death by gun (being 1 in 1 million-plus) isn't even close: Molly is far more likely to die in a swimming accident at Imani's house than in gunplay at Amy's".

The point they are really making is that there are risks that scare people and there are risks that kill people, and the two are very different. Depending on where you live in the world, for example, the risk of being buried alive in an earthquake-induced building collapse is thousands of times less than being run over by a bus. So, how much should we worry about earthquakes, tornadoes, or swine flu? How much time, money, and energy should we take to avoid the risks associated with each? And what exactly should we do to prevent the dangers posed by natural disaster, however remote or real they appear to be?

The second challenge with risk is in how it is perceived. An equally thought-provoking book called *Nudge* by Richard Thaler and Cass Sunstein explains the behavioural psychology involved. In it, they acknowledge that biased assessment of risk can, as in Molly's case, adversely influence how we prepare for and respond to crises. But it also suggests that we don't always see what we're looking at, despite being absolutely convinced that we can.

They demonstrate this *blunder of bias* by showing a drawing of two tabletops, one long and thin, the other short and wide. The funny thing is that both tabletops are identical in size, yet they look different because of the different perspective and visual cues used when they were drawn. The point here is that our judgement is often biased by such subtle shifts in perspective and the way we as individuals interpret contextual cues. Not only that, but Thaler and Sunstein go on to point out that we can be absolutely convinced of our own infallibility. Anyone seeing the drawing for the first time is utterly convinced that one table is shorter and wider than the other. It's the same when managing disasters: when everyone around a decision-making table is trying to reach consensus, personal convictions can be hard to shift even after the introduction of contrary evidence.

91   *Exposure is not the same thing as Vulnerability.*

At its most fundamental, risk involves the concept of avoiding harm, and in so doing requires us to make trade-offs between our perceptions of hazard, probability, and likely consequences. At its most sophisticated, it involves complicated statistical gymnastics such as *multivariate regressions*, *mortality risk indices*, and *loss exceedance curves*, all of which, one way or the other, attach numbers and values to things which cannot be easily numbered or valued to give the impression that the worst effects can somehow be avoided, or at least controlled, if only we understood them better.

Whether we really do understand them better or not, every minute of every day we come up with what we consider to be appropriately managed solutions to the hazards and perils that surround us given the potential rewards, whatever they might be.

Do we really know enough, though, to allow us to make these trade-off decisions? Did the people of Christchurch, New Zealand, know on the 22nd February 2011 when an earthquake devastated their town that six-to-eight-storey buildings collapse in earthquakes more often than those that are shorter or taller? Would it have made a difference to their daily lives if they had? Is it more important in a flood to know how to swim, or to know what to do if your brother is bitten by a snake? Is it important to know that many of those pulled smiling from the rubble of the Haiti earthquake in 2010 died later because dialysis was not available in sufficient quantities to treat the crush injuries they had sustained? Does it make a difference to know that, without vaccination, tetanus has the potential to kill just as many people as falling debris in an earthquake? Or that, without immediate use of third generation antibiotics, those who have ingested cholera into their lungs in a tsunami are likely to die later of pneumonia?

The extent to which we might be affected depends on four main factors, and it is these that are being considered when trade-off decisions are being made:

The nature of the hazard (H): how much devastation could this defined hazard potentially unleash?

Our exposure (E): how many people are potentially in harm's way?

Our vulnerability (V): have those in harm's way been sufficiently protected from measures taken beforehand to prevent or reduce the likely impact?

Our resilience (r): will those affected be able to adapt to, and cope with the consequences?

The simple way to understand disaster risk, then, is to see it as a product of the probability that a defined hazard event will impact on a known number of vulnerable people exposed to that event, mitigated by their capacity to cope with its effects.

These elements are sometimes put it into the form of a pseudo-equation of risk (R) which looks something like this:

$$\mathcal{R} = \frac{H(1/p \times m) + (V \times E)}{r}$$

Each of these products is made up of a variety of different factors. The first of these to consider is the *hazard* which is defined as a potentially damaging physical event, phenomenon, or human activity that may cause loss of life or injury, property damage, social and economic disruption, or environmental degradation. Examples include droughts, hurricanes, and earthquakes, all of which display physical characteristics to a greater or lesser degree of:

Probability: is this a ten-year or thousand-year event[110]?

Predictability: what is the speed of onset, and will early warning be possible?

Location: where will it take place?

Magnitude: how much energy will be unleashed, over how wide an area, and for how long?

---

[110] The theoretical 'return interval' is the inverse of the probability that the event will be exceeded in any one year. For example, a 50 year flood has a 0.02 or 2% chance of being exceeded in any one year. Slightly confusingly, this does not mean that a 100 year flood will happen regularly every 100 years despite the implication. In any given 100 year period, a 100-year-event may occur once, twice, more, or not at all, and each outcome has a probability that can be computed.

Hazards only result in *disasters* when they collide with the *vulnerability* of societies to which they are exposed i.e those people affected by economic, demographic, social, physical, environmental, or political factors such as:

Population Density: The population potentially exposed (PPE) might be living in dispersed rural villages, in urban high-rises, or in peri-urban slums. The population per square kilometre will be very different for each.

Period of Exposure: This does not just refer to those trapped under the rubble in earthquakes, but communities that are cut off from outside assistance, and for whom access to health care, food, and water is not possible without, say, helicopters or boats.

Displacement: Those who have had their homes destroyed might be supported by neighbours within their communities, or may have been obliged to move in with family members far away, or into temporary shelters where everyone around them is a stranger.

Demography: With more women than men typically affected by disaster, the proportion of men, women, boys and girls among the survivors will be different to what it was before. Much depends, for example on the time of day the disaster took place, and whether children were in school, or workers in factories. Those under five years of age and the elderly are particularly vulnerable. Minority groups, who might have been facing persecution before the event might find themselves being blamed. Levels of poverty may not have changed much, but disasters are great levelers as everybody is equally affected. Some will now have become single parents, female heads of household, or orphaned. Others will have lost contact with surviving family members

Health Status: Diseases which were endemic before the disaster and vaccination coverage rates will both have a direct and immediate bearing on whether mass immunisation is called for, and what response measures are to be prioritised. Nutritional status and physical disability are also useful to know as these vulnerabilities become more acute in the weeks and months after a disaster.

Climate: Whether the climate is hot or cold, and whether or not this will change over the next few months will have a major bearing on shelter and protection policies. Precipitation patterns of rain and snow and likely windspeeds of seasonal storms will have a bearing on what type of thermal insulation to provide in the forms of clothes, blankets, stoves, and winterized accommodation.

Infrastructure: Dwellings and key structures such as hospitals, mobile communications towers, shelters, airport runways, bridges, and power plants (and the electricity distribution grids that go with them) need to be able to withstand the shock of foreseen hazards if relief and recovery operations are to have a chance of getting communities back on their feet quickly.

Resilience: Communities are more resilient in the face of disaster than they are often credited for. But their ability to cope using their own resources, and their ability to adapt to their new situation cannot be assumed for long when cash and food runs short. Whether women and children have been taught CPR will have a direct bearing on how many people drown or die from snakebite in a riverine flood. Similarly, if men and women have been taught how to give first aid, far fewer people will die from their injuries, whatever the cause.

Perceived Risk: Perceptions about the risks facing those populations potentially exposed are usually at odds with the reality. Using evidence to explain these risks, and providing relevant stories of successful 'best practice' survival options from elsewhere will help communities and households engage in determining their own survival solutions.

Residual Risk: This refers to the risk that remains in unmanaged form, even when effective disaster risk reduction measures have been put in place.

In general, if a phenomenon such as climate change affects the frequency, intensity or duration of extreme weather events such as floods, droughts, storms and extreme temperatures, it can be expected that some locations might experience an increase in the number and duration of events, while others might experience a decrease. Some of the effects of these changes will tend to offset each other and/or be redistributed over space and time. For instance, an increase in deaths due to heatwaves in the summer at one location might be offset by a decline in deaths due to fewer or less intense coldwaves during the winter at the same or another location. Equally, climate change might redistribute the pattern of rainfall and drought in space and time.

For example, in contrast to expectations that climate change is resulting in more fires, regional increases in fire incidence seems to be counter-balanced by decreases at other locations, due to the interplay of temperature and precipitation. In other words, drier, more combustible zones are counterbalanced by wetter, less combustible ones elsewhere.

All regions of the world are experiencing increasing exposure simply due to population growth, yet some regions have managed to reduce their residual risk despite this increase in exposure, which means they have reduced their vulnerability. In the US, for example, exposure increased by 58% between 1970 and 2010, yet net risk remained the

The risk of dying in a natural disaster is only one-third of what it was.

same owing to an equal and opposite decline in vulnerability. Over the same period, risk was reduced by 300% across the Asia-Pacific region owing to a drastic reduction in vulnerability – more than 70% since 1970 – despite even larger exposures.

In recent decades, countries all over the world have strengthened their capacities to reduce the risk of their citizens dying from major hazards such as earthquakes, tropical cyclones and floods. Because of these efforts, and despite more and more people living in flood plains and along cyclone-exposed coastlines, mortality risk relative to population size is falling all over the world. In East Asia and the Pacific, for example, it is now only a third of what it was in 1980.

We assume that an expanding population means more people potentially exposed, and that these extra people are just as vulnerable as before. But they are not necessarily more vulnerable, and therefore not necessarily more at risk. As has already been mentioned, they might have adapted to the new realities, and become more resilient by taking robust measures to prevent, or at least mitigate, the threat posed by the hazard they know faces them; by building basement shelters, for example, in known tornado-prone areas, or seismic-resistant hospitals in areas of known earthquake risk; or by teaching each other how to treat physical injuries amongst their neighbours should the worst happen; drawn up and rehearsed evacuation plans; or pre-positioned stockpiles of food, water, and fuel.

Being able to anticipate disasters; making people aware of approaching calamity and what they have to do to survive it; and investing in shock-resistant infrastructure and social protection mechanisms, are all part of being resilient, as is the ability to adapt behaviour to changing circumstances. Everyone in the path of a tropical cyclone is exposed to the same hazard, but the young and healthy family who spent that little bit extra tying down their corrugated iron roof and protecting the water well is less susceptible to the hazard than the elderly widow next door who could not. Being poor, female, uneducated, disabled, or elderly also changes the risk profile, as these sub-groups are always disproportionately affected during natural disasters.

In practice, the picture is made more complex through politics, lack of information, dynamic movement within and between populations, and secondary shocks. Often, it is these secondary shocks that prove more debilitating than the original hazard event itself. Salt-water inundation, for example, may have rendered low-lying agricultural land infertile after a storm surge has drowned the cattle and washed away what was left of the family home after high winds had already blown the roof off. Later stresses such as polluted groundwater or rising food prices then begin to pile on top of the original shocks, accumulating slowly to become a shock in their own right.

Assessing relative risk means being able to qualify and, where possible, quantify a number of risk factors as each will play a role in determining how much risk a system, a process, a person, or a community can bear. Once we have done this, the question then arises as to which hazard poses the greatest risk, and how we weigh up that risk relative to the next so that preventive actions are correctly prioritised.

The fact that people suffer from the effects of naturally occurring events indicates a failure of development in its broadest sense ... the sad consequence of the country's failure to realise its true potential because policymakers have not taken the action required to protect their people.

Comparing tropical cyclone *Sidr* which struck Bangladesh in 2007 and tropical cyclone *Nargis* which struck Myanmar further down the Bay of Bengal in 2008, provides a good example for comparing the relative impact of risk reduction measures. Despite the fact that *Sidr* hit a larger population with stronger winds over a larger area, it resulted in thirty times fewer victims than did *Nargis*. This was put down at the time to the lack of early warning in Myanmar and a lackadaisical response by authorities more engaged in politics than protecting their people. In practice, and given that the international humanitarian response was more or less the same in both cases, it was the number of cyclone shelters and flood defences built, the accuracy, timeliness, and coverage of community-based early warning systems, the re-forestation of coastal mangroves, and the widespread penetration of first-aid training that accounted for the majority of the difference.

It is also noteworthy that, while cyclone *Sidr* kill fewer than 3,000 people, a similar strength cyclone in 1970 that followed more or less the same path killed nearly half a million, mostly from drowning. The difference was that in the intervening 38 years, Bangladesh had become better prepared. What this means is that Bangladesh, despite higher hazard risk exposure and appalling poverty, has drastically reduced overall mortality risk, whereas Myanmar has not.

The impact of natural hazard events also depends on how well prepared a community is to cope with it. Some are better able to withstand the shock and recover than others. The Haiti earthquake at the beginning of 2010 killed over 250,000 people and caused severe injuries to over 300,000 more. Yet an earthquake 100 times more powerful in Chile a few weeks later killed less than 3,000, almost 100 times fewer. Both these events took place in densely populated urban areas. The fact that one had complied with building codes and the other had not, clearly demonstrates that disaster risk management efforts are not made in vain.

92   *Coordination by consensus is not the best way to manage a disaster response.*

Almost ten years ago, a senior UK aid official, Hilary Benn, famously described humanitarian coordination like this:

> *"Imagine if, here at home, every time there was a fire, we had to hold a meeting of local and central government officials, politicians and community leaders before responding.*
>
> *First they have to go and look at the fire because they don't trust the alarm system.*
>
> *Then they have to decide with the landlord what they are allowed to do.*
>
> *Once that has been done, they then have to raise the money needed to buy fuel for the fire trucks, while simultaneously seeking competitive bids to find the lowest cost supplier.*
>
> *After that, they decide who should do the firefighting and then begin ringing round to see who might provide some semi-trained volunteer crew members.*

They are then given the cheapest equipment available and sent into harm's way without the required delegation of authority to act.

It sounds ridiculous doesn't it? But that's how things are working now in the international humanitarian system".

Things have changed considerably since then, especially in the area of resource mobilisation, mass casualty management, and urban risk reduction. Nevertheless, anyone working in the disaster management business today might give a wry smile but would still recognise this passage as containing some fundamental truths. Just ask them how happy they feel, for example, climbing into a UN helicopter built in the USSR over 30 years ago, which has had minimal maintenance since, and is being flown by vodka-swilling pilots from the lowest bidder, a private Ukrainian company. Or ask anyone working in the human resources department of an international aid organisation how easy it is to find experienced and qualified staff to 'surge' at a moment's notice into a disaster zone.

The primary purpose of coordination is to achieve maximum impact within the limits of resources available. The consequence of lack of coordination is the development of parallel response systems. Such parallelism duplicates services in one area, leaves other areas uncovered, and leads to inadequate inter-sectoral integration. Left to their own devices, chaotic or laissez faire humanitarian interventions cost more, achieve less, and lead to more adverse unintended consequences than those that are properly coordinated[111].

Poorly coordinated disaster responses cost more, achieve less, and lead to greater adverse outcomes.

Because humanitarian action cannot – and some would argue, should not – be anything other than an expression of civil society solidarity whose strengths lie in its very diversity, coordination cannot be carried out through any other method than by consensus. How consensus is reached is the art and science of coordination, and, as in a corporate boardroom, requires a subtle blend of facilitation, negotiation, and coercion.

The coordination of disaster response operations takes shape at up to four different geographic levels:

---

[111] For deeper insights into how coordination is conducted in practice, refer to www.clustercoordination.org.

International: This includes the UN Secretariat, national governments, headquarters of the participating agencies, and the donors;

National: This includes the 'host' government, national and sometimes international military and civil defence units, civil society groups, the private sector, the UN country offices, international organisation such as the Red Cross-Red Crescent, and the national representatives of donors and NGOs;

Sub-National (Field Hub): This includes local authorities, field staff from international humanitarian agencies, community based organisations, and beneficiaries. In larger countries, or in more widespread responses, field level coordination may involve yet another level below this.

Coordination also takes place in the disaster-affected country at two procedural levels:

Strategic: At this level the UN's Humanitarian Coordinator interacts with the host government and its disaster management agency, donors, the military and/or civil defence, and the heads of the main humanitarian agencies to ensure that oversight is maintained on the overall humanitarian strategy.

Operational: It is at this level that the day-to-day management of operational responses are coordinated, both within the clusters[112], and between them. Often, this will involve establishing loose associations between these sector groupings so that thematic areas common to each are properly addressed, with the UN's Office for Coordination of Humanitarian Affairs (OCHA) facilitating this process.

---

[112] First implemented in Pakistan in 2005 in response to humanitarian reform efforts, a cluster consists of groupings of UN agencies, The Red Cross, NGOs and other international organisations around a defined sector or service during a humanitarian crisis under the leadership of a single pre-determined agency. The cluster approach currently encompasses 11 sectoral areas of work, including logistics, health, food security, water-sanitation-hygiene, education, and nutrition as well as more thematic areas such as protection. For more detail, see www.humanitarianresponse.info

Management of national disaster response operations is conceptually very different to coordination of international humanitarian relief. The essential difference is that the government of a disaster-affected country has the authority to direct response and recovery activities within its territories, in furtherance of its legally bound mandate to protect its people[113]. International organisations coming in from abroad, on the other hand, are under no such obligation, and, although they must abide by national policies, are essentially free to respond as they see fit under a voluntary charter of humanitarian standards and guidelines[114]. The UN sits in the middle, and supports the government by coordinating international components of the relief effort until such time as the government has the capacity to resume, or take on its responsibilities in this regard[115]. In essence, government can direct, command and control, whereas the UN can only suggest, request, and cajole. Government can lead from the front, but, as they put it themselves, "The UN can only lead from behind".

Government can direct, command and control, whereas the UN can only suggest, request and cajole.

Because of such political complexities, the role of all humanitarian coordinators demands a super-human blend of technical knowledge, relevant experience, and leadership skills. As I once described to Sergio di Mello, the UN head in Baghdad just before he was tragically killed in the UN Canal Hotel bombing in 2003:

> "… coordination requires us all to combine the skills of magician, diplomat, chairman, composer, conductor, chief negotiator, information manager, reports officer, financial controller, and boy scout … all the while trying to embrace cultural and gender diversity knowing that half the room won't understand your jokes – that some will even be offended by them – and you are speaking to the other half in their third language."

(Author, Baghdad, August 2003)

---

[113] UN Security Council Resolution 46/182, December 1991

[114] These are the 'Humanitarian Charter and Minimum Standards in Humanitarian Response', commonly referred to as "SPHERE", and can be found at www.sphereproject.org

[115] Actually, although the UN has this international mandate under Security Council Resolution, in practice it is exercised in partnership with the Red Cross and NGO community through a semi-formal entity called the Inter Agency Standing Committee.

In practice, then, coordination of humanitarian aid is a messy and complex affair that suffers the chaos of uncertainty; insufficient and asymmetric information; and a host of actors with different mandates and different ways of doing things. It is the task of 'coordination' to take such complications into account when managing this complexity.

So, how is a disaster response actually coordinated? Are responsibilities allocated by sector? If so, who does the allocating? Does one group do Health, while another takes on responsibility for Water, and yet another covers Education? Does that mean that environmental sanitation engineers can't conduct health programmes? Does it imply that a doctor – whose whole being is constructed around saving the life of a single patient no matter what the cost – is the best person to conduct a public health campaign?

How about coordination by geographic region? Perhaps a single organisation could handle an entire neighbourhood or region? But that would assume they have the capacity and broad spread of skills required to work across multiple sectors ... in schools and in health centres, while running camps and sorting out problems connected with under-nutrition, unsafe water and disposing of solid waste. Most relief agencies, big and small, are specialised and don't have this broad range of skills.

As a result – and discounting the type of coordination used in refugee camp settings – coordination ends up being a messy combination of sectoral, thematic and geographical cooperation, and becomes as much a management art as an evidence-based science in the process.

This complexity is not helped by the unwillingness of many organisations to share their information. During the Indonesian earthquake response of 2006, the Emergency Shelter Cluster conducted an informal survey which demonstrated that under a half of all the aid agencies with relief operations in the field attended coordination meetings, even irregularly, and, of these, less than two thirds proactively shared their information. When asked why, almost all the agencies concerned said that they didn't know they had to. But the real reason is that they saw coordination as a bureaucracy-ridden, time-consuming, painful hassle, the benefits of which were hard to see from their perspective, at least over the short term. Something similar was seen during the typhoon *Yolanda* response in the Philippines in 2013/2014, where half of the 75 partner agencies in the Shelter Cluster admitted to being unaware of their responsibilities within the cluster approach[lxxiv].

✦

According to the International Feinstein Center, "Very few agencies conduct a formal or structured analysis of the various options, and base decisions on the evidence that points to the most appropriate response". They go on to say that there appears to be a high level of 'path dependence' in most decision making processes in the humanitarian sector. In other words, the range of options is limited by previously decided strategic priorities, the wishes of those providing the resources, and other such barriers[116]. Decision makers may be highly selective in their uptake and interpretation of evidence, too, with personal biases, rules of thumb, and mental models preventing individuals and organisations from responding to a situation in the way that evidence appears to demand. It is common for experienced aid practitioners to base decisions mainly on past experiences, instinct, and assumptions as a result, even in the face of contradicting evidence[lxxv].

93 *Information is as important as relief supplies.*

When disaster strikes, access to information is as important as access to food and shelter. Since 2005 when the Red Cross made this point, disaster-affected populations have become increasingly digital thanks to the widespread adoption of mobile technologies. Indeed, as a result of these mobile technologies, affected populations are increasingly able to source, share, and generate a vast amount of information. This has changed the way disaster risk is managed and completely transformed the landscape of disaster response.

This is as much to do with sideways-scanning infra-red spectrometers bolted onto satellites as it is to do with the humble mobile phone. Crisis mappers use digital data to assess flood risk, quantify earthquake damage, and track epidemics in real time. Aerial photography and satellite imagery have not just helped in rescue and relief operations, but have helped raise public awareness about what is unfolding, allowing for more evidence-based advocacy to prod politicians into action.

---

[116] 'www.clustercoordination.org' has listed 23 such barriers to engagement.

If new technologies are changing the environment in which disaster response is planned for and carried out, none are doing this more so than web platforms and social media as it is these that have created new opportunities for gathering information and providing early warning with and for communities. Crowd-sourced crisis mapping platforms such as *Ushahidi* and *Open StreetMap* are revolutionising the way disaster information is gathered, analysed, and made available.

Disaster information from social media can be deliberately malicious, so needs curating.

You-tube and *Twitter* in particular provide actionable information in real time as disasters unfold. They are especially useful when used together, as the combination of visual image and short, GPS-coded message, allows for attribution and verification of source, location, and time. These are important considerations in an information age that so often means misinformation.

During the Haiti earthquake response in 2010, a virtual community of on-line volunteers was grouped into teams under leadership of the University of Miami in Florida to capture, validate, geo-reference, collate, and analyse the raw information streaming in from the ground. This process included information coming in from side-scanning satellite imagery, some of which was infra-red, which allowed estimates to be made of how many people per building may have been trapped and could still be alive. This analysis was then reported to disaster responders back in Haiti a matter of hours after it had been received, allowing search and rescue efforts to focus on where they were likely to be needed most.

94 Investment in Disaster Risk Reduction is extremely cost-efficient.

In their annual letter to investors circulated in January 2015, the Bill and Melinda Gates Foundation, the world's largest philanthropic organisation by capitalisation, wrote about the economics of despair … except they preferred to use the term 'optimism'. "The lives of people in poor countries," they said "will improve faster in the next fifteen years than at any time in history."

They went on to talk about reducing infant mortality by half worldwide, eradicating polio and finding a vaccine for malaria – all of which represent international health challenges reliant as much on hope as experience – as well as the potential for mobile money transfer among the unbanked and education for the uneducated. Behind everything they were saying was the implicit acknowledgement that trade liberalisation and economic growth would achieve more than aid or philanthropy ever could.

According to the Copenhagen Centre on Consensus, a think tank, a free trade deal between China, Japan, South Korea, and the other countries in ASEAN would, for example, generate $3,438 for every $1 spent.

By comparison, a cost-benefit analysis conducted in 2013 in Ecuador concluded that, by eliminating recurring losses from floods and storms, every dollar invested in disaster risk reduction ultimately provides $9.50 in savings. Similarly, the European Union estimates that €1 ($1.18) spent on flood protection brings €6 in savings.

The Copenhagen group's analysis also showed how one dollar invested in controlling one of the world's biggest killer diseases, Tuberculosis, would reap $43 in savings and how $3.6 billion per year spent on global reproductive health services would generate benefits of $432 billion i.e $120 per dollar spent ... apparently demonstrating an even better return on investment.

And herein lies the humanitarian dilemma faced by national and local disaster planning authorities the world over: when resources are inadequate to prevent every possible type of emergency, which one should be prioritised over the other? And the answer to that question is unfortunately as much to do with the "Three P's" of local politics, power dynamics and patronage as it is to do with the sciences of disaster epidemiology and health economics.

95 *The private sector is not yet invested in humanitarian action to the scale it could be.*

Commercial enterprises, if they want to get involved at all, usually want to engage in areas of response that conform to their area of expertise, cost little in real terms, and are highly visible. This is because most are not in the business of philanthropy, but in business full stop. Which means that their legal obligation to maximise return on investment for the shareholder has only two motivations: either dumping of excess inventory, thereby looking good to employees, shareholders, and suppliers while writing off most of the actual costs incurred against tax as a 'charitable donation' [see *Disaster Misperception # 80*]; or seeking low-cost entry into emerging markets. Both of these motives result in duplication of effort, increased transaction costs all round and, in all probability, needs not being adequately met. This, at least, is the view of those that believe there is little place for the profit-making world in humanitarian action.

The less cynical will have noticed that commercial companies are increasingly visible during relief and recovery operations. Yet, corporations vary as to the level with which they have integrated the ethos of social responsibility. Some don't engage in it at all, and only a very few have actually developed long term relationships to address disaster response and recovery programming.

The private sector has equal interest in humanitarian outcomes where they operate.

The partnership between TNT and the World Food Programme (WFP) is one example of how the private and non-profit sector have come together to create a synergy where the whole has value in excess of its parts. This relationship has stood the test of time because the focus of the relationship is on a topic integral to the functioning of both organisations: logistics. While it may only seem logical for a company to align its core corporate priorities with its philanthropic or social engagement priorities, this is very often not the case.

According to Andrew Macleod, a former UN Operational Coordinator and Corporate Social Responsibility manager with an Australian mining conglomerate, companies have known for a long time how communities and corporate interests can go hand in hand. Most of them, especially those with overseas interests, understand that they don't operate in a bubble.

BHP Billiton, for example, ran a very effective anti-malaria programme in Mozambique where it operates an aluminium smelter. This programme reduced adult malaria infection from near 80% to less than 10%. But why would a multi-national corporation, one of the world's largest profit- driven enterprises, involve itself with the social issues faced by a poor African country? Of course, such a reduction in infection represents a huge win for the community. But it also had considerable impact on BHP's bottom line, as improved community health reduced absenteeism from 22% to 2%, increasing productivity so significantly that the direct returns more than covered the cost of the programme. In other words, the anti-malaria program did not just pay for itself, it was profitable. In addition, and although only indirectly beneficial to the company, the programme also reduced malaria transmission amongst their employee's children, which not only boosted school attendance – and therefore learning – but created much goodwill towards the company in the community … especially amongst its future 'second generation' recruits.

The Australian based bank ANZ offers another example as it expands throughout the Asia Pacific. Its community development work in places like Fiji, Samoa, and the Cook Islands focuses on financial literacy training programs. Cynics might well say that, in educating people about the workings of small business loans or mortgages, it is just expanding its market. On the other hand, who could deny that better informed people are better able to benefit from other services we take for granted in the developed world? There is an argument for saying that prospering alongside a community empowered by greater skills in budgeting, saving, and money management is not only logical, but ethical.

We will watch how things unfold with the increasing role being assumed by the Cash Management Industry consortium in humanitarian 'cash transfer programming'.

96 *The political economy of cash needs to be better understood.*

Instinctively, we tend to feel that earthquake and flood survivors need food, water and shelter rather than bags of banknotes which they can neither eat nor use to keep warm (banknotes are not made of normal paper, so don't burn very easily). Some people also feel that cash donations will be wasted – stolen, spent on alcohol and cigarettes, or syphoned off by unscrupulous middlemen – if given in place of physical relief items. Apparently not.

The private sector is set to transform humanitarian cash transfer programming.

The World Bank surveyed 19 randomised trials across the world studying cash transfers. Not one of them found evidence that spending on alcohol or tobacco increased by a statistically significant amount when relief commodities were replaced with cash. On the contrary, disaster survivors have better things to do with the money, and often spend it wisely or even invest it successfully. "Concerns about the use of cash transfers for alcohol and tobacco consumption," they concluded, "are unfounded."

Clearly there will be times when cash is useless because there is nothing to buy. But if disaster victims have money, entrepreneurs will scramble to solve logistical problems and supply them with things to spend the money on just as fast as the aid agencies can supply the same items, and probably faster.

Except for a few cases of *market failure* – such as when vitamins and vaccines are needed, for example – refugees are likely to understand their own needs best and just need some help to know which minimum standards and what product quality is acceptable. In the first days after a natural disaster, when there is no access to local supplies, shipments of food and medical supplies may still be vital. And some urgent problems, like treating severe malnourishment with therapeutic feeding, may require the special skills of humanitarian agencies. In scenarios like these, it seems likely that cash will complement rather than replace more traditional forms of aid..

Scientific scrutiny has challenged conventional wisdoms and prejudices. It turns out that cash is used wisely by recipients, and spurs entrepreneurialism rather than trapping people in dependency. A number of rigorous evaluations show that those who receive cash are more likely to start their own business, earn more and send their children to school rather than into work. And giving people cash, rather than food, clothes or livestock, allows recipients to choose what they need, as well as stimulating local markets.

Cash transfers disrupt the traditional model of humanitarian aid – where organisations do things on behalf of people, and derive revenue in the process – though, so remain comparatively rare. Figures are imprecise, but best estimates suggest that 6% of humanitarian aid was being handed over as cash in 2015.

In addition to the World Bank study, two rigorous reviews of economic development programmes in Kenya and Uganda conducted in 2013 by Daniel Masterson of Yale University and Christian Lehmann of the University of Brasilia, also revealed that giving people cash works.

This was the first scientifically rigorous evaluation of emergency cash for refugees, and it unveiled some striking findings:

In the winter of 2013/2014, 90,000 Syrian refugee families facing freezing conditions in the Lebanese mountains were given $100 a month through ATM cards by international aid agencies. For each dollar of cash assistance spent, they found that at least $2.13 was created in local markets, boosting the Lebanese economy. Strikingly, no inflationary impact was found; instead, supply moved to meet demand. In addition, it was found that households receiving cash assistance were half as likely to send their children out to work. Cash also increased access to education, and there was some evidence of reduced tensions within the household and between the refugee and host community.

This research does not mean there is a new humanitarian silver bullet, however: $100 a month does not remedy the trauma and loss of being driven from your country, after all. And there is still work to be done around the circumstances in which different forms of cash distribution work best, how to reach people securely, quickly and reliably, and how to ensure the costs of managing cash are kept down.

In the Philippines, a week after Typhoon Haiyan destroyed much of Tacloban, aid agencies' noble intentions didn't always match the need. In some places, agencies provided a surfeit of cooking utensils, but no food to put in them. When road routes re-opened, tankers brought water from other parts of the Philippines, but no generators for a city without power. Instead, people charged their mobile phones from the batteries of army trucks guarding the water deliveries. At that point, could cash have more efficiently matched the supply of local markets to the demand of survivors?

In low-income societies, people are familiar with cash. They trust it. This doesn't change when disaster strikes. For it's just when dazed survivors realise that modern world conveniences have disappeared, when there is no power, no water, and no food, that they turn to physical currency, cash they can feel and trust.

This is slightly inconvenient for those who think that cash means digital, and digital means going cashless. Why? Because most digital mobile money transfer models, including M-Pesa which we will come on to discuss, rely on the use of physical currency. This has implications for government, the cash management industry, and aid agencies, especially when disaster threatens.

Overall, cash transfer programming offers substantial benefits for beneficiaries, governments, and financial service providers alike. Government finances will be improved because of the reduced burden on subsidies, reduction in 'leakages', and increased political legitimisation which results when the people see "their money" transferred faster, more reliably, more efficiently, and with less opportunity for corruption.

All this having been said, cash transfers are not a 'silver bullet' for eliminating suffering or rectifying the current inefficiencies in aid delivery, but they can go a long way to improving lives and restoring livelihoods in the wake of disaster. Despite this, many in the aid world are unaware of the broad range of societal benefits offered by cash and cling to a number of misperceptions about the usefulness of cash transfers in times of crisis:

Cash Misperception # 1: Cash is redundant. To paraphrase Mark Twain, 'Reports of the death of cash have been greatly exaggerated.' Despite political moves to embrace the utopia of a cashless society, cash remains by far the most used payment instrument across the world.

This cash is made available to the general public primarily through ATMs. By the end of 2014 there were over 3 million ATMs around the world, a figure which is predicted to increase to over 4 million by time of the ATM's 50th anniversary in mid-2017. This means a new ATM is being installed somewhere in the world every three minutes.

Cash Misperception # 2: M-Pesa is the mobile money model to emulate. M-Pesa (*M* stands for mobile and *Pesa* means 'money' in Swahili) is the iconic mobile banking service that led to copycat businesses around the globe. Essentially, it is an electronic payment and store-of-value system accessible through mobile phones which enables the user to send money in electronic form, store money on a mobile phone in an electronic account, and deposit or withdraw money in the form of hard currency.

Lack of in-depth understanding of how the M-Pesa mobile money model actually works in practice, however, has resulted in a situation which is not necessarily in the best interests of those affected by disaster, nor for those for whom financial inclusion represents their best opportunity of clawing their way out of poverty. This is because most digital mobile money transfer models, including M-Pesa, are not virtual, but rely on the use of physical currency. With M-Pesa, it is estimated that over 90% of all mobile payments involve 'cash in' and/or 'cash out' at some point in the cash cycle[lxxvi]. Equity Bank in Nairobi estimates that 98% of the value of all financial transactions in Kenya today are still made in cash. Equally significant is that, though proximity to bank agents in Kenya has increased since 2013, 80% of users still access financial services either through their branch (41%) or via an ATM (38%)[lxxvii].

In light of M-PESA's impressive success and widespread use, it is also perhaps surprising to note that since this mobile money system was introduced, both the velocity (rate of cash use) and volume of currency in circulation in Kenya have actually increased. It is also interesting to note that, according to the ECB[lxxviii], "Most forms of electronic payments seem to be competing for volume with forms of payment other than cash."

Cash Misperception # 3: Cash is apolitical. Moves for entire countries to go cashless are essentially political acts, and are driven in part by a legitimate desire to increase transparency, reduce corruption, and minimise opportunities for tax evasion. But they are also driven by a less legitimate desire to increase the profits of those involved in digital payments. Countries such as Sweden, Denmark, Rwanda and Nigeria have all declared their intent to go 'cashless' (or at least not force retailers to accept physical currency). To achieve this goal, access to cash first has to be restricted. This is done by introducing legislation that limits the use of cash at point-of-sale, reduces the number of ATMs and bank branches, and by allowing charges for ATM withdrawals to remain artificially high.

Bearing in mind Misperception # 1, this tells us is that access to cash is being deliberately restricted in the face of an increasing demand for cash from the general public. It is fair to ask why any industry would actively limit access to a product which is apparently in growing popular demand? This trend will not serve those affected by disaster well, either in the short or the long term. The humanitarian sector should strive to ensure that the full range of payments options are properly considered. Apart from anything else, the 'dignity, humanity and agency' logic of moving from in-kind aid delivery to cash transfers demands that recipients should have the freedom to decide their own priorities and choose their own solutions.

Cash Misperception # 4: Cash is inefficient. There are a number of attributes that distinguish cash from other payment instruments. Firstly, cash is legal tender. That is to say it is a medium of exchange recognised by a country's sovereign and legal system as being valid for meeting financial obligations, both personal and national. Non-cash methods of payment do not comprise legal tender, and are therefore 'un-secured'.

Furthermore, non-cash payment methods are not public goods. As Thierry Lebeaux, CEO of ESTA, a trade association, puts it, "Cash is public money generating public revenue, while electronic money is private money generating private revenue." Promotion of non-cash payments leads to the transfer of risk and shifting of costs to the recipient while creating additional revenue streams for all those involved in the transaction.

It is also worth noting that digital money doesn't recirculate, while physical currency does. This means that, while digital money is creating revenue for those involves in the transaction, it exerts no leveraging affect within local communities. According to a study by the UK's Overseas Development Institute published in 2015, every dollar distributed in the form of humanitarian cash transfers, on the other hand, exerts a 'multiplier' effect within the local economy, generating in the region of $2.4's worth of additional transacting.

Cash Misperception # 5: Cash is insecure. Cash is more secure than supposed. The insecurity of cash is relative and dependent on the online insecurities that come with paying electronically. Of course there are disadvantages in carrying cash around, especially where law and order has broken down. Logic would suggest that those affected by disaster might regard the use of cash as less safe than making card payments or paying electronically by mobile smart phone as a result. But they shouldn't, and for one simple reason: the risk of having their money stolen through cyber-fraud is thousands if not hundreds of thousands of times greater than the risk of being mugged, even in a refugee camp.

Cash Misperception # 6: Cash is inconvenient. Ready cash is a 'safe haven' that forms the foundation for the way we operate socially as well as economically, especially in uncertain economic times. Cash is simple to stockpile prior to a hazard event occurring, and is resistant to systems failures and power outages once it has. Those lucky enough to have early warning of impending disaster – when hurricane or tsunami warnings have been issued, for example – always try to stock up on cash as one of their first priorities if they have the time. ATMs along the Florida and New Jersey shorelines had to be replenished at four times the normal rate as Hurricane Matthew and Super-Storm Sandy approached, and the mayor of Tacloban in the Philippines not only asked the banks to stockpile large quantities of cash but got them to build walls around their ATMs as the storm-surge in front of Typhoon Haiyan approached in December 2014.

The experience of New Zealand's response to the Christchurch earthquake of 2011 explains why cashless payments systems are not applicable in the context of natural disasters. According to Alan Boaden[lxxix], Head of Currency at the Reserve Bank of New Zealand, "Access to physical currency is an immediate priority in times of national emergency, even in a country where 75% of transactions are normally made with electronic payments. In fact, when electronic retail payment systems are not working, electronic payment becomes a vulnerability, not a strength." In terms of lessons learning, he went on to suggest that "local authorities need to work closely with banks and cash-in-transit companies in high-risk areas prior to these types of natural hazards occurring." According to Ecuador's Minister of Finance, it was much the same during Ecuador's response to its earthquake in April 2016. "People are comfortable with cash," he said, "They trust it, and it was our job to invigorate recovery by making sure they had access to it."

Cash Misperception # 7: Cash is expensive. Banknotes have to be printed, stored, and distributed. All this requires insurance, security, machinery, staff, real-time tracking, and linked up IT systems. However, the ECB concluded in 2015 that "cash is less expensive than electronic payments, both for society as a whole and for retailers." This goes against conventional thinking, particularly by those in favour of mobile payments. "On average," the report says, "cash payments show the lowest social costs per transaction ... while merchants would be better off if transactions currently executed with debit cards were instead carried out using cash."

Cash Misperception # 8: Cash is simple. Conducting cash transfers at scale in a disaster zone is a highly complicated and complex undertaking. There is no one-size-fits-all approach for the optimisation of cash management. The availability of, and access to non-cash payment infrastructure – as measured by the number of debit cards issued, point-of-sales terminals available, or percentage of population with a bank account, for example – differs widely per country. The optimal cash cycle also depends on many country specific factors, including culture, geography, the regulatory environment, and the efficiency with which physical currency is recirculated in society.

Cash Misperception # 9: Cash has few indirect societal benefits. For generations, physical money has served a societal role in educating children on both the value of money and how to manage or save it. For largely psychological reasons, this cannot be replicated by non-tangible forms of payment. Cash allows consumers to exert control over their spending habits. A psychological phenomenon known as the 'dissociation effect' ensures that digital-only consumers over-spend by anywhere between 20% and 40%. This not only has short-term

238

implications for the individual beneficiary, but has longer-term implications for aid agency and donor budgets. In addition, humanitarian cash transfers in times of disaster represent not only a more efficient way for donors to donate but also a more efficient way to provide relief to survivors i.e more can be done with less.

When discussing the cost-benefit of any one particular payment instrument over another, the discussion should not be limited to the quantifiable only. Qualifiable elements such as ease-of-use, convenience, access, and availability all need to be factored in, as do other types of non-quantifiable components such as impacts on culture and gender equality.

Cash is also more than a convenient method of payment. For those who are illiterate or for people who find it difficult to manage an electronic budget – and that includes the vast majority of those affected by disasters around the world – cash has a number of important symbolic values: It gives them dignity; it affords choice; and it puts them in charge.

The social impact of the visual imagery printed on banknotes should not be ignored, either. As the later story from Libya makes clear, banknotes are part of the glue of society. As with a flag or a national anthem, they provide a vivid symbol of a country's sovereignty and provide people with a living link to their cultural and historical roots. Many people in society, old and young alike, feel comforted by the presence of physical currency.

Cash Misperception # 10: ATMs are unsuitable for humanitarian action. As has been pointed out already, ATM penetration is increasing in low-income societies, not reducing. Rural ATM networks in the Southern Americas, across Africa and Asia, and from India to the Philippines are expanding. In part this is because governments are keen to stimulate financial inclusion and reduce disaster risk, and have understood the role that ATMs can play in societies in crisis. Like the commercial banks, they recognise that technology – particularly biometric technology – has enabled the ATM's transformation from 'automated teller' to stand-alone 'branchless bank'; that remote operations are increasingly feasible; and that an adequate return on investment is now possible, not just in revenue terms but for society at large.

Decision-makers are unduly swayed by the media.

Natural disasters appear to be just like shark attacks in that they kill and maim without warning, and without apparent discrimination. They also affect us emotionally when they unfold with high drama on our TV screens. But, despite the fact that we know from evidence elsewhere in this book that early warning of impending disaster is almost always possible and that disasters are very discriminating, the media somehow messes with our ability to analyse what is going on correctly. Warren Meyer, writing in his blog in July 2012, gave the following example:

> *"Let's take a step back to 2001 and the 'Summer of the Shark" in the United States. The media hysteria began in early July, when a young boy was bitten by a shark on a beach in Florida. Subsequent attacks received breathless media coverage, up to and including near nightly footage from TV helicopters of swimming sharks. Until the 9/11 attacks, sharks were the third biggest story of the year on the three major broadcast networks' news shows.*
>
> *Throughout this coverage, Americans were left with a strong impression that something unusual was happening; that an unprecedented number of shark attack were occurring that year; and the media dedicated endless coverage to speculation by various 'experts' as to the cause of this sharp increase.*
>
> *Except there was one problem. There was no sharp increase in attacks. In the year 2001, five people died in 76 shark attacks. However, just a year earlier, 12 people had died in 85 attacks. The data showed that 2001 was actually quite a slow year for shark attacks."*

Today's media agenda is like the ocean, so vast and wide we cannot absorb the information being flung at us in the never-ending waves of breaking news. Topics lurch in an apparently random torrent of inaccuracy from one disaster to another and back again, interrupted only by reports about the weather. In its quest to inform and entertain – and thereby improve ratings, and increase advertising spend[117] – the

---

[117] Competition, especially between 24-hour news channels with an audience to win, is ferocious and deluding. Getting there first can mean instant fame for the journalist on

process ineluctably reduces subject matter to the depth of a car park puddle. With little time or energy to delve deeper, our numbed brains fail to separate fact from fiction, and we end up with a spinning head full of half-truths and misconceptions. This risks diminishing the complex nature of what a natural disaster is, and what it does. As the Netflix TV series *Newsroom* put it so well, it is time to challenge this superficiality, and introduce more evidence-based rigour into media reporting about natural disasters.

The tornado that tore through the US town of Moore, Oklahoma in May 2013 causing a shocking swathe of devastation nearly 1.5 kms wide and over 25 kms long is a good example. Given the number of people living in harm's way, it was remarkable that only 24 people were killed by the 320 kph winds. Over 34 TV crews arrived within a matter of hours to broadcast the carnage, the debris of obliterated houses forming a more realistic film set than Hollywood could ever devise. For two days, news channels nationwide and around the world were saturated with coverage of the chaos, and then, just as suddenly as the temporary studios had arrived, they were gone, leaving a bewildered community to pick up the pieces of their shattered world.

Such saturation coverage fuels a false perception among the public of the risk they face from natural hazards like this. While this might be a good thing in terms of waking up local authorities to the preventive action needed – in this case making it mandatory to build basement shelters and enhance early warning systems – it does nothing to convey to the public the relatively low frequency of these types of events ... information needed so that informed choices can be made about where and how to live, and what mitigation measures are worth investing in.

The introduction of evidence-based rigour into media reporting about natural disasters is long overdue.

Clive James, the sardonic Australian TV commentator, once said "it's in the nature of the business", adding, "anyone who has ever been involved in making factual television is all too well aware of how the fictional element creeps in, just by what you choose to shoot, then by what you say to camera – which, in the adrenaline of the moment, is often not what you meant to say exactly – and then by what, in the editing, you choose to discard".

---

the ground, a bonus for the anchor in the studio, and advertising fortune to the station's owner.

But every new disaster in a digital age of social media poses challenges, not least challenges of veracity. Tweeting alleges facts which turn out not to be facts at all. And, with even the poorest having access to a mobile camera-phone nowadays, we are all more and more exposed to the gruesome sights and sounds of disasters unfolding as they happen. These jerky and poor quality shots are then stirred by a sensationalist media who, to feed the 24-7 demand for news, will repeat each tale of woe in horrific detail giving the false impression that more people are dying than actually are; that less is being done to help them than actually is; and the whole response is being managed less efficiently than it could be.

Against this barrage of mis-information, many decisions are taken by politicians unencumbered by any knowledge of what they are facing. This is not their fault, as they are, after all, politicians, not professional disaster managers. But because these same disaster managers have failed to get their message across, it is the media who fill the information vacuum. And they fill it with recycled half-truths more often than they should, mostly because it takes a great deal of money and effort to do otherwise. Perhaps the disaster risk management profession has been unprofessional in failing to educate them?

During the hurricane *Katrina* response in New Orleans, political leaders and disaster managers relied too heavily on the media as a credible source of information. As a US House of Representative's report put it at the time:

> *"We focused assets and resources based on situational awareness provided to us by the media ... frankly. And the media failed in their responsibility to get the story right.*
>
> *We sent forces and capabilities to places they didn't need to go in numbers far in excess of what was required, because they kept running the same footage over and over ... and the impression to us that were watching was that conditions were not changing.*
>
> *Accurate reporting was foremost among Katrina's many victims. If anyone rioted, it was the media. Many stories were at best unsubstantiated, at worst simply false."*

This is not just an American phenomenon. After the Asian tsunami of 2004, relief agencies identified water quality as critical, and the displaced were housed in small well-spaced camps rather than in large, overcrowded facilities. These two preventive measures in Sri Lanka further mitigated the already unlikely potential for a cholera outbreak. Heightened media attention, however, encouraged rumours and triggered investigations ultimately with negative findings. In spite of the lack of risk factors and absence of evidence, around mid-April 2005 a cholera immunisation campaign targeting 150,000 people began using a new oral vaccine of unproven efficacy. Every individual more than two years old received two doses at two week intervals.

As discussed in Disaster Misperception # 57, there is no evidence that indicates a heightened risk of cholera epidemic following sudden-onset disasters due to natural hazards in general, and this was even less the case in Sri Lanka given the pre-existing profile of the disease.

In the evaluations which followed, it was found that the media's sensationalist reporting influenced decision-makers who were not emergency health professionals into carrying out an expensive and futile campaign; that the funds used could have been applied to more important interventions elsewhere; and that risk assessment based on epidemiological evidence should always inform response measures.

As the world's media increasingly relies on the repetition of compelling visual imagery to gain and retain viewers, there is a corresponding focus on mega-disasters. This 'CNN effect' is nothing new and sees a few select mega-disasters get the lion's share of attention while hundreds of smaller disasters are overlooked completely. There are many small and medium-sized disasters, as well as enormous slow-onset chronic disasters, where access to the people affected, to information, and to the media gives a false impression of what is going on.

In Haiti in 2010, the earthquake occurred in an urban setting in the poorest country of the Western hemisphere. In Pakistan the "slow-motion tsunami" that was the 2010 flood took place not just over enormous swathes of land over months but in a volatile political environment. It also affected more people than the 2004 Indian Ocean tsunami, the 2010 Haiti earthquake and the 2005 Pakistan earthquake combined. While all this was going on, and almost unnoticed by the international media, massive floods in China affected nearly 7 times as many people as the floods in Pakistan and topped the list of natural disasters in 2010 in terms of affected population.

Television is a visual electronic medium which, when it covers disasters, focuses on the 'right now' drama of what Professor Katherine Fry in her book *Constructing the Heartland* calls "the beautiful and the horrid". Certain types of natural disaster are considered newsworthy just because of the pure drama of the collision between nature and human endeavour which TV is uniquely able to convey ... volcanoes spewing lava, earthquakes collapsing buildings, landslides carrying away whole mountainsides. The number of people affected, and the economic consequences are secondary.

But TV does not just capture and relay drama. TV creates drama in the way language is employed; the way subjects, images, camera shots, and computer graphics are chosen; and the way sequences are massaged and edited together. News segments are becoming more dense, faster paced, and graphics are becoming better designed. Words are few and secondary to the visual imagery. Moving pictures move people in ways that print media cannot, but leave out a lot of important information in the process, filling in the gaps with sensory information that "excites the eye". The viewer's focus is trained on the movement of the moment, not the descriptive and considered.

Politicians and disaster officials are not impervious to this, and, as the earlier story demonstrates, fully admit to making operational decisions as the disaster unfolds based as much on TV news coverage as on direct feedback from first responders on the ground. Given the limitations and agendas of the medium, this has major implications for the way disasters are portrayed and disaster risk is managed before, during, and after the event[118].

98 *It is possible, indeed necessary, to put a value on human life.*

After the terrorist attacks on Paris in November 2015, an outpouring of grief and solidarity erupted in the twitter-sphere. People from all corners of the globe cried, sent flowers, and daubed their Facebook profiles in the tricolour of France. Attacks in Nigeria, Kenya, Yemen and the Lebanon in the weeks leading up to this massacre killed more people on each occasion than the 132 murdered in Paris. Yet these incidents went largely unnoticed and provoked no public outcry. Why the difference?

Because some people – perhaps most people – perceive a French life to be 'worth' more than a Yemeni, Nigerian, Kenyan or Lebanese one. It

---

[118] The news media have several responsibilities when reporting on natural disaster, and guidelines exist for news reporters, editors, producers and other TV executives to follow by way of fulfilling their public service and ethical obligations. They can be found at www.isdr.org

doesn't matter that Paris might be more familiar to them, or that they love everything French because they once munched a baguette in the Côte D'Azur; the fact is, the 'value' of a human life is a relative measure, not an absolute one.

At the same time, not everything that counts can be counted, and not everything of value can be valued. Nevertheless, to arrive at the right choice when it comes to preventing avoidable death and destruction requires assigning 'value' to human life. This suddenly makes things more difficult as putting a value on human life is abhorrent to many, and the ethical issues it raises are always controversial. But ignoring the issue implicitly considers people as useless, passive victims … and it would be equally unethical and unfortunate if property were to be protected but lives were not. This, anyway, is the argument put forward by the insurance industry for which such decisions are their bread and butter.

The humanitarian imperative says that intervention should take place according solely to need … implicitly suggesting that this should be regardless of cost. Unfortunately, we live in a world of scarcity which makes such lofty ambition unrealistic. Disaster risk managers don't have the luxury of not having to choose between competing priorities, and have to make life and death decisions all the time. They do this by preferring actions that demonstrate the highest cost-to-benefit ratio … or, at least, they should.

Deep ethical and philosophical factors have to be considered when attaching value to human life. This is especially true when decisions affect others, as almost all do when considering disaster preparedness and response priorities. Preventing a disaster befalling one group may not reduce the risk for everyone; it may simply shift the risk to others who will be adversely affected, even if these are fewer in number, have less earning potential, and their possessions have lower value.

Building an embankment, for example, diverts flood water from one place to another, and in doing so may reduce death and destruction upstream while merely increasing it later downstream. Such prevention measures also skew the probability distribution in as much that those protected by the embankment from smaller flood events face a far greater risk should the embankment fail … a result that becomes more and more likely over time as rivers silt up, flow rates from increased snowmelt and rainfall rise, and maintenance budgets reduce.

The *Value of Statistical Life* (VSL) is often used in cost-benefit analysis. Despite the obvious moral flaws and biases involved, the VSL has been estimated at $960,000 in Santiago, Chile (based on 1992 purchasing power parity and annual inflation since then of 2.38 percent), $413,000 in Taiwan, and $250,000 in rural Thailand. Another analysis suggests that VSL would be 60 times annual income in low-income societies[lxxx] which suggests numbers as low as $150,000 in some countries of Sub-Saharan Africa[119]. By way of comparison, the compensation paid to the families of US soldiers killed in Afghanistan is $600,000.

But the VSL concept has limitations because what is 'lost' when someone dies cannot be captured; it cannot reflect the 'value' put on pain and suffering, for example. How is the loss of the head of the family costed versus the loss of a daughter? How does the loss of five goats and two cows compare against the destruction of a water well?

In practice, disaster managers don't use VSL but do their cost-benefit analyses by calculating the injuries avoided or deaths averted in terms of *Disability Adjusted Life Years* (DALYs)[120]. In essence, the costs of the programme, minus its non-health benefits, can be divided by the DALYs saved to calculate a cost per DALY avoided. The big advantage of this approach is that it provides a way of comparing costs across different policies, strategies, programmes, and places at different times. This encourages consistency in decision making, and allows for more objective planning when it comes to project prioritisation.

The concept of 'life years lost' was used for the first time to make such comparisons at the macro level in the ISDR Global Assessment Report on Disaster Risk Reduction in March 2015 when it stated, "42 million life years were lost (due to disasters) every year between 1980-2012, a setback to human development on a par with the (global) toll wrought by Tuberculosis."

At the more local level, the table overleaf [lxxxi] was used in Haiti when planning the cholera control response in September 2010 to advocate for measures other than vaccination, an unproven and expensive technology which is itself not entirely without risk.

The challenge for planners when using tables like this is to interpret what the data is saying. The data alone is not enough; it is providing information across a range of options which have to be understood not only in terms of knowing the implications of each, but understanding

---

[119] Based on Sierra Leone where mean per capita income per month is estimated at $210 (Source: CIA Handbook, 2011)

[120] One DALY can be thought of as one lost year of healthy life. Quality Adjusted Life Years (QALYs) can also be used.

their inter-dependencies. It is not just a question of, "washing hands with soap is better than vaccination."

Interventions against Diarrhoeal Disease	Cost-Effectiveness ratio ($ per DALY averted)
Cholera Immunisation	1,658 - 8,274
Measles Immunisation	257 - 4,565
Oral Rehydration Therapy	132 - 2,570
Breastfeeding Promotion	527 - 2,001
Latrine construction	270
Water supply by truck	233
Hygiene Promotion	3

Another possible solution is to use 'microlives' and 'micromorts'. A microlife is one millionth of an adult lifespan – about half an hour – and a micromort is a one-in-a-million chance of dying. According to Tim Harford, the 'undercover economist' for the Financial Times, The National Health Service in the UK uses analysis that prices a microlife at about £1.70 which allows the UK's Department of Transport to spend £1.60 to prevent a micromort. "In a world where life-and-death trade-off's have to be made and faced squarely, this is a less horrible way to think about it all," he says. "A human life is a special thing; a microlife, not so much."

Assigning such figures might seem crass, but such valuations are routine in our daily lives, not least by insurance companies who have to determine how much coverage they'll allow customers and at what level the premiums should be set.

That said, it was Kant in 1785 who said that "no pricing structure does justice to the dignity of human life". Since some of the benefits of disaster risk reduction programmes are therefore priceless, any monetary value of total benefits will necessarily be incomplete.

Assigning value to human life also leads to the ethically embarrassing conclusion that the poor count for less because they earn less, and cannot afford to pay as much to reduce life-threatening risks. In other words, human lives are not valued at the same rate in developed and developing countries. As uncomfortable as it may be, the reality is that we don't actually think of all people as equal. If we did, there would be many more properly functioning hospitals and health clinics in developing countries.

99 Politicians are legally accountable for the impact of natural hazard events.

According to the still-dominant view of natural disaster, these hazard events are understood by scientists, the media, and technocrats as primarily accidents – unexpected, unpredictable happenings – that are the price of doing business on the planet. Seen in this way, as freak events removed from people's everyday interactions with the environment, they are positioned outside the moral compass of our culture. As a result, no one can be held accountable for them.

Furthermore, there is an argument that natural disasters not only bear a strong human component, but that those in power — politicians, local municipal authorities, and corporate executives — have tended to view these events as purely natural in an effort to justify a set of responses that makes them as leaders seem indispensable.

An 'Act of God' is a legal term for an event considered outside human control, and for which no single person or entity can be held responsible. Until recently, 'Acts of God' have therefore been insurable 'accidents' and valid excuses for non-performance of a contract.

In tort law, an 'Act of God' is a naturally occurring phenomenon that either could not realistically have been predicted or, if it could have been, the consequences could not have been realistically prevented.

In contract law, an 'Act of God' may be interpreted as an implied defence under the rule of impossibility or impracticability. If so, the promise is discharged because of unforeseen occurrences, which were unavoidable and would result in insurmountable delay, expense, or other material breach. Such an indemnification may be no excuse, and in fact may be the central risk assumed by the promisor – e.g. flood insurance – the only variables being the timing and extent of the damage. In more and more cases, failure by way of ignoring obvious risks due to "natural phenomena" will not be sufficient to excuse performance of the obligation, even if the events are relatively rare.

So, foreseeable results of unforeseeable causes may still raise liability.

For example, if members of the public are electrocuted when a storm-surge downs power lines through which current is still passing, liability may be found if the local authority did not adequately compel the utility company to take reasonable care to protect against such an eventuality by, say, investing in automatic isolator switches.

This scenario took place in New York during the passage of Super-Storm Sandy in 2012 and again in Tacloban, Indonesia during the passage of Typhoon Yolanda in 2013. In both cases, the Mayors are being sued for billions of US dollars by victims' families. Legal observers suggest they will not be found liable. But Mayors and insurance companies around the world are paying close attention, as more and more becomes known about the risks posed by natural hazards and how their likely impacts can be prevented.

Epilogue

IT JUST MAY BE THAT THE world of mountaineering provides the perfect metaphor for what is happening to the planet disaster-wise.

A freakish unseasonal avalanche in the French Alps in July 2012 killed nine climbers, and another buried four more in Alaska at more or less the same time. Both 'natural hazards' occurred in places where avalanches don't usually happen, and especially not at that time of year; a situation which has scientists and mountain guides alike agreeing that patterns from the past can no longer be relied upon for determining risk when out climbing. Tucker Chenowath, Chief Ranger at Mount McKinley in Alaska said at the time that, "Abnormal is the new normal. Extremes appear to be becoming more extreme. And the chances of having an average year appear to be reducing".

"In a strange kind of way," he went on, "wild places like Mount McKinley seem to be getting wilder ... or at least harder to predict".

Since November 2011, at least 34 people in the US alone have been killed by avalanches, and three of the four worst years for fatalities since 1950 have occurred in the past five years, according to the US National Information Centre in Colorado.

Sharper seasonal variations of ice, snow and temperature are being repeated elsewhere across the mountaineering world, from the Himalayas to the Andes, which climatologists say are driven by higher levels of energy in the atmosphere. As a result, climbers have to think twice about what conditions they might expect one year to the next – or even one day to the next – in places they have been climbing for decades. The chances of having an average year are reducing.

Compounding the consequences of this apparent shift is that the biggest changes in the mountains are happening not at the upper elevations, where the risks and challenges are usually the greatest, but much lower down, where wider, more frequent, and faster temperature swings are weakening hitherto unseen fractures in glacial ice and rock. A weather station on Mount McKinley recorded a temperature range from 21°F above zero to 13°F below over a single 48 hour period in 2012, with 60 cms of snow falling in-between. This violent fluctuation is rare at any time, but especially in July.

Venturing into high and wild places has always carried its dangers, of course, and mountain weather, as even a casual day hiker knows, is invariably capricious. But, when more and more people are seeking adventure in zones of more variable risk – as they are – the frequency with which man collides with nature can only rise. And disaster is sure to follow when it does.

Climbing mountains could never be considered a sport for the risk averse, but, given the range of mitigation measures that climbers take – from equipment, to training, to planning, to evacuation procedures – could it be that the whole balance of risk – the hazard, the exposure, and the climber's vulnerability – has swung in favour of the mountain, and has reached the point where we have to analyse risk in a new, more evidence-based, light?

It should not be possible, or acceptable, for large numbers of people to die in natural disasters.

For those of us who are not mountaineers, we have seen the future. It's laid out for us in apocalyptic films such as *Mad Max*, *Legion*, and *The Book of Eli*. Because of our rapaciousness, the world's resources deplete to the point that society implodes. Anyone with a tattoo, a gun, and some ammunition survives, while everyone else dies.

Disaster movies, on the other hand, don't confront us with our fallibility in quite such brutal fashion, and, in showing us how nature intends to kill us, comfort us in the knowledge that the extinction of our species is somehow not our fault. Disasters are 'natural' accidents, unexpected and unpredictable happenings removed from our everyday interactions with ourselves and the environment is the sense they convey.

Furthermore, while the heroes survive, these freak events remain positioned outside the moral compass of our culture, and, as a result, no one can be held accountable for them. We forge on, eyes wide shut, aware but oblivious of our responsibilities. This is probably what John Holmes, a former UN bigwig, was implying when he said in 2010, "we are, to a certain extent, sleepwalking our way into disaster".

The 'four drivers of the apocalypse' – poverty, population growth, urban migration, and ecological change – are changing the world's risk profile. In an article in February 2011, The Lancet, a respected UK medical Journal, concluded that, "Natural disasters will be more frequent in coming years if unplanned urbanisation and environmental degradation continue ... and if it there are increases in weather-related events." They went on, "future emergency responses need to be better aligned with longer-term perspectives looking at key socio-economic investments, infrastructure and preparedness planning for disaster if more lives are to be saved".

The article was right on a number of levels: In the modern world, it should not be possible, or acceptable, for large numbers of people to die in natural disasters such as earthquakes, volcanic eruptions, or landslides. These are well understood phenomena, and the science has existed for some time for us to understand how they happen, and when and where they might strike. And yet, sudden manifestations of these forces of nature continue to kill thousands, or even hundreds of thousands, of people at a time.

So, if we know what to do, why are there so many avoidable tragedies on our TV screens? Why do some schools become death traps during earthquakes? Why are so many trees chopped down on already unstable slopes, making it almost inevitable that a mud-slide will result the next time it rains hard? Why were 20 million people washed out of their mud-brick homes in Pakistan in 2010 when extensive flooding was forecast days in advance? And why is it that the less than 2% of the $24 billion spent on humanitarian assistance every year is devoted to reducing disaster risk?

Some of the answer lies in the shifting demographics; the simple fact that the planet has more people on it now, and even though the number of people vulnerable to hazard events has declined proportionately, this smaller proportion of the larger total means more people are exposed overall.

Another part of the answer lies in the weather. Despite there being no evidence for this at the moment, we are told that weather-related events – hurricane-force winds, storm-surges, floods and, to a certain extent, landslides and droughts – are going to increase in magnitude, if not in frequency. Such events will inevitably impact on the vagaries of human nature to result in disaster.

But perhaps the fact that risk reduction programmes are extremely complex in nature and complicated to put into practice has a lot to do with it too. Engineering solutions are expensive, especially when outcomes are so uncertain. Mayors and Ministers are no different to the rest of us in tending to discount low-probability-high-impact hazards, and seem reluctant to invest in disaster risk management as a result. Despite the magnitude of disaster costs, and the proven cost-benefits, reducing disaster risk is often perceived as less of a priority than mending the street lights or filling in the potholes. There are few votes in spending money on preparing for something which may not happen.

There is also a perverse political incentive. Political leaders have always understood the symbolic power of responding to disasters, especially natural disasters. Saving lives and assisting disaster victims is a moral, humanitarian, and political imperative that few would contest. As such, disaster relief is a powerful tool for leaders, enhancing their political profile and facilitating patronage. In contrast, the incentives for reducing disaster risk, a public good, are far less visible and far less obvious. The benefits also take longer to accrue than democratic election cycles allow.

In an ideal world, though, national and local authorities would prevent as much at risk as is cost-efficient, reduce or transfer what they can of the remaining risk, and then, recognising that there will always be residual risk, prepare for it. You would think that such an approach by those authorities whose job it is to protect us – our elected officials and public servants – would be obligatory. But it isn't.

Ultimately, it comes down to economic fundamentals and on deciding how much risk we can afford to accept. But the costs of ignoring disaster risk are substantial. Not making decisions on reducing urban disaster risk is to accept high numbers of deaths, extensive damage, disruption to business, prolonged economic decline, and lost opportunity for years, if not generations.

A paradigm shift is needed from post-disaster compensation for reconstruction and recovery to pre-disaster investment in risk management and adaptation. This requires investment in enhanced early warning systems, better land-use planning, the establishment of sustainable insurance systems, and the building of resilient infrastructure such as hazard-resistant hospitals, schools, transportation systems, ports, energy grids, water treatment plants, and communications systems. It also requires the much cheaper, but much more difficult expedient of informing the people, so that we may be made aware of the risks facing us and know what options are available to confront those risks ourselves.

While this shift relies on political and technical innovation, it is the economic dimension that will ultimately be the foundation for change by developing incentives and market mechanisms to align actions among national and local governments, the private sector, and civil society toward greater resilience. Working with communities to enable them to prepare for, cope with, and adapt to, future hazards at the local level is the key.

To achieve this, all of us need to take greater responsibility for protecting ourselves and those around us. However, we also need to demand greater accountability than we do now from our elected representatives for reducing our vulnerability to so-called natural hazards in the first place.

The traditional discourse from those whose livelihoods depend on disasters continuing to occur is that the pace at which we are creating exposure to hazard risk has become greater than the pace at which we are reducing our vulnerability to it.

Disaster Epidemiology provides decision-makers with the evidence they need to confront hard choices.

But when some of the long-held myths are unpacked, something else suggests itself: We know what to do, but we're just not doing it.

Scepticism might linger over the true nature of climate change, its causes and effects, and more attention is already being paid to slow-onset disasters driven by such things as over-fishing, de-forestation, dependence on certain crops, sea-level rise, and excessive extraction of groundwater. But, as the response to typhoon *Yolanda* so cruelly demonstrated to the people of the Philippines at the end of 2013 and the *Ghorka* Earthquake to the people of Nepal in 2015, resources are never enough. And it is here, in this vortex of competing priorities and misinformation, that the discipline of disaster epidemiology provides decision-makers, opinion-formers, and disaster planners with the evidence they need to confront hard and potentially unpopular choices.

It is true that responses to natural hazard events are better organised and more systematic nowadays as people become more aware of the risks facing them and the mitigation options available. After all, as Professor Myles Allen of Oxford University once put it, "people deserve to know how much natural disasters affect them ... and we have the methods to answer that question".

Local authorities the world over, as well as elected officials, foreign diplomats, the media, NGOs, and the first responders that work with them, have no option but to sit up and take note, as citing an "Act of God" and being unaware of what disaster epidemiology is telling us all, will no longer suffice as a plausible defence against inaction.

Glossary

DEFINITIONS THAT RELATE TO natural disasters are from the international agreed glossary of basic terms related to 'disaster risk management'. (See www.emdat.be and www.isdr.org)

Note: *Certain words used regularly in public health settings and international conventions have distinct and very different connotations in other areas.*

Accountability

Accountability is a concept in ethics and governance often used synonymously with such concepts as responsibility and liability, and with the expectation of an individual being called to account. In leadership roles, accountability is the acknowledgment and assumption of responsibility for actions, products, decisions, and policies including the administration, governance, and implementation within the scope of the role or employment position. It encompasses the obligation to report, explain and be answerable for consequences of actions taken or not taken. Only individuals, not organisations, can be held to account.

Adaptation

The adjustment in natural or human systems in response to actual or expected climatic stimuli or their effects, which moderates harm or exploits beneficial opportunities.

Affected Population
Those who, at least for a time, either lost their homes, crops, animals, livelihoods, or their health because of the disaster.

Agent
A pathogen, toxin or substance that causes disease or other health effects by infection, poisoning or other means.

Attack Rate
In epidemiology, an attack rate is the cumulative incidence of infection in a group of people observed over a period of time during an epidemic. Quantitatively, it is the number of exposed people infected with the disease divided by the total number of exposed people. As an example, if there are 70 people taken ill out of 98 in an outbreak, the attack rate is 70 ÷ 98 = 0.714 or about 71 %. The term should probably not be described as a rate because its time dimension is uncertain. For this reason, it is often referred to as an attack ratio.

Biological Hazard
Process or phenomenon of organic origin or conveyed by biological vectors, including exposure to pathogenic micro-organisms, toxins and bioactive substances that may cause loss of life, injury, illness or other health impacts, property damage, loss of livelihoods and services, social and economic disruption, or environmental damage.

Case Fatality Ratio
In epidemiology, the case fatality rate is the ratio of deaths within a designated population of people with a particular condition, over a certain period of time. An example of a fatality rate would be 9 deaths per 10,000 people at risk per year. This means that within a given year, out of 10,000 people formally diagnosed with a disease, 9 died.

Climate Change
The climate of a place or region is changed if over an extended period (typically decades or longer) there is a statistically significant change in measurements of either the mean state or variability of the climate for that place or region.

Communicable Diseases
Communicable Diseases are illnesses caused by micro-organisms transmitted from an infected person or animal to another person or

animal. All infectious diseases are, by definition, communicable but the same is not true the other way around. Some diseases can be spread only indirectly, usually through contaminated food or water, e.g., typhoid, cholera, and dysentery. Still other infections are introduced into the body by animal or insect carriers, e.g., rabies, malaria, and encephalitis. These are communicable but not infectious diseases.

Contingency Planning
A management process that analyses specific potential events or emerging situations that might threaten society or the environment and establishes arrangements in advance to enable timely, effective and appropriate responses to such events and situations.

Coping Capacity
The means by which people or organisations use available resources and abilities to face adverse consequences that could lead to a disaster. In general, this involves managing resources, both in normal times as well as during crises or adverse conditions. The strengthening of coping capacities usually builds resilience to withstand the effects of natural and human-induced hazards.

Consensus Management
Is the antithesis of a 'macho', top-down management style based on hierarchical (often military) models comprising levels of authority, unity of command, line control, and staff function. It is instead based on a participatory approach where the representation is collective, rather than individual. This style of management does not imply dilution of responsibility or accountability, rather the transferring of authority to a network or partnership. These relationships may be 'formalised' using 'Memoranda of Understanding', or equivalent, but nevertheless remain fluid and dynamic.

Coordination
The management science of realising maximal allocative efficiencies where the contrary forces of inter-dependence and competition interact. Clusters assume a 'coordinating' function that oscillates between facilitation and cooperation. Its role is to complement, and, where government is dysfunctional or non-existent, to supplement government capacity to lead and manage sectoral aspects of crisis; to act independently as 'honest broker' in advising all stakeholders of appropriate technical and managerial (best-) practices; and to facilitate

consensual decision-making (including through enhanced information management systems).

We **coordinate** in an effort to reach common goals with no duplication and no gaps. We **cooperate** when we agree not to work at cross-purposes (by sharing knowledge, learning and building consensus, for example), and have an intention to help each other as need arises. And we **collaborate** when we have an intended result in mind – something we all want to create.

Cost Benefit Analysis

This refers to the process of quantifying costs and benefits of a decision, program, or project over a defined period, and making a comparison with its alternatives in order to make a rational decision. For example, when considering its emergency shelter distribution plan for the earthquake response in Yogyakarta, Indonesia in 2006, IFRC had to decide whether to provide one tarpaulin for every affected family or two per family as suggested in the Cluster's 'strategic operational framework' (SOF). Either half the affected people received adequate shelter materials or the entire affected population received half of what was needed. A second distribution would be required if opting for the latter, a decision which would more than double operational overheads. Such decisions about how to prioritise the allocation of scarce resources are made every day by relief planners. This example also shows that, though employed mainly in financial analysis, a CBA is not limited to monetary considerations only; it often includes those environmental and social costs and benefits that can be reasonably quantified.

Critical Infrastructure

Physical and information technology facilities, networks, services and assets that, if disrupted or destroyed, would have a serious impact on health, safety, security or economic well-being or the effective functioning of governments. This infrastructure relates to: information and communication; electric power generation, transmission, and distribution; oil and gas storage and distribution; banking and finance; transport; water supply; and emergency assistance.

Crush Injury (linked with Compartment Syndrome)

Crush injury begins with direct pressure on muscle cells which causes them to switch to anaerobic metabolism which generates large amounts of lactic acid. This process occurs during the first hour after suffering the crush. The force of the crush also compresses blood vessels, resulting in loss of blood supply to muscle tissue. Normally, muscle can withstand approximately four hours without blood flow before cell death occurs. These mechanisms cause the injured muscle tissue to generate and release a number of substances that become toxic when released back into the body's general circulation. The crushing force actually serves as a protective mechanism, preventing these toxins from reaching the central circulation. Once the patient is extricated and the force is released, however, the toxins are free to travel around the body and exert their effects systemically. They can affect organs far from, and not involved in, the local crush injury, with the leakage continuing for as long as 60 hours after release.

Crush Injury Syndrome is often accompanied by Compartment Syndrome. Muscle groups are surrounded by tough layers of fascia tissue that form compartments. When the muscle tissue in these compartments swells, the pressure within the compartment increases. This leads to further muscle damage. Also, any blood vessels or nerves that travel through that compartment will be injured.

Diminishing Returns

This is the concept in economics that says if one factor is increased while other factors are held constant, the resulting increase in output will level-off after some time and then decline despite the continuing input. In the humanitarian world, an example might be when the (marginal) cost of reaching an isolated village at the top of the mountain takes up so much time, money, and effort, that the gain in terms of improved health outcomes for the villagers is considered no longer worth it when compared to how many extra villages could be reached for the same effort and at the same cost in the valley. In everyday experience, this law is expressed as "the gain is not worth the pain."

Disability and Quality Adjusted Life Year (DALY & QALY)

DALYs and QALYs are complementary concepts which allow like-for-like comparisons to be made across time and space concerning burdens of disease or the impact of disaster.

QALYs are years of healthy life lived, whereas DALY's are years of healthy life lost. Both approaches multiply the number of years by the quality of those years. QALYs use utility weights of health states. DALYs use 'disability weights' to reflect the burden of the same states. DALYs combine information about morbidity and mortality in numbers of healthy years lost (to disease or disaster). Each state of health – loss of an arm due to snakebite, for example – is assigned a disability weighting on a scale from zero (perfect health) to one (death) by an expert panel. To calculate the burden of a certain disease or disaster-related injury, the disability weighting is multiplied by the number of years lived in that state and is added to the number of years lost due to that state. Future burdens are discounted at 3% per year, and the value of the lifetime is weighted so that years of childhood and old age count for less.

For example, the disability weight of deafness is 0.67, hence a utility weight of 0.33 (=1- 0.67). Disregarding age weighting and discounting, and assuming a life expectancy of 80 years, a deaf man aged 50 represents 0.67x50=33.4 QALYs gained and 0.33x50+30x1=46.6 DALYs lost

Disaster

A serious disruption of the functioning of a community or a society causing widespread human, material, economic or environmental losses which exceed the ability of the affected community or society to cope using its own resources.

Disaster Risk

The potential disaster losses, in lives, health status, livelihoods, assets and services, which could occur to a particular community or a society over some specified future time period. Disaster risk comprises different types of potential losses which are often difficult to quantify. Nevertheless, with knowledge of the prevailing hazards and the patterns of population and socio-economic development, disaster risks can be assessed and mapped.

Disaster Risk Management

The systematic process of using administrative decisions, organisation, operational skills and capacities to implement policies, strategies and coping capacities of society and communities to lessen the impacts of natural hazards and related environmental and technological disasters. This comprises all forms of activities, including structural and non-structural measures to avoid (prevention) or to limit (mitigation and preparedness) adverse effects of hazards, as well as coordination of response actions.

Disaster (Risk) Reduction

The conceptual framework of elements considered with the possibilities to minimise vulnerabilities and disaster risks throughout a society, to avoid (prevention) or to limit (mitigation and preparedness) the adverse impacts of hazards, within the broad context of sustainable development. The disaster risk reduction framework is composed of the following fields of action, as described in ISDR's 2002 publication Living with Risk: A Global Review of Disaster Reduction Initiatives:

- Risk awareness and assessment including hazard analysis and vulnerability/capacity analysis.
- Knowledge development including education, training, research and information.
- Public commitment and institutional frameworks, including organisational, policy, legislation and community action.
- The application of measures including environmental management, land-use and urban planning, protection of critical facilities, the application of science and technology, partnership and networking, and financial instruments.
- Early warning systems including forecasting, dissemination of warnings, preparedness measures and reaction capacities.

The October 2005 earthquake and the July-August 2010 floods in Pakistan demonstrated that years of development efforts can be wiped out more or less overnight by disasters. Moreover, it is the most vulnerable, those already with the least access to services and resources that bear the greatest impact of disasters. If DRR is not systematically integrated into plans, programmes and practices, this pattern is likely to continue with greater intensity and frequency due to increased exposure, poor development practices, environmental degradation and climate change. Disasters will thereby continue to seek out the most vulnerable, and ensure that they remain so!

Disasters are not only tragedies but also opportunities to do things differently and introduce good practice. Recovery efforts must avoid creating new risks and exacerbating existing ones. Recovery is an important opportunity to build back better and enhance the resilience towards future disasters.

The strategic and conceptual challenges are to 1) make a clear distinction between hazards and risk, 2) adopt a multi-hazard approach, 3) perceive disasters as failures of development, and 4) expand the emergency focus from preparedness and response to include prevention and mitigation.

Disease Surveillance
The ongoing, systematic collection, collation, analysis, and interpretation of data on specific health events for use in planning, implementing, monitoring, evaluating and learning lessons from public health programmes.

Drought
Period of deficiency of moisture in the soil such that there is inadequate water required for plants, animals and human beings.

Early Warning
The provision of timely and effective information, through identified institutions, that allows individuals exposed to a hazard to take action to avoid or reduce their risk and prepare for effective response. Early warning systems include a chain of concerns, namely: understanding and mapping the hazard; monitoring and forecasting impending events; processing and disseminating understandable warnings to political authorities and the population, and undertaking appropriate and timely actions in response to the warnings.

Endemic
An infection is said to be endemic in a population when that infection is maintained in the population without external inputs. For example, chickenpox is endemic (steady state) in the UK, but malaria is not.

Environmental Health
The intentional modification of the natural and built environment to reduce risks to human health or to provide opportunities to improve health.

Epidemic
The occurrence of more cases of an infectious or communicable disease than would be expected in a defined community or geographic area over a given period of time.

Epidemiological Investigation
A process used to identify how suspected human cases of a disease occurred, to assess the clinical impact of the disease or condition, and to determine the risk that infected or contaminated people or their environment may represent for others.

Exposure

People, property, systems, or other elements present in hazard zones that are thereby subject to potential losses. Measures of exposure can include the number of people or types of assets in an area. These can be combined with the specific vulnerability of the exposed elements to any particular hazard to estimate the quantitative risks associated with that hazard in the area of interest.

False Negative

A result that appears negative when it should not. An example of a false negative would be if a rapid diagnostic test designed to detect Malaria returns a negative result, but the person actually does have the disease.

False Positive

A result that indicates a given condition is present when it is not. An example of a false positive would be if a rapid test designed to detect malaria returns a positive result for presence of parasites, but the person does not have malaria.

Famine

Catastrophic food shortage affecting large numbers of people due to climatic, environmental and socioeconomic reasons.

Feasibility Study

In humanitarian terms, this is an analysis and evaluation of a proposed project to determine if it is:

- technically feasible with respect to the quality, quantity, and appropriateness of the technology available
- feasible within the allocated budget
- constrained by socio-cultural realities or physical access
- can be completed within the timeframe foreseen given known logistical constraints, and
- will confer the intended benefit on the target disaster-affected population.

Flood

Significant rise of water level in a stream, lake, reservoir or coastal region.

Fujita Scale

The Enhanced Fujita (EF) Scale represents likely tornado damage by aligning wind speed with historical storm damage in five categories:

EF-0:   65-85 mph (105-137 km/h), minor damages, tree branches broken.

EF-1:   86-110 mph (138-178 km/h), roofs stripped, mobile homes pushed off foundation or overturned.

EF-2:   111-135 mph (179-218 km/h), considerable damage, mobile homes demolished, trees uprooted.

EF-3:   136-165 mph (219-266 km/h), roofs and walls torn down, trains overturned, cars thrown.

EF-4:   166-200 mph (267-322 km/h), well-constructed walls leveled, cars thrown and small missiles generated.

EF-5:   >200 mph (>322 km/h), homes lifted off foundation and carried considerable distances, cars thrown as far as 100 meters.

Geological Hazard

Natural earth processes or phenomena that may cause loss of life or injury, property damage, social and economic disruption, or environmental degradation. Geological hazards include internal earth processes of tectonic origin, such as earthquakes, geological fault activity, tsunamis, volcanic activity and emissions, as well as external processes such as mass movements: landslides, rock slides, rock falls or avalanches, surface collapses, expansive soils and debris or mud flows. Geological hazards can be single, sequential or combined in their origin and effects.

Geographic Information Systems (GIS)

An analysis that combines relational databases with spatial interpretation and outputs often in the form of maps. A more elaborate definition is computer programmes for capturing, storing, checking, integrating, analysing and displaying data about the earth that is spatially referenced. Geographical information systems are increasingly being utilized for hazard and vulnerability mapping and analysis, as well as for the application of disaster risk management measures.

Hazard

A potentially damaging physical event, phenomenon or human activity that may cause loss of life or injury, property damage, social and economic disruption, or environmental degradation. Hazards can include latent conditions that may represent future threats and can have different origins: natural (geological, hydro-meteorological or biological) or induced by human processes (environmental degradation and technological hazards). Hazards can be single, sequential or combined in their origin and effects. Each hazard is characterised by its location, intensity, frequency and probability.

Hazmat Suit
An garment impermeable to hazardous materials designed to protect the wearer, and usually combined with an independent breathing apparatus. In the humanitarian world, it is generally used by emergency health personnel responding to outbreaks of unknown communicable diseases in areas endemic for haemorrhagic fevers.

Hurricane (synonym: Tropical Cyclone, Typhoon)
Large-scale closed circulation system in the atmosphere above the Western Atlantic with low barometric pressure and strong winds that rotate clockwise. Maximum sustained wind speed of 64 knots (119 km/hr) or more (See 'cyclone' for the Indian Ocean and South and Eastern Pacific and 'typhoon' for the Western Pacific).

Category	Wind speed (km/hr)	Effects
1	119-153	No real damage to buildings; some coastal flooding.
2	154-177	Some roofing, door and window damage; considerable damage to vegetation.
3	178-209	Destruction of mobile homes; more inland flooding damage.
4	210-249	Erosion and flooding of inland areas; roofs torn off.
5	>250	Complete roof failures and some complete building failures; flooding and landslides; usually mass evacuation.

Hydro-Meteorological Hazards
Natural processes or phenomena of atmospheric, hydrological or oceanographic nature, which may cause loss of life or injury, property damage, social and economic disruption, or environmental degradation.

Hydro-meteorological hazards include: floods, debris and mud floods; tropical cyclones, storm surges, thunder/hailstorms, rain and windstorms, blizzards and other severe storms; drought, desertification, wildland fires, temperature extremes, sand or dust storms; permafrost and snow or ice avalanches. Hydro-meteorological hazards can be single, sequential or combined in their origin and effects.

Hyperthermia
A condition that occurs when core body temperature rises above 105°F or so. Other factors such as obesity, hypertension, and heart disease can contribute to such deaths, as can the taking of antipsychotic or diuretic medications, which can affect the body's ability to regulate heat.

Immunisation (synonym: Vaccination)
Protection of susceptible individuals from communicable disease by administering living modified agents, a suspension of killed organisms or an inactivated toxin. Temporary passive immunization can be produced by administering antibody in the form of immunoglobulin in some conditions.

Infectious Diseases
These are not quite the same as communicable diseases as, to be 'infectious', human to human or animal to human transmission is assumed either by direct or indirect contact with infected persons. Most such diseases are spread through contact or close proximity because the bacteria or viruses are airborne; i.e., they can be expelled from the nose and mouth of the infected person and inhaled by anyone in the vicinity. Such diseases include diphtheria, measles, mumps, whooping cough, and influenza. Skin diseases can also infect another person and are therefore infectious.

Information Management
Techniques in data collection, synthesis, transmission, presentation and analysis.

Intensity
A measurable force. Earthquake intensity describes the severity of a seismic event in terms of its effects on the earth's surface, including on humans and their structures. Several scales exist, but the one most commonly used is the Modified Mercalli scale.

Landslide
In general, all varieties of slope movement, under the influence of gravity. More strictly refers to downslope movement of rock and/or earth masses along one or several slide surfaces.

Marginal Cost
This refers to the increase or decrease in the total cost of a production from making, procuring, or distributing one additional unit of an item. It is computed in situations where breakeven point has been reached: the fixed costs have already been absorbed by the already produced items and only the direct (variable) costs have to be accounted for. Marginal costs are variable costs comprising labour and materials plus an estimated portion of fixed costs (such as administrative overheads and expenses). The concept of marginal cost is of critical importance where maximum efficiency in allocation of scarce resources is required – as is the case in humanitarian operations – as opposed to 'effective' allocation where life must be saved whatever the cost.

Mass-Casualty Management
The medical response to an event in which the number of casualties is large enough to disrupt the normal course of emergency and health care services. Activities include pre-hospital emergency care, hospital reception and treatment, and redistributing patients to other hospitals when necessary.

Mitigation
Structural and non-structural measures undertaken to limit the adverse impact of natural hazards, environmental degradation and technological hazards.

Moral Hazard
Moral hazard occurs when a party insulated from risk behaves differently than it would behave if it were fully exposed to the risk. Moral hazard arises because an individual or institution does not take the full consequences and responsibilities of its actions, and therefore has a tendency to act less carefully than it otherwise would, leaving another party to hold some responsibility for the consequences of those actions. For example, a person with insurance against automobile theft may be less cautious about locking his or her car, because the negative consequences of vehicle theft are (partially) the responsibility of the insurance company.

Economists explain moral hazard as a special case of information asymmetry; a situation in which one party in a transaction has more information than another. In particular, moral hazard may occur if a party that is insulated from risk has more information about its actions and intentions than the party paying for the negative consequences of the risk.

Non-Food Items (NFI)
A term commonly used by humanitarian agencies to refer to relief commodities that are not food. In the shelter sector, these would include such items as cooking sets, rubble removal kits, blankets, clothes etc. but not tents, plastic or corrugated iron sheets which would probably be referred to as shelter items. In the health sector, unspecified non-medical supplies such as intravenous giving sets (also referred to as 'medical consumables') are sometimes – mistakenly – referred to as NFIs.

Opportunity Cost
This is the benefit or value of something that must be given up to acquire or achieve something else. Since every resource (land, money, time, human effort etc.) can be put to alternative uses, every action, choice, or decision has an associated 'opportunity' cost of another action not taken. In the health sector, for example, not conducting a polio vaccination catch-up campaign will allow the money saved to be used for supplying more bed nets instead, but there will be a cost years later in terms of death and disability (as measured by 'disability adjusted life years' -- DALYs) for those who contracted polio as a result of not having been vaccinated when younger.

Pandemic
An epidemic that is spreading through human populations simultaneously in different parts of the world, and is a long-term phenomenon. A widespread endemic disease that is stable in terms of how many people are getting sick from it does not constitute a pandemic.

Pathogen
A biological agent that causes disease or illness in its host.

Preparedness

Activities and measures taken in advance to ensure effective response to the impact of hazards, including the issuance of timely and effective early warnings and the temporary evacuation of people and property from threatened locations.

Prevention

Activities to provide outright avoidance of the adverse impact of hazards and means to minimize related environmental, technological and biological disasters. Depending on social and technical feasibility and cost/benefit considerations, investing in preventive measures is justified in areas frequently affected by disasters. In the context of public awareness and education, related to disaster risk reduction changing attitudes and behaviour contribute to promoting a 'culture of prevention'.

Recovery

The restoration, and improvement where appropriate, of facilities, livelihoods and living conditions of disaster-affected communities, including efforts to reduce disaster risk factors.

Relief

Relief refers to the emergency food, shelter, health, water, sanitation and support services provided over a typically three to nine month period in the immediate aftermath of a natural disaster. By contrast, development refers to the longer-term aid aimed at creating self-sufficiency and sustainability within a community. Provision of chlorine tablets to purify contaminated water would be an example of the former, while drilling boreholes to create wells would be an example of the latter.

Residual Risk

The risk that remains in unmanaged form, even when effective disaster risk reduction measures are in place, and for which emergency response and recovery capacities must be maintained.

Resilience

The capacity of a system, community or society potentially exposed to hazards to adapt, by resisting or changing, in order to reach and maintain an acceptable level of functioning and structure. This is determined by the degree to which the social system is capable of organizing itself to increase its capacity for learning from past disasters for better future protection and to improve risk reduction measures.

Retrofitting
Reinforcement or upgrading of existing structures to become more resistant and resilient to the damaging effects of hazards.

Retrofitting requires consideration of the design and function of the structure, the stresses that the structure may be subject to from particular hazards or hazard scenarios, and the practicality and costs of different retrofitting options. Examples of retrofitting include adding bracing to stiffen walls, reinforcing pillars, adding steel ties between walls and roofs, installing shutters on windows, and improving the protection of critical facilities and equipment.

Richter Scale
A numerical scale for expressing the magnitude of an earthquake on the basis of seismographic oscillations. The more destructive earthquakes typically have a magnitude of above 5.5. It is a logarithmic scale and a difference of 1 represents an approximate thirtyfold difference in magnitude. Note that, as with tropical cyclones, magnitude is not the same as 'intensity'.

EARTHQUAKE MAGNITUDE: RICHTER SCALE	
Category	**Effects**
<3.5	Generally not felt, but recorded
3.5 - 5.5	Felt, but rarely causing any damage
5.6 – 5.9	Slight damage to well-constructed buildings, heavy damage to poorly constructed buildings
6.1 - 6.9	Damage to inhabited areas up to 100 km from epicentre
7.0 - 7.9	Major earthquake that may cause serious damage in a very wide area
8.0 - 8.9	Serious earthquake that causes damage hundreds of kms away from the epicentre
>9.0	Rare great earthquake causing major damage over 1,000 kms from the epicentre

Risk
The probability of harmful consequences, or expected losses (deaths, injuries, property, livelihoods, economic activity disrupted or

272

environment damaged) resulting from interactions between natural or human-induced hazards and vulnerable conditions. Conventionally risk is expressed by the notation Risk = Hazards x Vulnerability. Some disciplines also include the concept of exposure to refer particularly to the physical aspects of vulnerability. Beyond expressing a possibility of physical harm, it is crucial to recognize that risks are inherent or can be created or exist within social systems. It is important to consider the social contexts in which risks occur and that people therefore do not necessarily share the same perceptions of risk and their underlying causes.

Samaritan's Dilemma
Providing external emergency assistance to low-income countries that have neglected to invest in their own protective measures.

Tornado
Violently rotating and most violent weather phenomenon. It is produced in a very severe thunderstorm and appears as a funnel cloud extending from the base of a cumulonimbus cloud to the ground.

Tropical Cyclone
A tropical cyclone is the generic term for a non-frontal synoptic scale low-pressure system over tropical or sub-tropical waters with organized convection (i.e. thunderstorm activity) and definite cyclonic surface wind circulation.

The words "hurricane" and "typhoon" are simply different names for a "tropical cyclone." As a general rule, these cyclones are given the name "hurricane" in the Western hemisphere (the North Atlantic Ocean, the Northeast Pacific Ocean east of the dateline, or the South Pacific Ocean east of 160E), and the term "typhoon" is applied in the Eastern hemisphere (the Northwest Pacific Ocean west of the dateline).Where wind-speeds are lower than 33 metres per second, such cyclones are called "tropical depressions".

At some point, increasing wind-speeds turn a "depression" into a "storm", at which point they are given a local name according to a sequenced list maintained by the World Meteorological Organization.

Tsunami
Series of large wave-like energy pulses generated by sudden displacement of seawater (caused by earthquake, volcanic eruption or submarine landslide); capable of propagation over large distances and

causing a destructive surge on reaching land. The Japanese term for this phenomenon, which is observed mainly in the Pacific, has been adopted for general usage.

Vaccination (synonym: Immunization)
Protection of susceptible individuals from communicable disease by administering living modified agents, a suspension of killed organisms or an inactivated toxin. Temporary passive immunization can be produced by administering antibody in the form of immunoglobulin in some conditions.

Vector Control
Control of animals and insects that act as intermediaries in the transmission of disease. These might be ticks for tick-borne typhus, mosquitoes for malaria and dengue fever, flies for trachoma, or rats for pneumonic plague. Counter measures include fogging, residual spraying, and baiting.

Vulnerability
The characteristics and circumstances of a community, system or asset that make it susceptible to the damaging effects of a hazard. There are many aspects of vulnerability, arising from various physical, social, economic, and environmental factors. Examples may include poor design and construction of buildings, inadequate protection of assets, lack of public information and awareness, limited official recognition of risks and preparedness measures, and disregard for wise environmental management. Vulnerability varies significantly within a community and over time. Note that vulnerability is identified as a characteristic of the element of interest (community, system or asset) which is independent of its exposure.

Zoonosis
A zoonotic disease is an infectious disease transmitted between animals and humans (or vice versa), sometimes involving an intermediate vector. Of 1,415 pathogens known to infect humans, approximately two-thirds are zoonotic in origin.

Explanatory Notes

THERE ARE THREE BROAD GENERIC categories for disasters: Natural, Complex, and Technological. *Absolute Disaster* only deals with those in the 'natural' category which is divided into five sub-categories which in turn cover 12 disaster types and, although not all are shown here, more than 30 sub-types.

To keep things simple, I have considered weather-related events to mean extreme hydro-meteorological events directly related to wind and water i.e windstorms, storm surges, heatwaves, and floods. Technically, wet mass movements such as landslides and snow avalanches should all be included in this category, but climate-related disasters such as wildfires and droughts should not, as they are considered to be indirectly related to the weather. Clearly, though, all are related to climate one way or the other.

I have considered geophysical disasters to be earthquakes, volcanic eruptions, and dry mass movements such as rockfalls, debris flows, and sinkholes, even though some could be considered 'wet' mass movements.

As was made clear at the beginning of the book, communicable diseases (epidemics) have been included as a sub-category despite not being recognised as such in official EM-DAT data.

CATEGORY		DEFINITION	MAIN TYPE
	Geophysical	Event originating from solid earth	Earthquake Volcano Landslide (dry mass) Tsunami
Hydro-Meteorological	Meteorological	Event caused by short-term atmospheric processes	Storm Storm surge inundation (coastal) Tornado Cyclone / Hurricane
Hydro-Meteorological	Hydrological	Event caused by deviation to normal water cycle and/or flow	Flood (General & Flash) Landslide (wet mass) Avalanche
Hydro-Meteorological	Climatological	Event caused by long-term atmospheric processes	Drought Wildfire Extreme temperature (cold / hot)
	Biological	Event caused by exposure to germs and toxins	Epidemic Insect infestation
	Non-terrestrial	Event caused by hazard originating from space	Radiation Asteroid

✦

The statistics quoted throughout are taken from the Emergencies Database (EM-DAT) at the World Health Organisation's Centre for Research on the Epidemiology of Disasters (CRED) at the Université catholique de Louvain in Belgium, or the United Nations' International Strategy for Disaster Reduction (UN-ISDR) unless otherwise specified. For more, see www.cred.be

✦

The World's Disaster Databases Catalogue of the United Nations Development Program's Global Risk Information Platform (GRIP) website lists 46 disaster databases of which only five provide worldwide multi-risk data, one of which is EM-DAT. The others are the

GLIDE number database (Asian Disaster Reduction Centre), the Disaster Database Project (University of Richmond), National Catastrophe Service (Munich Re), and Sigma (Swiss Re). Two additional databases, the Lloyds Casualty Week, and the Aon Benfield Impact Forecasting's Global Catastrophe Recap also provide useful aggregated information.

On a global basis, the impact of different types of natural disaster display fat-tailed distributions. This means that comparatively few events result in most of the loss of life. This, in turn, can mean that mode, mean, and median figures might not be faithfully representing what is actually going on. Here, the 'mean' is used.

Using average deaths per event is not very useful in epidemiological terms, mostly because it tells you almost nothing about distribution patterns over space and time. But such figures do provide insight into the changing scale of impact within a particular category of hazard, and allow for comparison between one type of hazard and another.

Similarly, global statistics are aggregated and therefore tell you little about local impacts.

Where the term *decadal average* is used, reference is being made to the annualised average over the last ten years for which data are available (2005-2014) unless otherwise specified.

The book is designed more for dipping into than reading from cover to cover. This means that some points are made more than once as they are relevant to more than one disaster misperception.

All sums are quoted in US Dollars unless otherwise stated.

Preparedness and Mitigation Measures by Hazard Type

The following bullet points refer to response and preparedness measures and longer-term prevention and mitigation measures that ideally should be considered when planning disaster risk reduction activities. Every single one reflects a lesson learned during a recent disaster, and each one has been learned the hard way. They are separated by sector for convenience. Recommendations on where to find additional information online are also included.

GENERAL (and applicable to all)	
Response & Preparedness	**Prevention & Mitigation**
• Agree definitions – for what constitutes an 'affected person' for example – and contextual baselines	• Enact legislation and regulation at the appropriate jurisdictional levels, including for mandatory evacuation
• Place evacuation route signs along roadways clearly indicating the direction inland or to higher ground	• Enforce building codes in critical high-use and high-occupancy buildings and use of appropriate materials, especially in zones of high seismic risk
• Establish an early warning system using flags, whistles, sirens, local radio, and, crucially, bulk mobile phone SMS	• Have a contingency plan in place at a national and local level for people to evacuate in time
• Conduct regular evacuation exercises and ensure community participation	• Strengthening the ability of local communities to respond to disasters will save many more lives than an equivalent amount of resources spent on deploying expensive international assets
• Prepare personal 'grab bags'	
• Store as much water as possible, and have a large supply of chlorine disinfection tablets	• Conduct hazard risk mapping for each hazard type and make these available to communities
• Avoid mass graves unless epidemic threatens	• Educate people and raise

	awareness of risks facing them
	• Humanitarian agencies should be prepared to supplement national emergency obstetric and post-natal care services
	• In mass casualty events, increase the proportion of anaesthetists, nephrologists, mental health specialists, and general physicians

- www.adb.org/disaster/lessons
- www.understandingrisk.org
- www.preventionweb.org
- www.odi.org.uk/hpg
- www.ifrc.org/Global/Publications/disasters/WDR/wdr2010/WDR2010-English-2.pdf
- Geographic information system maps - www.maplecroft.com
- Disaster risk reduction, including satellite imagery from UNOSAT - www.unisdr.org
- Disaster risk management programmes ongoing in selected at risk countries - www.gfdrr.org
- Disaster epidemiology and burden of disease - www.cred.be
- Data on capital loss trends - www.munichre.com

BIOLOGICAL	
Response & Preparedness	**Prevention & Mitigation**
• Immunise for Tetanus where coverage is low	• Augment cold storage for dead bodies and stockpile body bags and tags • Victim identification (by DNA testing, dental records and photography) is critical to recovery • Know patterns of drug resistance in disaster-prone areas
• Indian government guidelines – www.ndma.gov.in/ndma/guidelines/biological • Health library for disasters – http://helid.desastres.net	

TSUNAMI	
Response & Preparedness	**Prevention & Mitigation**
• The first sign of an impending tsunami is often a seemingly innocuous receding of the sea. Depending on the slope of the sea-shore, the water may recede to the horizon. If you see either this or a large wave coming towards you, run and scramble to the highest point that you can, shouting a warning to others as you do so. This should be solid ground (a hill), a concrete building, or a tree in that order of priority. Stay there, as the initial wave will not only not recede but may be followed by three of four more of equal or greater severity at intervals of up to twenty minutes. These waves may also 'rebound' and come from the opposite direction. • Equipment and facilities for post-disaster tetanus control needs to be mobilised immediately.	• Map hazard risk given local bathymetry, and its anticipated high-tide maximum run-up • Clearly designate shelter and ground higher than 10 metres above sea level which can be reached immediately • Reinforce ground floors of multi-storey buildings e.g by attaching vertical structures on sea-facing vertical supporting columns that allow water to swirl around and which take the brunt of any debris impact • Move homes and buildings away from the shoreline or up (on stilts) above the anticipated ingress height • Protect essential infrastructure such as schools and hospitals, roads, harbours, power plants, and telecommunications towers banking and place generators at higher levels if possible • Install seawalls • Ensure that natural barriers – dunes, mangroves and coral reefs – are protected as they help mitigate impact on shore • Keep tsunami indigenous knowledge and practices alive in local memory • Integrate tsunami education in the school curricula and rehearse tsunami drills at least

	twice every year
	• Make sure people know that when seawaters recede noticeably, everyone must head for high ground or upper floors of buildings constructed with reinforced concrete
	• Include third-line antibiotics in primary health emergency response kits

- Tsunami – www.tsunami.noaa.gov and www.ioc-unesco.org
- Flood resistant housing – www.practicalaction.org/flood-resistant-housing-drr

EARTHQUAKE	
Response & Preparedness	**Prevention & Mitigation**
• Wear some form of facemask during an earthquake to prevent dust inhalation, and when exposed to dust and asbestos during clean-up operations	• Focus on retrofitting schools and hospitals to become seismic resistant, enforcing safer building codes, and educating the population on how to respond when tremors occur
• Wear stout shoes as puncture wounds can cause Tetanus	• Research following the Sichuan earthquake of May 2008 indicated a general lack of multi-disciplinary health teams, and an absence of preparedness training for medical staff
• If indoors, stay there and do not run outside where falling debris can often inflict more harm than collapsing buildings. The possible exception is if you are in a one-storey bungalow in a remote area. In this situation, it's a judgement call but you should consider exiting if you physically can	• Provide portable and/or mobile primary and secondary health clinics before spending limited funds on establishing temporary tertiary facilities which are under-used
• If in a high-rise hotel do not run downstairs or try	• Support higher levels of disability management. Spinal and crush injuries require mandatory training and appropriate equipping of first responders whose use of spinal

to take the lift. Move into a doorway or corner of a room nearest the centre of the building as these are structurally the strongest places in the building. Next best is to lie down next to – not under – a stout piece of furniture

- Be aware of the strong likelihood of after-shocks and be ready to run away from landslides. In the Pakistan earthquake of 2005, landslides claimed almost as many lives as collapsing buildings
- When everything has gone quiet, render what first aid you can. Don't let people smoke because gas lines are likely to have been ruptured. Post-earthquake fire killed three times more people than collapsing buildings during the Kobe earthquake in Japan
- If water is readily available damp down debris as, in developing countries, there will probably be asbestos in the dust. And inhaled asbestos will kill as surely as a falling roof tile, just more slowly
- In contexts where affected areas are isolated or cut off, it may be better to

boards and neck braces must be considered an integral part of evacuation and transportation

- Lessons learned from the Christchurch, New Zealand hospital during the 2011 earthquake:
  - expect patients to arrive by unusual means without pre-hospital care
  - manual registration and tracking of patients is required
  - patients will be reluctant to come into hospital buildings
  - expect complete loss of electrical power
  - manage the many willing helpers
  - control the media by limiting access and providing regular press briefings
  - integrate atypical providers of acute injury care into response plans
- Detection and treatment of crush injury syndrome, both on site at the time of extrication and afterwards, should receive much greater emphasis. Include more nephrologists in planning and response teams
- More orthopaedic and plastic surgeons are needed in medical relief teams (not necessarily as part of a field hospital) together

send helicopters than field hospitals
• Include more nephrologists in disaster planning and on disaster medical teams
	with external fixators and associated surgical and medical supplies
	• According to Public Health England, immediate health needs after an earthquake include:
	   ○ adequate quantity and quality of water
	   ○ appropriate shelter and protection from the elements
	   ○ prevention and treatment of diarrhoeal, respiratory, and vector-borne illnesses
	   ○ provision of health services to prevent maternal and infant deaths
	   ○ prevention of violence and further unintentional injury
	   ○ treatment of kidney failure due to crush injuries
	   ○ prevention of deaths from infected wounds
	   ○ prevention and treatment of inflamed lung tissue caused by inhalation of concrete dust

• Earthquakes and Megacities Initiative – www.emi-megacities.org/home • US Geological Service, Earthquake Hazards Program – http://earthquake.usgs.gov • UN search and rescue – http://insarag.org • World Health Organisation guidelines on use of field hospitals – http://paho.org/disasters	

VOLCANO	
Response & Preparedness	**Prevention & Mitigation**
• Educate and raise awareness on volcano risk, especially if the volcano has a history of pyroclastic eruption	• Integrate volcano risk in land-use planning: volcano risk can be substantially reduced by limiting the development of infrastructure in hazardous areas • Install a monitoring system to observe volcanic behaviour
• European Volcanic Society – http://www.sveurop.org • Michigan Technological University Volcanoes Page – http://www.geo.mtu.edu/ volcanoes • US Geological Survey – http://volcanoes.usgs.gov	

LANDSLIDE & AVALANCHE	
Response Preparedness	**Prevention & Mitigation**
	• Do not allow building in areas of known landslides and avalanche risk • Stabilise slopes by geo-engineering, including: o reducing the amount of water infiltrating the soil by covering with an impermeable membrane o placing gabion cage rock berms at the toe of the landslide o pinning rock faces and/or covering them in steel mesh • For soil slopes, install an acoustic or fibre-optic monitoring system and link to rainfall monitoring to alert of impending collapse • Integrate landslide risk assessment into urban planning strategies

	• Secure towns, villages and tunnels at the bottom of slopes with concrete retaining walls and protection • Reinforce river protection with wooden dams of limited height in streambeds or gulleys liable to potential debris flow • Plant trees and prosecute illegal logging as forested areas provide protection against the release of avalanches and landslides • Devise early warning systems based on local precipitation and temperature models • Construct V-shaped barriers up-slope of critical infrastructure

• International Consortium on Landslides (ICL) – www.iclhq.org
• International Society for Soil Mechanics and Geotechnical Engineering (ISSMGE): www.issmge.org
• Kyoto University Research Center on Landslides – http://landslide.dpri.kyoto-u.ac.jp
• www.fema.gov/hazard/landslide
• USGS Landslide Hazards Program – http://landslides.usgs.gov/learning/faq
• http://durham.ac.uk/international_landslide_centre
• Avalanche Center – www.avalanche-center.org
• Oracle ThinkQuest: Natural Disasters – http://library.thinkquest.org/NatDisasterPages
• Swiss Federal Institute for Forest, Snow and Landscape Research – www.slf.ch

NON-TERRESTRIAL	
Response & Preparedness	**Prevention & Mitigation**
	• Faraday cages should be built around all critical point transformers. • Stockpile transformers

• Asteroids – http://impact.arc.nasa.gov
• Solar flares – http://solarstormwarning.com

FLOOD & STORM SURGE

Response & Preparedness	Prevention & Mitigation
• Learn the elevation level of your property and whether the land is flood-prone. This will help you know how your property will be affected when storm surge or tidal flooding are forecast • Identify levees and dams in your area and determine whether they pose a hazard to you • Snakebite trays should be available in each Hospital and Rural Health Centre in areas at risk of flooding • Educate about the risk of nocturnal snake bites • Establish a system of motorcycle volunteers for rapid referral	• Consider construction of: • Flood-resistant housing which incorporate materials such as concrete, stone, ceramic or brick for foundations, plinths, and lower walls • Dykes to channel water away from vulnerable communities • Gabion cage spurs made of local stones, tightly packed together in 'gabion' wire boxes, extend out into the river, altering the pace and direction of its flow. Spurs can be locally and easily maintained, and on average can act as a form of flood defence for around 7-8 years • Sea walls. Mangroves, trees and coral reefs should be protected as they act as natural wave breakers and reduce the speed of seawater, wave strength and wind force in coastal storm surges; wetlands and forests can serve as flood control systems, storing large amounts of floodwater, and should also be preserved • A watch tower means villagers can see the waters rising to dangerous levels. They are able to sound a siren which can be heard up

	to 3 kms away. This also means that neighbouring villagers can come to help
	• Fit rain/flood gauges to monitor how quickly the waters are rising
	• A bridge to create an escape route for the community at risk
	• Construct emergency (cyclone) shelters with toilets and clean water pumps are built on higher ground. There are extra rooms to give women privacy. Outside of monsoon season, the shelter can be used as a school
	• Stockpile emergency materials, including life jackets and flat-bottomed metal boats
	• Flood risk assessment should be integrated into urban planning strategies
	• Avoid building directly on the coastline, where storm surges may cause flooding
	• Review anti-venom procurement policy as many anti-venoms are inappropriate and/or ineffective

• Association of State Floodplain Managers: www.floods.org
• UNISDR Guidelines for Reducing Flood Losses: www.unisdr.org/eng/ library/isdr-publication/flood-guidelines/isdr-publication-floods.htm

DROUGHT & TEMPERATURE EXTREMES	
Response & Preparedness	Prevention & Mitigation
• Young children and the elderly, especially those living on their own, are most at risk. They may be unaware of becoming overheated and not drinking enough liquid to remain hydrated. Become a 'good neighbour' and check up on such people	• Develop and install efficient drip irrigation technologies which reduce over-watering and evaporation • Introduce drought-tolerant crops • If potentially at risk, register with the integrated global drought early warning system (GDEWS) • Where possible, collect surface water (e.g build sand dams)
• Aon Benfield Hazard Research Centre at University College, London – http://drought.mssl.ucl.ac.uk/drought • UK National Health Service – http://health4 work.nhs.uk • Intergovernmental Panel on Climate Change – www.ipcc.ch	

WILDLAND FIRE	
Response & Preparedness	Prevention & Mitigation
• Conduct community-based fire risk minimisation activities • Provide community alerts through fire danger rating systems; these systems forecast the potential for fire, based on recent rainfall, temperature, wind speed, and fuel on the ground • Conduct community risk communications programmes outlining the risks of wildfires, especially as people are often responsible for igniting them • Develop firefighting capacities	• Limit development in high wildfire risk areas • Create buffer zones between human habitation and susceptible forests by clearing undergrowth • Create firebreaks between homes and any forested or bush land areas, if a natural firebreak (such as a road or a river) does not exist • Avoid building in high-risk areas bordering forests, grasslands, or bush lands • Use fire-resistant building materials • Use traditional and advanced methods of

	prescribed burning for sustainable agriculture and flora and fauna management, including fuel management and restoration of fire regimes

- Global Fire Monitoring and Community Action: www.fire.uni-freiburg.de
- UN Forestry Management: www.fao.org/forestry/firemanagementstrategy

WINDSTORM	
Response & Preparedness	**Prevention & Mitigation**
• Stay indoors, as the principal storm threat is from flying debris, especially corrugated iron sheeting • When a tornado approaches, below ground is the safest place to be. If there is no basement, head to the bathtub. Get away from windows. Tornadoes can make windows suddenly shatter as if they were exploding. It's a myth that opening windows can somehow equalize the pressure. Most deaths and injuries from tornadoes are from falling rubble so, unlike an earthquake, get under a stout table. Wear a helmet. A cushion will do. Even straw can puncture your skin. Wrap yourself in a blanket as such puncture wounds, when infected, are extremely difficult to treat and can become a significant cause of post-disaster mortality long after the twister has moved on.	• Incentives should be provided to property owners in marginal areas to adapt buildings to threats posed by rising sea levels and increasingly powerful storm events • For urban planners, the task is to discreetly integrate prevention and preparedness measures into traditional planning efforts. Storm water drainage systems, for example, should be separated from sewage systems. • Among natural disasters, tropical cyclones are uniquely amenable to risk reduction through a combination of planning, technology, and behaviour change. Effective forecasting, early warning, first aid training, evacuation and sheltering

- Avoid mobile home settlements in tornado-prone zones
- Learn community hurricane evacuation routes and how to find higher ground. Determine where you would go and how you would get there if you needed to evacuate.
- Make plans to secure your property:
  - Cover all of your home's windows. Permanent storm shutters offer the best protection for windows. A second option is to board up windows with 5/8" marine plywood, cut to fit and ready to install. Tape does not prevent windows from breaking.
  - Install straps or additional clips to securely fasten your roof to the frame structure. This will reduce roof damage.
  - Be sure trees and shrubs around your home are well trimmed so they are more wind resistant.
  - Clear loose and clogged rain gutters and downspouts.
  - Install a generator for emergencies.
  - If in a high-rise

are primary approaches to reducing unnecessary death and suffering. Application of secondary prevention and mitigation approaches such as protecting wells, surface water ponds, and pit latrines from water intrusion also play a substantial part in subsequent efforts to reduce diseases transmission and increase resilience, especially where coastal inundation is likely

building, be prepared to take shelter on or below the 10th floor. • Consider building a safe room.	
• Atlantic Oceanographic & Meteorological Laboratory – www.aoml.noaa.gov/hrd • www.fema.gov/hazard/tornado/index.shtm • NOAA US Tornado Climatology – http://ncdc.noaa.gov/oa/climate/severeweather/tornadoes • Tornado Project – www.tornadoproject.com	

Acronyms

ACT	Artemisinin-based Combination Therapy
ADB	Asian Development Bank
ALNAP	Active Learning Network for Accountability and Performance in Humanitarian Action
ARI	Acute Respiratory Infection
ATM	Automated Teller Machine
CBO	Community Based Organization
CDC	US Centres for Disease Control and Prevention
CERF	UN Central Emergency Response Fund
CFR	Case Fatality Rate
CMR	Crude Mortality Rate
CRED	WHO Collaborating Centre for Research on the Epidemiology of Disasters
DALY	Disability Adjusted Life Year
DFID	UK Department for International Development
DNA	Deoxy-Ribose Nucleic Acid
DPT	Diptheria, Pertussis, Tetanus
DRM	Disaster Risk Management
DRR	Disaster Risk Reduction
ECHO	European Commission Humanitarian Aid and Civil Protection Department
EM-DAT	Emergency Events Database (CRED)
ERF	Emergency Response Fund
GAR	Global Assessment Report
GDP	Gross Domestic Product
GLOF	Glacial Lake Outburst Flood
GNI	Gross National Income
FAO	UN Food and Agriculture Organization
FEMA	US Federal Emergency Management Agency
GIS	Geographic Information Systems
GPS	Global Positioning System
HCT	Humanitarian Country Team (UN/IASC)
HFA	Hyogo Framework for Action
HDI	Human Development Index
HIV-AIDS	Human Immunodeficiency Virus – Acquired Immuno Deficiency Syndrome

IASC	Inter-Agency Standing Committee
ICRC	International Committee of the Red Cross
ICU	Intensive Care Unit
IDMC	Internal Displacement Monitoring Centre
IFRC	International Federation of Red Cross and Red Crescent Societies
IOC	Intergovernmental Oceanographic Commission
IOM	International Organisation for Migration
IPCC	Intergovernmental Panel on Climate Change
IRIN	Humanitarian News and Analysis (UN-OCHA)
ISDR	International Strategy for Disaster Reduction
LDC	Least Developed Country
LHD	Low Human Development
LSE	London School of Economics
MDR-TB	Multi-Drug Resistant Tuberculosis
MRSA	Multi-Drug Resistant Staphylococcus Aureas
NASA	US National Aeronautical and Space Agency
NDMA	National Disaster Management Authority
NEO	Near Earth Object
NGO	Non-Governmental Organisation
NOAA	US National Oceanic and Atmospheric Administration
NRC	Norwegian Refugee Council
NWS	US National Weather Service
OCHA	UN Office for the Coordination of Humanitarian Affairs
OECD	Organisation for Economic Co-operation and Development
OFDA	Office of US Foreign Disaster Assistance
OPD	Out-Patient Department
PPE	Population Potentially Exposed
RNA	Ribose Nucleic Acid
SARS	Severe Acute Respiratory Syndrome
TB	Tuberculosis
UN	United Nations
UNDP	United Nations Development Programme
UNEP	United Nations Environment Programme
UNICEF	United Nations Children's Fund
UNOSAT	United Nations Operational Satellite Applications Programme
UK	United Kingdom

US	United States of America
USAID	US Agency for International Development
USAR	Urban Search & Rescue
USGS	US Geological Survey
VSL	Value of Statistical Life
WASH	Water, Sanitation and Hygiene
WFP	UN World Food Programme
WHO	UN World Health Organisation
WMO	UN World Meteorological Organisation

Acknowledgements

MANY FRIENDS AND COLLEAGUES were called upon for their technical input and support during the research, development, writing, editing, and publishing of this book as well as the online quiz which goes with it. I am indebted and grateful to them all, and would like to take this opportunity to thank them here, especially: Debby Guhar-Sapir, Regina Below, Roger Lewis, Ben Verbeke, Madalene O'Donnell, Tom and Ant Colborne Malpas, Lewis Sida, Dave Petley, Lizzy Berryman, Tony Redmond, Pascal Peduzzi, Margareta Whalström, Brian Kelly, Andrew Macleod, Jesper Lund, John Douglas-Menzies, Robert Scott Moncrieff, Jane Hampson, Quentin and Isabell Browell, Anissa Toscano, Simon Little, Jonathan Ashmore, Joseph and Jules Ashmore, and Bob McKerrow.

Five additional people deserve particular mention, as, without their support, none of this would have been feasible:

John Adlam of the UK Government's Department for International Development for persuading the Crown Agents' Foundation to stump up the initial research grant.

Dr. Peter Walker, then Director of the International Feinstein Center at Tufts University, who kindly offered me a Visiting Research Fellowship to facilitate my researches.

Dr. Katherine Fry of Brooklyn College at the City University of New York, who never lost patience while supporting me physically and emotionally through the whole process.

Dave Hodgkin of Benchmark Consulting who provided much-needed impulsion when my researches began to wander off message.

Dr. Richard Garfield of the US Centres for Disease Control and Prevention in Atlanta and Columbia University who provided technical advice on the Health-Related section, as well as helping in getting the message out there.

About the Author

JAMES SHEPHERD-BARRON IS ONE OF THE world's most experienced international disaster management consultants. He has been directly involved in 27 disaster responses[121] over the past 20 years, and has worked with the widest possible range of international aid agencies[122] and governments at director and ministerial level. He is also one of a handful of qualified disaster epidemiologists. This is a unique combination.

James is also an experienced coordinator, having led Health, Shelter, Water-Sanitation-Hygiene, and Early Recovery Clusters[123] in nine of the world's largest disaster responses, most recently during the 2013-2014 Typhoon Haiyan response in The Philippines and the 2015 Earthquake response in Nepal. In the past few years, he has also acted as senior humanitarian adviser for the UK government's Department for International Development in Libya, Turkey (for the Syria crisis), and

---

[121] Croatia, Bosnia, Burundi, Rwanda, Albania, Kosovo, Iraq, Chad, Sudan, Pakistan, Indonesia, Georgia, Bangladesh, Myanmar, India, Thailand, Libya, Turkey, Syria, Honduras, Haiti, Philippines, Sierra Leone, Liberia, Nepal

[122] European Commission (ECHO), UK Government (DFID), Red Cross (IFRC), International Organisation for Migration (IOM), United Nations (OCHA, UNICEF, UNDP, WHO), CARE International.

[123] He has been a Cluster Coordinator a record nine times for Health, Shelter, Water-Sanitation-Hygiene, Protection, and Early Recovery.

Nepal, and was Special Adviser to Sierra Leone's Minister of Health during the early phases of the Ebola crisis.

When not coordinating, writing or lecturing, James advises international aid agencies and governments on how to build resilience and reduce risk posed by natural hazards ... and then on how to manage response and recovery operations when all else has failed, and disaster has ensued.

He has an MSc in International Health and Epidemiology, and was awarded an honorary doctorate in public health by the government of Albania following his work during the Kosovo crisis in the late 1990's. He has been a 'visiting research fellow' at the Feinstein International Center at Tufts University, and was CARE International's first Global Director of Emergency Response. He currently advises and co-chairs the Cash Management Industry's 'Cash Access in Crises Committee'.

Index

References

i   Shepherd-Barron et al: Cholera Lessons Learned -Guidelines for control of diseases of epidemic potential; Sierra Leone Ministry of Health, December 2012.

ii   UNICEF-Bangladesh: Annual Report, 2007

iii   Brookings Institution, London School of Economics: Review of Natural Disasters in 2010, April 2011

iv   UK Government Foresight Project, 2012

v   IFRC World Disasters Report, 2007.

vi   Spence et al: Human casualties in earthquakes; Advances in Natural and Technological Hazards Research, Vol.29,2011

vii   Goklany: Death and death rates from extreme weather events, 1900 to 2008; Journal of American Physicians and Surgeons, Vol.14 (4), 2009

viii   Internal Displacement Monitoring Centre (IDMC) of the Norwegian Refugee Council, June 2012

ix   Guha-Sapir and Hoyois: Reducing Risks of Future Disasters – priorities for decision makers; Report produced for the UK government Foresight Project, 2012

x   IFRC World Disasters Report, 2011

xi   From data provided by Ubyrisk Consultants and published in the Red Cross-Red Crescent Magazine, Issue 2, 2011

xii   Wisner and Gaillard: Handbook of Hazards and Disaster Risk Reduction; Routledge, 2011

xiii   Jennings: Time's Bitter Flood – Trends in the number of reported natural disasters; Oxfam GB Research Report, 2011

xiv   International Federation of Red Cross and Red Crescent Societies: World Disasters Report, 2000

xv   Development Asia Bulletin, January-March 2011

xvi   UN Department of Economic and Social Affairs: World Fertility Patterns in 2009; 2011

xvii   Rush: The Impact of Natural Disasters on Poverty in Indonesia; University of Hawaii, 2013

xviii   Dercon and De Weerdt: Risk-sharing networks and insurance
         against illness; Journal of Development Economics, Vol.81 (2),
         2006
xix   Coburn et al: 1992
xx   Petley: Global patterns of loss of life from landslides; Geology,
         published online on 1 August 2012 as doi 10.1130/G33217.1
xxi   Guzzetti: Landslide fatalities and the evaluation of landslide
         risk in Italy; Engineering Geology, Vol.43, 2000
xxii   Simon Winchester, Newsweek, March 2011
xxiii   UN-ISDR: Global Assessment Report on Disaster Risk
         Reduction, 2009
xxiv   Kremer et al: Giant Lake Geneva tsunami in AD 563; Nature
         Geoscience, Vol.5, 2012
xxv   Kellet and Sparks: Disaster Risk Reduction – spending where it
         should count: Global Humanitarian Assistance Briefing Report,
         2012
xxvi   World Health Organisation: Monsoon Flood in Bangladesh;
         South East Asia Regional Office Site Report, 2007
xxvii   Sharma et al: Clinico-epidemiological features of snakebite: a
         study from eastern Nepal; Tropical Doctor, Vol.34, 2004
xxviii   Amaral et al: Tourniquet ineffectiveness to reduce the severity
         of envenoming after snake bite in Belo Horizonte, Brazil;
         Toxicon, Vol.36, 1998
xxix   Ho and Park: Tropical Cyclone Threat in East Asia; Article
         5592, environmentalresearchweb.org, January, 2014 [accessed
         2nd June 2014]
xxx   Laframboise and Loko: Natural Disasters – mitigating impact,
         managing risks; International Monetary Fund working paper
         WP/12/245, October 2012
xxxi   Below et al: Documenting drought-related disasters – a global
         reassessment; The Journal of Environment and Development,
         Vol.16, No.3, 2007
xxxii   Sheffield et al: Little change in global drought over the past 60
         years; Nature, Vol.491, 2012
xxxiii   Trenberth: National Centre for Atmospheric Research; 2010
xxxiv   Sousounis et al: Tropical Cyclones Risk Models-circular symmetry
         revisited; Proceedings of the 30th American Meteorological Society

Conference on Hurricanes and Tropical Meteorology, Ponte Vedra Beach, Florida, April 14-20, 2012

xxxv   From a discussion between the author and the area coordinator for the World Health Organisation in Tacloban, January 2014

xxxvi   Holle: Annual rates of lightning fatalities by country; 10th International Lightning Detection Conference, April 2008

xxxvii   Flannigan et al: Presentation at the 5th International Wildland fire conference, May 2011

xxxviii   Lehsten et al: Climate fire interactions; CRC press, 2010 [DOI: 10.1201/b 10275-31]

xxxix   ISDR Global Assessment Report on Disaster Risk Reduction, 2009

xl   www.ncdc.noaa.gov/sotc/index.php. Accessed July 2012

xli   Arino et al: Global night-time fire season timing and fire count trends using the ATSR instrument series. Remote Sensing of Environment, Vol.116, January 2012

xlii   Steffan et al: Heatwaves - hotter, longer, more often; Australian Climate Council, 2014

xliii   Pielke: Statement to the Sub-committee on Environment of the Committee on Science, Space and Technology of the United States House of Representatives; December, 2013

xliv   Mandelbaum et al: Management of tornado casualties; Trauma Journal, Vol.6, 1966

xlv   Glass et al: Injuries from the Wichita Falls tornado – implications for prevention; Science, Vol.207, 1980

xlvi   Beelman: Disaster planning – report of tornado casualties in Topeka; Journal of the Kansas Medical Society, Vol.68, 1967

xlvii   World Health Organisation: Disease Control in Humanitarian Emergencies, 2007

xlviii   Floret et al: Negligible risks for epidemics after geo-physical disasters; Journal of emerging infectious diseases, Vol.12, No.4, April 2006

xlix   Briët et al: Maps of the Sri Lanka malaria situation preceding the tsunami and key aspects to be considered in the emergency phase and beyond; Malaria Journal, Vol.4 (8), 2005

l   Guha-Sapir and van Panhuis: Health Impact of the 2004 Andaman Nicobar Earthquake and Tsunami in Indonesia; Prehospital and Disaster Medicine, Vol.24 (6), 2009

li   Tulloch et al: Artemisinin-resistant malaria in the Asia-Pacific region; The Lancet, Vol.381, Issue 9881, 2013

lii   Nadjafi et al: Archives of Iranian Medicine; Vol.12, No.4, July 2009

liii   Taitelman et al: Prevention of acute renal failure in traumatic rhabdomyolysis; Archives of Internal Medicine, Vol.144, 1984

liv   Bartels and Van Rooyen: Medical complications associated with earthquakes; The Lancet, Vol.379, Issue 9817, 2012

lv   Morgan: Infectious disease risks from dead bodies following natural disasters; Panam Salud Publica, 2004

lvi   Lim: Wound infections in tsunami survivors – a commentary; Singapore Annual of Academic Medicine, Vol.34 (9), 2005

lvii   Potera: In disaster's wake - tsunami lung; Environmental Health Perspectives, Vol.113 (11), 2005

lviii   Park: Preventive and Social Medicine; 1997

lix   Niederman: Preparing for the Unexpected - Lessons Learned About Respiratory Infection from the Japanese Tsunami of 2011; Chest Journal, Vol.143, No.2, 2013

lx   www.un.org/news/briefings/docs/2005/050929_nabarro.doc (accessed 26 June 2014)

lxi   Suttle et al: Do viruses control the oceans?; Natural History Magazine, Vol.108, 1999

lxii   Radio interview with the Chief Medical Officer, Public Health England, BBC Radio Four, 21st May 2013

lxiii   International Journal of Tuberculosis and Lung Disease, 2012

lxiv   Pan American Health Organisation (PAHO): Disasters, Issue No.114, 2010

lxv   Von Schreeb et al: Foreign field hospitals in recent sudden-onset disasters; Prehospital and Disaster Medicine, Vol. 23 (2), 2008

lxvi   Oxfam International: Growing a Better Future – food justice in a resource constrained world; 2011 [www.policypractice.oxfam.org.uk/publications/download?id= 432326; accessed 20 February 2013]

lxvii   Koch: OECD development Centre, policy insights No.73, 2008

lxviii   Bengtsson et al: Improved response to disasters and outbreaks by tracking population movements with mobile phone network data – a post-earthquake geospatial study in Haiti; 2011 (doi:10.1371/journal.pmed. 1001083).

lxix Sack et al: Four year study of the epidemiology of vibrio cholerae in four rural areas of Bangladesh; Journal of Infectious Diseases, Vol. 187, 2003

lxx Hiruma: Tsunami Lung; American Journal of Respiratory Critical Care Medicine, Vol.187, Issue 1, 2013

lxxi OECD, 2008 and

lxxii Wharton School of Economics, 2012

lxxiii Kenny: Why Do People Die in Earthquakes? - The Costs, Benefits and Institutions of Disaster Risk Reduction in Developing Countries; World Bank Policy Research Working Paper No.4823, 2009

lxxiv Typhoon Haiyan shelter cluster weekly conference call, April 2014

lxxv The International Feinstein Center: The use of evidence in humanitarian decision making; ACAPS Operational Learning Paper, 2013

lxxvi Dan Littman, Federal Reserve Bank of Cleveland; personal communication, 4 October 2016

lxxvii Central Bank of Kenya: Household Financial Access Survey, February 2016

lxxviii ECB: Consumer Cash Usage – a cross-country comparison; Working Paper Series No.1685, June 2014

lxxix Boeden: Demand For Cash After a Natural Disaster; Singapore International Currency Conference, October 2011

lxxx Cropper et al: Willingness to pay for mortality risk reductions – does latency matter?; Journal of Risk and Uncertainty, Vol.32 (3), 2008

lxxxi Jamison et al: Disease Control Priorities in Developing Countries; Unicef, 2006

www.ingramcontent.com/pod-product-compliance
Lightning Source LLC
Chambersburg PA
CBHW031424270326
41930CB00007B/569

* 9 7 8 0 9 9 2 7 2 0 1 2 4 *